圖書館服務英文
Library Service English

李文瑞　策劃
文藻外語學院・圖書館團隊　著
謝慧貞・王愉文　英譯
Sandi Edwards　英文審定

致　謝

謹以此書
獻給在文藻校園全力推動國際化的李文瑞校長
及
所有在圖書資訊領域服務的伙伴

推薦人❶
台灣大學圖書館館長　陳雪華

　　本書中以中英對照方式呈現圖書館多元化服務，以情境對話方式設計面對面會話、e-mail、電話、即時訊息，並列出圖書館常用英文詞彙、書末附上圖書館服務所需的各種文件與表格等，內容完備極具參考價值，對圖書館國際化有莫大的助益。

推薦人 ❷
中興大學圖書館館長　詹麗萍

　　這是一本由文藻外語學院圖書館員合力編製的工具書，集結了館員多年來的雙語服務經驗，對於想提昇英文程度、增進服務能力的圖書館同道極具參考價值。更可貴的是，這是館員在繁忙的工作中努力擠出時間完成的一本書，其中蘊藏了無限服務的熱忱和分享的精神。

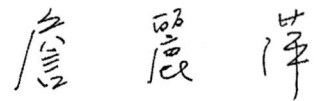

推薦人❸
南台科技大學圖書館館長　楊智晶

　　是什麼樣的書，能讓我們每天經手近千本圖書的圖書館員們引領期盼，雀躍三尺？

　　文藻外語學院，有著各國語言、文化之校園特質，在此工作的圖書館員，每人至少需具備2種以上的外國語言之能力。文藻王愉文館長暨圖書館團隊充分發揮了技專校院圖書館之外語特色，再加上熱誠且實務經驗豐富之館員知識彙集，才能成就此非常完善的圖書館實務工具書，真實的反映圖書館服務之內容。在此鄭重的推薦給各類型的圖書館同道，以及欲了解圖書館專業翻譯用語的人士。

FOREWORD

校長 序

　　1999年文藻改制學院，過去10年對師生而言，文藻圖書館的發展可以用「飛躍」兩個字來形容：圖書資料預算、館藏量及館員人數均增加了一倍左右，館舍空間則由原有的3層半，擴充至目前的8層；其他如服務品質的提升、推廣活動的卓著成效等，各方面都表現出轉型為一座外語大學圖書館的旺盛企圖心。

　　文藻校園像是一個小小的聯合國，英、法、德、西、日及其他國籍的教師占所有教師人數的1/10，加上華語中心來自30餘國的外籍學生、每年數百位前來參觀的外籍訪客，對文藻圖書館而言，以英語服務外籍人士是日常的重要工作之一。在校園中，圖書館公認是非常國際化的單位，外籍師生也因為圖書館的各項英語服務而倍感溫馨。

　　《圖書館服務英文》（Library Service English）一書的出版一方面可以視為文藻圖書館多年來雙語服務成果的累積，另一方面也可以看作是館員自我鞭策的計畫，他們自動自發地編製了完整的自學教材，希望藉此雙語服務的水準可以更為提升，不可否認地，文藻的同學也因此多了一本獨立自學的實用教材。

本書的內容涵括了圖書館各面向的服務，從流通作業到技術服務，從面對面的對話到MSN，從email到緊急廣播，對從事圖書館實務的館員而言，這是一本非常完備的工具書；對圖書資訊系所的師生而言，書中的內容除了可以提升學生的專業英文程度外，更可以在學生未踏出校門前，培養他們的溝通工具與國際視野。

　　過去幾年，台灣各大學國際化的腳步加快，各校外籍教授及學生人數普遍增加，國際交流也日益頻繁；但平心而論，各校對如何服務這些遠地來的師生及訪客，並未有廣泛且有系統的課程訓練或研習，在圖書館服務方面也不例外。身為台灣唯一外語學院的圖書館工作者，文藻的圖書館同仁盡其全力出版此書，藉此拋磚引玉，期待未來有更多相關主題的研究出版。

文藻外語學院校長

李文瑞

2009.5.25

ACKNOWLEDGEMENT

館長 序

　　《圖書館服務英文》這本書最早的內容雛型是2003年5月館員共同完成的「100句辦公室英文」。當時校內由上而下推動辦公室英文，對許多單位而言，可能只是一項校方政策，但對圖書館同仁而言，卻是一件志業的萌芽。真正認真地思考要出版一本書是在2007年初，這時離校內推動辦公室英文已經過了三年多，難得的是全體館員興致不減。

　　文藻圖書館包括館長共11位同仁，撰寫及翻譯的過程，對每一位館員來說，正是持續不斷的學習過程。收集整理常用辭彙、揣摩情境、撰寫對話、搜尋參考資料、開會討論、英譯、校對、洽談授權引用、尋找合適的審定者及出版公司等工作，在每個人繁忙的館務工作夾縫中緩慢進行。每完成一小部分，心中的喜悅與成就感便增加一分，同時堅持下去的決心也增長一分。一次次和慧貞及育群的三人小組會議中，我們確定了中文初稿；後續的英譯工作因為慧貞優秀的英文能力及專業素養，進行得頗為順利。

　　當初在設想本書的內容方向及會話腳本時，我們決定針對台灣大專校院圖書館的現況及未來3-5年可能的發展來撰寫；部分內容亦適用於專門圖書館，公共圖書館及高中圖書館則需要斟酌使用。鑑於台灣圖書館發展大致追隨美國模式，本書內容的英譯部分，不論是館務用語或表達方式，均依照美國圖書館慣用辭彙及方式翻譯。

　　是文藻多元文化的校園孕育了這樣的一本書；是李文瑞校長的國際化理念在幕後推動、激勵了書的撰寫與出版；由於蘇其康副校長的指引與協助，在最後階段本書才得以順利送審定及出版；本校產官學合作處則在出版合約書方面提供全程協助。

英文初稿完成時，很幸運地，大學同學君徽引介了她在美國德州Rice University圖書館的同事、參考部主任Ms. Sandi Edwards為我們逐字審定；學養深厚、實務經驗豐富，並且認真仔細的Ms. Sandi Edwards為書的英文內容，不論是專業辭彙或文法用字方面做了許多修正與建議。感謝Dr. Carol Hughes和Mr. Steve Shaw的慷慨授權，書的附錄中我們引用及中譯了University of California, Irvine圖書館的Podcast圖書館導覽腳本及Prairie View A&M University圖書館的線上問卷題目作為範本。

最後要感謝華藝數位公司的熱心幫忙，出版《圖書館服務英文》紙本及電子書的同時，也同意我們將電子書收入文藻機構典藏，供文藻師生永久無償使用。洽談出版的過程中，透過華藝鍾瑞珍小姐的引介，幾個月來與華藝學術出版事業部張芸總編輯聯繫，在在感到她們對學術出版的熱誠與專業。

我以身為文藻圖書館一份子為榮，也慶幸我們終於完成了這本書。

文藻圖書館館長

王愉文

2009.5.15

PREFACE

英文審定者 序

I was pleased to be asked to contribute a preface for this eminently practical and valuable guide for library staff training in the English language.

As I was reviewing the well-selected, thought-out array of service, collection and facility scenarios included in this book I was struck by how familiar it all seemed to me – suddenly Taiwan did not seem so distant a country. While some of the lesser details may vary it is clear that there exists a universality of purpose that underlies all library endeavors – the goal to provide excellent customer service, relevant & accessible collections and comfortable, safe and flexible facilities.

Key to achieving this goal is a well-prepared and highly motivated staff. This guide will provide libraries in Taiwan with a useful tool in preparing staff for the challenges of a continually evolving library workplace.

The librarians at Wenzao Library are to be commended for their dedication and thoroughness in bringing this book to a successful completion. They have produced an important primer for library staff training that will remain pertinent for some time to come.

美國德州萊斯大學圖書館參考服務部主任

Sandi Edwards

2009.5.2

圖書館服務英文 章節目次
《Library Service English》 Table of Contents

校長序 Foreword	008
館長序 Acknowledgement	010
英文審定者序 Preface	012

第一章 大學圖書館常用詞彙 Glossary of Common Library Terms — 021
  1. 圖書館行政 Library Administration — 022
  2. 閱覽流通典藏業務 Public Services, Circulation & Collection Services — 024
  3. 圖書資料類型 Library Materials — 027
  4. 空間區域與設備 Library Spaces & Facilities — 030
  5. 多媒體空間及設備 Multimedia Spaces & Equipment — 033
  6. 資訊科技與設備 Information Technology & Facilities — 034
  7. 書目資料 Bibliographical Data — 036
  8. 資料狀態 Status of Materials — 038
  9. 編目分類業務 Cataloging & Classification — 039
  10. 期刊業務 Serials Management — 041
  11. 採購業務 Library Acquisitions — 042
  12. 電子資料庫 Electronic Databases — 043
  13. 利用教育/推廣活動 User Education & Outreach Programs — 044
  14. 數位圖書館 Digital Library — 045
  15. 其他 Miscellaneous — 046

第二章 認識圖書館 Learn About Library Services — 047
  Unit 2.1 進出圖書館 Access the Library — 048
  Unit 2.2 開放時間 Opening Hours — 050
  Unit 2.3 空間配置 Library Spaces — 052
    2.3.1 詢問書庫樓層 Location of Stack Areas — 052
    2.3.2 詢問行政辦公室 Location of Library Offices — 054

第三章 借還圖書資料 Borrow or Return Library Materials — 057
  Unit 3.1 申辦借書證 Library Card Application — 058
    3.1.1 學生借書 Student Borrowing Privileges — 058

3.1.2 教職員眷屬借書　　060
Faculty, Staff, & Family Members Borrowing Privileges

3.1.3 退還保證金 Security Deposit Refund　　062

Unit 3.2 借還資料 Borrow or Return Library Materials　　064

3.2.1 辦理外借手續 Borrow Library Materials　　064

3.2.2 借閱冊數上限 Maximum Number of Checkouts　　066

3.2.3 郵寄還書 Return Checkouts in the Mail　　068

3.2.4 誤將他館的書還到自己學校的圖書館　　070
Drop Books from Other Libraries in the Book Return by Mistake

3.2.5 誤將自己學校圖書館的書還到他館　　072
Return Library Checkouts to Other Libraries by Mistake

Unit 3.3 續借 Renew Checkouts　　074

Unit 3.4 預約 Place a Hold　　078

3.4.1 線上預約 Place a Hold Online　　078

3.4.2 無法預約，疑難排除 Problems with Online Reservation　　080

Unit 3.5 催還 Recall Borrowed Materials　　082

Unit 3.6 逾期 Overdues　　086

3.6.1 沒收到圖書館電子郵件通知　　090
Library Notices via Email Not Received

3.6.2 逾期處理費 Library Overdue Fines　　090

Unit 3.7 遺失、損壞圖書資料 Lost or Damaged Library Materials　　092

3.7.1 遺失圖書 Deal with Lost Books　　092

3.7.2 找到遺失的圖書 Lost Books Found　　096

3.7.3 損壞及污染資料 Deal with Damaged Books　　098

3.7.4 賠書 Replace Lost or Damaged Books　　102

3.7.5 賠書款 Replacement Bill　　104

3.7.6 遺失視聽資料 Lost Media Materials　　106

Unit 3.8 宣稱已還書 Claim a Return　　110

第四章　取得圖書館找不到的資料　　115
Access Materials Not Available in Local Library

Unit 4.1 館際合作／文獻傳遞　　116
Interlibrary Loan & Document Delivery Services

4.1.1 國內費用及時限 Services for Domestic Libraries　　116

　　　　　4.1.2 國外費用及時限 Services from Overseas Libraries　　120
　　　　　4.1.3 到他館借書　　124
　　　　　　　Walk in and Borrow Books from Other Libraries
　　Unit 4.2 尚未上架的資料 Materials Not Available on Shelves　　126
　　　　　4.2.1 一般讀者詢問 Inquiry from Library Patrons　　126
　　　　　4.2.2 介購者詢問　　130
　　　　　　　Inquiry from a Patron Requesting Library Purchase
　　　　　4.2.3 過期期刊送裝訂 Back Issues Sent To Be Bound　　134
　　Unit 4.3 推薦訂購 Library Purchase Recommendations　　138
　　Unit 4.4 尋書 Search Service for Missing Books　　142

第五章　線上借閱服務 Online Services　　147
　　Unit 5.1 查看個人借閱狀況 View Personal Library Account　　148
　　　　　5.1.1 忘記密碼 Forget Password　　148
　　　　　5.1.2 借閱紀錄異常 Cannot Access Personal Account　　150
　　　　　5.1.3 更改個人資料 Update Personal Information　　152
　　Unit 5.2 線上續借或預約 Renew or Place a Hold Online　　156
　　　　　5.2.1 如何續借及預約　　156
　　　　　　　Steps for Online Renewals and Reservation
　　　　　5.2.2 無法續借及預約　　160
　　　　　　　Problems with Online Renewals and Reservations
　　Unit 5.3 研究小間申請 Request a Study Carrel　　164

第六章　查詢館藏資源 Search Library Collection & Resources　　169
　　Unit 6.1 以資料性質區分 Search by Material Types　　170
　　　　　6.1.1 館藏圖書資料 Library Materials　　170
　　　　　　　6.1.1.1 以圖書類別詢問館藏樓層　　170
　　　　　　　　　Location of Specific Subjects in Collection
　　　　　　　6.1.1.2 尋找多媒體資料　　172
　　　　　　　　　Search Multimedia Resources
　　　　　　　6.1.1.3 排架方式 Arrangement of Library Materials　　174
　　　　　6.1.2 查詢期刊文獻 Find Journal Articles　　178
　　　　　6.1.3 查詢新聞資料 Find Newspaper Articles　　180
　　　　　6.1.4 查詢學位論文 Find Theses and Dissertations　　182

6.1.5 查詢研究報告 Find Research Papers 📄	186
6.1.6 考古題 Old Exam Questions 🔊	190
Unit 6.2 以工具類型區分 Library Research Tools	**192**
6.2.1 館藏目錄 Library Catalog	192
6.2.1.1 以作者為檢索點 Search by Author 📄	192
6.2.1.2 以主題為檢索點 Search by Subject 📄	194
6.2.2 聯合目錄 Union Catalog 📄	196
6.2.3 電子資料庫 Electronic Databases 📄	200
6.2.4 電子期刊 E-Journals 📄	202
6.2.5 電子書 E-Books 🔊	206
6.2.6 專利文獻 Patent Information 🔊	210
6.2.7 網際網路 Internet Resources 📄	212
Unit 6.3 校外連線使用 Remote Access 🔊	**216**

第七章 使用媒體資源中心 Use of Library Media Resources Center	**219**
Unit 7.1 不得攜入提袋、背包、食物及飲料 📄	**220**
Bags, Food and Drinks Are Not Allowed in the Center	
Unit 7.2 視聽資料借用 Borrow Media Materials 📄	**222**
Unit 7.3 預約小團體欣賞室 Reserve Small-Group Viewing Room 📄	**224**
Unit 7.4 設備故障 Facilities Out of Order 📄	**226**
Unit 7.5 資料轉錄 Media Materials Conversion 📄	**228**
Unit 7.6 校外使用隨選視訊系統 Remote Access to Video-On-Demand 📄	**230**

第八章 使用館內硬體設備（電腦、電話、影印機、印表機、掃描器……）	**233**
Use of Library Facilities (PCs, Phones, Photocopiers, Printers, Scanners, etc.)	
Unit 8.1 無線上網 Wireless Internet Access	**234**
8.1.1 登入帳號密碼 Log in 📄	234
8.1.2 訊號接收不良 Poor Connection Quality 📄	238
Unit 8.2 卡式或投幣式影印 Photocopy Services 📄	**240**
Unit 8.3 使用電腦 Use of PCs	**242**
8.3.1 無法使用IMS Instant Message Service Not Available 📄	242
8.3.2 特殊軟體需求 Specific Software Needs 🔊	244
8.3.3 無法將資料存在電腦中 📄	246
Problems with Saving Files on Library PCs	

第九章　教師服務 Faculty Services　　　　　　　　　　249
Unit 9.1 教師指定參考資料 Course Reserves 　　　　　250
Unit 9.2 委託代借 Proxy Borrower Request 　　　　　252
Unit 9.3 支援課程—安排圖書資源利用說明 　　　　　258
　　　　Library Instruction for a Class
Unit 9.4 專案計畫用圖書資料送交圖書館 　　　　　　262
　　　　Submit Books Acquired for Research Projects to the Library

第十章　技術服務業務用語 Technical Services　　　　267
Unit 10.1 索取目錄 Request for Publisher Catalogs 　　268
Unit 10.2 詢價、下訂及催貨 Price Quotes, Place and Claim an Order　270
　　10.2.1 詢價 Quotation 　　　　　　　　　　　　　270
　　10.2.2 下訂及確認訂單 Place and Confirm an Order 　272
　　10.2.3 催貨 Claim an Order 　　　　　　　　　　　274
　　10.2.4 詢價及決定不下訂 　　　　　　　　　　　　278
　　　　　Decide Not To Order after Requesting a Quotation
Unit 10.3 視聽資料採購 Acquire Media Materials 　　　280
Unit 10.4 寄錯及更換圖書 　　　　　　　　　　　　　284
　　　　 Receive Wrong Items and Request Exchange
Unit 10.5 瑕疵書更換 Request Replacement of Defective Books 　286
Unit 10.6 發票金額錯誤 Incorrect Total Amount of Payment 　288
Unit 10.7 遲未付款 Late Payment 　　　　　　　　　　290
Unit 10.8 資料庫議價 　　　　　　　　　　　　　　　292
　　　　 Negotiate Subscription Fees for Electronic Databases
Unit 10.9 期刊催缺 Claim Journals Not Yet Received 　　296
Unit 10.10 期刊停刊處理 Journal Ceases Publication 　　300
Unit 10.11 國外贈書 Gift Books from Overseas 　　　　　304
Unit 10.12 外文書編目 Catalog Books in Foreign Languages 　306

第十一章　特殊狀況處理 Specific and Unexpected Situations　311
Unit 11.1 違規行為 Conduct Violating Library Rules　　312
　　11.1.1 攜帶食物入館 Bring Food into the Library 　　312
　　11.1.2 在館內打手機 　　　　　　　　　　　　　　316
　　　　　Use Mobile Phones in the Quiet Reading Area

　　　　11.1.3 上色情網站 Link to Porn Websites 　　318
　　　　11.1.4 玩電腦遊戲 Play Computer Games 　　320
　　　　11.1.5 攜未借圖書出館 　　322
　　　　　　　Take Out Books without Checking Out
　　Unit 11.2 緊急狀況 Emergency Situations 　　326
　　　　11.2.1 地震 Earthquake 　　326
　　　　11.2.2 火災 Fire Alarm 　　328
　　　　11.2.3 颱風臨時閉館 Typhoon 　　330
　　　　11.2.4 防空演習 Air Defense Exercise 　　332
　　　　11.2.5 停電 Power Outage 　　334

第十二章 讀者抱怨處理 Library Patron Complaints　　337
　　Unit 12.1 逾期處理費 Overdue Fines 　　338
　　　　12.1.1 逾期處理費 Overdue Fines 　　338
　　　　12.1.2 賠償視聽資料 Media Resources Replacement 　　342
　　Unit 12.2 圖書採購太慢 Takes Too Long To Acquire Books 　　346
　　Unit 12.3 開館時間太短 Short Library Hours 　　348
　　Unit 12.4 服務態度不佳 Bad Service Attitudes 　　354
　　Unit 12.5 施工噪音 Noise Due to Construction Work 　　358
　　Unit 12.6 區域封閉時間延長 　　362
　　　　　Extend Closure of Certain Library Areas
　　Unit 12.7 燈光閃爍 Light Bulb Blinking 　　366
　　Unit 12.8 遺失錢包 Wallet or Purse Stolen 　　368
　　Unit 12.9 校外讀者太多 Too Many Walk-in Visitors 　　372
　　Unit 12.10 館內有可疑人士 　　374
　　　　　Suspicious Looking People in the Library

第十三章 其他 Miscellaneous　　379
　　Unit 13.1 如何捐書 Donate Books 　　380
　　Unit 13.2 教師授權機構典藏 　　382
　　　　　Institutional Repository Project for Faculty Publications
　　Unit 13.3 寫作輔導中心 Writing Center 　　386

參考資料 Reference　　390

附錄 Appendix 393
I. 表格舉隅 Sample Service Request Forms 394
  1. 眷屬借書證申請表 Faculty and Staff Spouses & Dependents Application Form 394
  2. 長期借閱申請表 Request Form for Long-Term Loan Period 395
  3. 委託代借申請表 Proxy Borrower Authorization Form 397
  4. 教師指定參考資料申請表 Course Reserves Request Form 398
II. 導覽腳本 Library Tour Script 400
III. 問卷調查 Sample Survey 408
IV. 公告舉隅 Sample Library News Items and Announcements 418
  1. 自動化系統主機維護 Maintenance on Library Server 418
  2. 國定假日閉館 Closed on National Holidays 419
  3. 消毒閉館 Closed for Sanitization 420
  4. 其他 Miscellaneous 421
V. 標示舉隅 Sample Library Signs 423
  1. 影印機／印表機故障 Copier / Printer Out of Order 423
  2. 網路斷線 Network Disconnected 423
  3. 電梯維修 Elevator under Maintenance 423
VI. 活動辦法 Library Events 424
  1. 換書活動 Book Swap & Raffle 424
  2. 講座活動 Lecture 428
VII. 感謝狀 Certificates of Appreciation 430
  1. 義工 Volunteer 430
  2. 捐贈 Gift 431
VIII. 授權書 Author Permission Forms 432
  1. 演講活動錄影授權書 Video & Audio Recording Permission Form 432
  2. 機構典藏作者授權書 Permission Form for Institutional Repository 434
IX. 電子郵件通知 Announcements via Email 436
  1. 電子資料庫試用 Free Database Trials 436
  2. 展覽活動通知 Announcement for an Upcomping Exhibition 438
X. 圖書館管理營運辦法 Library Policies 440
  1. 圖書館借書規則 Borrowing Policies 440
  2. 圖書委員會設置辦法 Library Committee 446
  3. 媒體資源中心使用規則 Media Resources Center Circulation Policies 448

本書圖示： 對話用語　電話用語　email用語　廣播用語　IMS（Instant Message Service）用語

chapter 1
第一章

大學圖書館常用詞彙
Glossary of Common Library Terms

Library Service English

1. 圖書館行政 Library Administration

任務宣言	mission statement
策略規劃書	strategic plan
館藏發展政策	collection development policy
館訊	library news / library newsletter
圖書館電子報	library e-newsletter
圖書（諮詢）委員會	library (advisory) committee
圖書（諮詢）委員	library (advisory) committee member
圖書館顧問	library consultant
館務會議	library staff meeting
營運管理辦法	rules and regulations
圖書館使用規則	library code of conduct
知識管理	knowledge management
館長	library director / dean of the library
副館長	deputy director / associate dean of the library
館長秘書	director's secretary
館員	librarian / library staff
組長	section head / division head / department head
工讀生	student assistant
志工	volunteer
組	section / division / department
行政組	administrative services department
編目組	cataloging department / bibliographic services department
採訪組	acquisitions department

chapter 1

典藏（管理）組	collection management department
流通組	circulation department
期刊組	serials department
參考服務組	reference services department
視聽組	audio-visual department
多媒體服務組	multimedia services department
資訊服務組	information services department
數位資源組	digital resources department
技術服務組	technical services department
系統服務組	systems services department
推廣組	outreach services department
讀者服務組	public services department
特藏組	special collections department
人力資源組	human resources department
資訊架構館員	information architect
學科館員	subject librarian
徵求館員／徵人啟事	employment opportunities in the library / job posting
值班	on duty
週末輪值	rotate weekend shifts

大學圖書館常用詞彙 Glossary of Common Library Terms

2. 閱覽流通典藏業務 Public Services, Circulation &

流通台	circulation desk
學生證	student ID card
校友證	alumni library card
教職員證	faculty or staff ID card
臨時閱覽證	visitor card
館際合作借書證	reciprocal borrowing card
身份證件	personal identification card
退休職員	retired staff
退休教師	retired faculty
榮譽教授	professor emeritus
持有效證件的讀者	authorized users
開放時間	library (opening) hours
借期	loan period
借書	check out books
還書	return books
預約（書）	reserve (a book) / place a hold on (a book)
續借	renew (v.) ; renewal (n.)
到期日	due date
圖書館通知單	library notices
逾期	overdue
逾期處理費	overdue fines
預約催還	request to recall a book / request for recall
可外借	circulating
不可外借	non-circulating

chapter 1

Collection Services

薦購單	purchase request form
還書箱	book return / book drop
自助借書機	self-checkout system
書架	stack
密集書架	compact shelves
高密度書架系統	high density mobile shelving storage system
自動化書庫	automatic storage and retrieval system
書庫	stacks
上架	reshelve (v.)
索書號	call number
館藏	holdings (n.)
館藏發展	collection development
文獻傳遞	document delivery services
館際合作	inter-library loan (ILL)
門禁系統	entrance guard system
安全系統	security system
贈書	gifts
新書展示	new books display
館藏目錄	online catalog / online public access catalog (OPAC) / WebOPAC
聯合目錄	union catalog
修補／裝訂	bind (v.) ; bindery (n.)

大學圖書館常用詞彙 Glossary of Common Library Terms

淘汰	weed
淘汰政策	weeding policy
遠端認證	remote access authentication (n.)
常問問題集	frequently asked questions (FAQs)
緊急編目服務	rush cataloging request

3. 圖書資料類型 Library Materials

期刊／雜誌	periodical / magazine
現期期刊	current periodicals (or issues)
過期期刊	back issues
裝訂期刊	bound periodicals
學術期刊	scholarly (or academic) journal
一般雜誌	popular magazine
學報	university (or college) journal
參考工具書	reference works (or collection)
地圖	map
地圖集	atlas
百科全書	encyclopedia
字典	dictionary
名錄／指南	directory
摘要	abstract
索引	index
電子資料庫	electronic databases
電子資源	electronic resources
電子書	ebook / E-book / Ebook /eBook
電子期刊	e-journal
電腦檔	computer file
互動多媒體資料	interactive multimedia
兒童文學	children's literature
兒童圖畫書／繪本	picture book
青少年讀物	juvenile collection / teen and young adult books
留學資料	study abroad material

政府出版品	government document
手稿	manuscript
小冊子	pamphlet
珍善本書	rare book
袖珍書／口袋書	pocket book
罕用資料	lesser-used (or low-use) materials
孤本	unique copy
教師出版品	faculty publication
教師指定參考資料	course reserves
考古題	past exam papers (or questions)
學位論文	theses and dissertations
畢業紀念冊	class yearbook
視聽資料	audio-visual material
多媒體資料	multimedia collection
多媒體組件	kit
錄音資料	sound recordings
錄影資料	video recordings
音樂CD	music CD
光碟片	disk
幻燈片	slide
幻燈捲片	filmstrip
錄音帶	audio cassette
錄影帶	video cassette
透明投影片	transparency
圖表	graphic / chart

地球儀	globe
實物	realia
遊戲	game
玩具	toy
點字本	braille
模型	model
樂譜	music scores
顯微鏡單片	microscope slide
閃示卡	flash card
工程圖	technical drawing
活動卡	activity card
簡介／摺頁	leaflet
拓片	diorama
藝術品原件	art original
複製藝術品	art reproduction
靜畫資料	graphic materials
微縮資料	microform

4. 空間區域與設備 Library Spaces & Facilities

中文書庫	Chinese Collection Stacks
外文書庫	Foreign Collection Stacks
西文書庫	Western Collection Stacks
東方語文書庫	Asian Collection Stacks
罕用書庫	Library Annex
密集書庫	Compact Shelving
待上架區	Sorting Area (or Room)
服務台	Information Desk / Service Desk
流通台	Circulation Desk
參考諮詢台	Reference Desk
研究諮詢台	Research Help
期刊區	Periodicals Area
參考資料區	Reference Collection
檢索區	Information Access Area
閱報區	Newspapers Area
自修室	Study Hall
新書展示區	New Books / New Arrivals
線上目錄區	OPAC / WebOPAC
指定參考資料區	Course Reserves Area
資訊交流區	Information Commons
媒體資源中心	Media Resources Center
特藏區	Special Collections
互動學習區	Interactive Learning Area
語言學習區	Language Learning Area
合作學習區	Collaborative Learning Area
教育訓練室／資訊素養教室	Training Room

chapter 1

遠距教室	Distance Learning Room
研究生自修室	Graduate Study Room
個人閱覽桌／研究小間	Study Carrels
靜讀區	Silent Reading Area
討論區	Discussion Area
影印區	Photocopy Area / Photocopying Area
媒體製作室	Media Production Studio
手機室	Cell Phone Room
機房	mechanical room
儲藏室	storage room
會議室	meeting room
國際會議廳	international conference room
學者中心	Scholar Center / Faculty Club
校史室（館）	University Archives
展覽藝廊	gallery
飲食區	Food Friendly Zone
咖啡輕食區	Library Cafe (or Café)
洗手間（男，女）	restroom (Ladies, Men)
自助借書機	self-checkout system
置物櫃	lockers
（運）書車	book truck / book cart
飲水機	water dispenser / water fountain
碎紙機	shredder
傘架	umbrella rack
影印機	photocopier

大學圖書館常用詞彙 Glossary of Common Library Terms

影印卡	copy card / vendacard
投幣式影印機	coin-operated photocopier
卡式影印機	card-operated photocopier
網路印表機	networked printer
影印／列印卡販賣機	vendacard dispenser (or machine or encoder)
[含加值功能]	
換幣機	change machine
公告欄	bulletin board
電子看板／跑馬燈	electronic display board
直立式公告牌	poster stand
LCD數位看板	LCD advertising display
桌燈	desk lamp
插座	plug-in / receptacle
筆筒	desk tidy / desk organizer
便條紙	scratch paper

5. 多媒體空間及設備 Multimedia Spaces & Equipment

隨選視訊系統	video on demand (VOD)
錄放影機	video player
DVD光碟機	DVD player
幻燈機	slide projector
數位攝影機	digital video camera
數位相機	digital camera
數位錄影機	digital video recorder (DVR)
藍光雷射光碟片[2種規格]	Blu-ray disc (BD) / HD-DVD disc
電子書閱讀器（軟體）	ebook reader
液晶電視	LCD TV
電漿電視	plasma TV
耳機	headphones / earphones / headset
無線耳機	wireless (or cordless) headphones (or earphones or headset)
耳掛式耳機	clip-on headphones (or earphones or headset)
耳塞式耳機	ear-buds
藍牙耳機	bluetooth headphones (or earphones or headset)
噴墨印表機	ink-jet printer
彩色雷射印表機	laser color printer
多功能印表機	multifunctional printer
相片印表機	photo printer
熱感應印表機	thermal printer
大（小）團體觀賞室	large-group (small-group) viewing room
音樂欣賞室	music appreciation studio
新資料展示區	new arrivals

6. 資訊科技與設備 Information Technology & Facilities

區域網路	local area network (LAN)
無線寬頻數據機	access point (AP)
伺服器	server
無線網路	wireless
網卡	network interface card (NIC)
無線網卡	wireless network interface card (WNIC)
外掛程式	plug-in
編碼	encode
網路交換器	switch
網路線	RJ45 (Cross-over Network Cable)
再生卡	restore card
集線器	hub
USB集線器	USB hub
喇叭	speaker
鍵盤	keyboard
手寫板	computer writing pad
滑鼠	mouse
射頻識別	radio-frequency identification (RFID)
（雷射）印表機	(laser) printer
掃瞄器	scanner
螢幕	monitor / screen
監視器	watchdog
銀幕	screen
網路攝影機	webcam
電腦廣播教學系統	screen broadcasting software
投影機	projector

chapter 1

手提電腦	notebook / laptop
隨身碟	USB (Universal Serial Bus) flash drive
讀卡機	card reader
圖書館網站	library website
圖書館部落格	library blog
館員網頁	library staff home page
無障礙網路空間	web accessibility

7. 書目資料 Bibliographical Data

作者	author
編輯者	editor
繪者	illustrator
翻譯者	translator
書刊名／題名	title
副題名	subtitle
分類號	classification number
作者號	author number
索書號	call number
國際標準書號	International Standard Book Number (ISBN)
國際標準叢刊號	International Standard Serial Number (ISSN)
國際標準樂譜號	International Standard Music Number (ISMN)
條碼	barcode
出版者	publisher
出版年	publication year
出版地	place of publication
經銷地	place of distribution
經銷者	distributor
印製地	place of manufacture
印製者	manufacturer
版本	edition
修訂版	revised edition
刷次	impression
面頁數	pages
冊數	volumes

chapter 1

高廣／尺寸	dimensions
附件	accompanying material
集叢	series
附註／一般註	note
內容註	contents note
摘要註	summary
學位論文註	dissertation note
並列題名	parallel title
劃一題名	uniform title
封面題名	cover title
卷端題名	caption title
逐頁題名	running title
書背題名	spine title
精裝	hard bound / hardback / hardcover
平裝	paperback / softback / softcover
贈書	gifts
補篇	supplemental
資料類型	material type
機讀編目格式	Machine Readable Cataloging Format (MARC)
書目紀錄	bibliographic record
主題／標題	subject

大學圖書館常用詞彙 Glossary of Common Library Terms

8. 資料狀態　Status of Materials

外借中	on loan / checked-out
預約中	on reserve / on hold
新書展示中	on display
編目處理中	in processing / in-process material
採（訂）購中	on order
待上架	waiting to be shelved / sorting
館藏地	location
洽該館藏地	check location
在館內	available
已登收	order received / newly acquired
宣稱已還	claim returned
遺失	missing / lost
遺失賠書中	replacement
遺失待罰款	billed for lost
遺失已罰款	lost and paid
預約架上	on holdshelf
裝訂中	in binding / at the bindery / in bindery
報廢	withdrawn
修補中	at repair
尋書中	on search
傳送中	(in) transit / transferred
限館內閱覽	library use only
限教師借閱	for faculty only
辦公室專用	library office use

9. 編目分類業務 Cataloging & Classification

編目館員	cataloging (or catalog) librarian
分類	classifying
編目	cataloging
中文圖書分類法	Classification Scheme for Chinese Libraries (CCL)
美國國會分類法	Library of Congress Classification (LC)
杜威十進分類法	Dewey Decimal Classification (DDC)
中文主題詞表	List of Chinese Subject Terms
美國國會標題表	Library of Congress Subject Headings (LCSH)
機讀編目格式	Machine Readable Cataloging Format (MARC)
中文機讀編目格式	Chinese MARC Format
國際標準書目著錄	International Standard Bibliographic Description (ISBD)
都柏林核心集	Dublin Core
中文編目規則	Chinese Cataloguing Rules (CCR)
英美編目規則第2版	Anglo-American Cataloguing Rules, 2nd ed. (AACR2)
克特作者號碼表	Cutter-Sanborn Three-Figure Author Table
預行編目	cataloging in publication (CIP)
抄錄編目	copy cataloging
原始編目	original cataloging
記述編目	descriptive cataloging
回溯編目	retrospective cataloging
主題編目	subject cataloging
書目紀錄功能需求	Functional Requirement for Bibliographic Records (FRBR)

權威控制	authority control
主題分析	subject analysis
主題標目	subject headings
編目工作手冊	cataloging procedures manual
編目委外作業	outsourcing of cataloging / cataloging outsourcing
緊急編目	rush cataloging
全國圖書書目資訊網	National Bibliographic Informational Network (NBINet)
書標	label
活頁目錄	loose-leaf (or notebook) catalog
珍善本書	rare book
袖珍書／口袋書	pocket book
罕用資料	lesser-used (or low-use) materials
孤本	unique copy

10. 期刊業務 Serials Management

已催缺	claimed (adj.)
裝訂中	in binding / at the bindery / in bindery
退款	refund (n. v.)
訂購	subscribe (v.) ; subscription (n.)
催缺	claim missing issues
續訂	renew (v.) ; renewal (n.)
詢價／訪價	inquiry / quotation
停訂	subscription cancelled
索贈期刊	donated journals
停刊	publication ceased / cessation
因缺刊而延長期數	extend the subscription to compensate for the missing issues
發票編號XXX的刊物已經寄送	shipped with invoice no. xxx
合刊	merger
尚未出版	not yet published
補寄／補刊	replacement copies
刊期重複	duplication
延遲出刊	delay
送裝訂	sent to bindery (or for binding)
現期期刊	current periodicals (or issues)
過期期刊	back issues
裝訂期刊	bound volumes (of periodicals)

11. 採購業務 Library Acquisitions

圖書資料薦購	purchase recommendation
薦購單	purchase recommendation form
結匯	exchange foreign currency
匯出匯款申請書	outward remittance application form
匯票	money order / bill of exchange
緊急採購	urgent purchase
請款核銷	auditing expense
驗收	acceptance for goods (or services)
預支	prepay (v.) ; prepayment (n.)
代理商	vendor
發票	invoice
公播版	public performance rights
授權書	author permission form
絕版	out of print (OP)
缺貨	out of stock (OS)
尚未出版	not yet published
取消出版	publication plan cancelled
政府採購法	government procurement method
會計年度	fiscal year
預算	budget
公開招標	open tender (n.) ; put something out to tender (v.)
投標	tender for (v.)
一般訂購	firm order
長期訂購	standing order
閱選採購	approval plan
統購	blanket order

12. 電子資料庫 Electronic Databases

電子資料庫	electronic databases
電子期刊	e-journals
電子書	e-books
校外連線	remote access
試用資料庫	free database trial
教育訓練課程	library workshop
布林檢索	boolean searching
切截查詢	truncation searching
整合查詢	federated search
萬用字元	wildcard
書目管理軟體	personal bibliographic software
RSS	Really Simple Syndication
使用統計	usage statistics (or report)

13. 利用教育／推廣活動 User Education & Outreach Programs

資訊素養	information literacy
利用教育	user education program
電腦技能	computer skills
智慧財產權	intellectual property rights
著作權	copyright
創用CC	Creative Commons
抄襲剽竊	plagiarism
專利	patent
圖書館週（活動）	library week (events)
影展	film festival
書展	book fair
專題展	feature exhibition
讀書會	study circle / reading club / booktalk
有獎徵答	trivia questions
導覽	library tour
主題指引	subject guide / pathfinder
書目指導	bibliographic instruction
線上報名	online registration
線上自學系統	online tutorial
虛擬圖書館導覽	virtual library tour

14. 數位圖書館 Digital Library

數位典藏	digital collection
機構典藏	institutional repository (IR)
元資料	metadata
永久使用	perpetual access
都柏林核心集	Dublin Core
網址	uniform resource locator (URL)
永久網址	durable URL / permalink
開放原始碼軟體	open source software
注意英文字母大小寫	case sensitive
行動裝置	mobile device
數位行動圖書館	m-library
圖書館遠距服務	distance library service ［註：專指針對網路大學或遠距教學課程學分班學生所提供的服務］

15. 其他 Miscellaneous

書目格式	citation style
APA格式	APA style
MLA格式	MLA style
Chicago格式	Chicago manual of style
財產標籤	ownership label
謝函	thank-you letter
緊急逃生門	emergency exit
火警逃生門	fire exit
火警及緊急疏散	fire and emergency evacuation procedures
煙霧偵測器	smoke detector
火警廣播	fire alarm announcement
停電廣播	power outage announcement
地震廣播	emergency earthquake announcement
無障礙網路空間	web accessibility
無障礙空間	barrier-free access
無障礙設施	accessibility equipment
科技輔具／適性科技	adaptive technology
視障專用電腦	computer for the visually impaired
導盲磚	directional tactile paving / truncated domes / detectable warnings

第二章
chapter 2

認識圖書館
Learn About Library Services

Library Service English

Unit 2.1 進出圖書館

情境：A同學和她的朋友站在圖書館門禁前猶豫著不知如何進館，B館員走向她。

B館員：請問有什麼需要幫忙的嗎？
A同學：我是剛到華語中心報到的學生，請問我要怎麼樣才能進入圖書館？
B館員：您只要有學校核發的學生證，把它放在感應區，門禁系統感應後，就可以進來了。
A同學：謝謝！那麼，我的朋友不是這裡的學生，他可以進來嗎？
B館員：可以的，但是我需要看一下他的證件。
A同學：他的證件在這裡。
B館員：好的，證件沒問題。麻煩他在這台電腦上輸入居留證號碼和姓名，這樣就可以進來了。
A同學：可是，我以前去的圖書館都沒有這樣管控？這裡為什麼要這麼嚴格？
B館員：因為我們學校位在市中心，來往的人比較多，周圍環境也比較複雜，為了大家的安全，我們需要有進出館讀者的紀錄。如果是本校教職員生，必須刷卡入館；如果是校外人士，一定要登錄個人資料換證才能進來，萬一有問題，我們比較容易追查和掌握狀況。
A同學：原來是這樣，我了解了，謝謝！
B館員：不客氣！也謝謝您的諒解。

Unit 2.1 Access the Library

Situation: Student A and her friend are standing in front of the library security gate. They look confused, so Librarian B approaches them.

Librarian B: Is there anything I can do to help you?
Student A: Yes, I'm a new student at the Chinese Learning Center. What should I do to enter the library?
Librarian B: You just need to have your university card ready and put it on the sensor panel. Once your card is validated, the gate will be unlocked.
Student A: Thanks! What about my friend? He is not a student here. Can he get into the library too?
Librarian B: Sure! May I have a look at his ID card?
Student A: Here it is.
Librarian B: Alright, it looks fine. Please type his personal information like his ARC No. and full name into the computer. The gate will unlock and then he can get in.
Student A: The library I used to go to did not have this kind of access control. Why is it so strict here?
Librarian B: This university is located in the downtown area, where a variety of people come and visit; therefore it becomes a more complex situation. To make the facility a safer place, we ask all of our patrons to either scan their Love River ID cards or to register personal information to obtain a visitor's card. This process helps us to identify and keep track of the visitors if problems should occur.
Student A: Alright, I see. Thanks.
Librarian B: You're welcome! And, thank you for your understanding.

Unit 2.2 開放時間

情境：A同學不知道圖書館開放時間，打電話到圖書館詢問。

B館員：喂，愛河大學圖書館，您好。
A同學：喂，您好。我想請問圖書館開放的時間。
B館員：目前週一到週五上午8:00開到晚上11:00，週末則是上午8:00到下午8:00。國定假日閉館。寒暑假的開館時間比較短。我們的網站上有開館時間表，您可以上去看看！
A同學：好的，我知道了，謝謝。
B館員：不客氣。

Unit 2.2 Opening Hours

Situation: Student A doesn't know the library's hours and makes a call to the library to ask about the opening hours.

Librarian B: Hello, this is Love River University Library. How can I help you?

Student A: Hello, I'd like to know the library's opening hours.

Librarian B: The library is open from 8 a.m. to 11 p.m. Monday through Friday, and from 8 a.m to 8 p.m. on weekends. It is closed on national holidays. During winter and summer breaks, the opening hours are shorter. You may check the library website for further information.

Student A: Alright, thank you!

Librarian B: You're welcome.

Unit 2.3 空間配置

2.3.1 詢問書庫樓層
情境：A同學想知道圖書館有沒有德文書，因此詢問館員。

A同學：您好，我上禮拜才來愛河，對圖書館很陌生，請問圖書館裡有德文書嗎？

B館員：有的，您可以在5樓的西方語文區找到德文書。我們的排架方式是把所有歐洲語文的書，依主題而不依語言排列。您有沒有特別要找哪一本書？可以用館藏目錄先查出索書號，這樣比較容易在書架上找到書。

A同學：沒有，我沒有特別要找那一本書，只是想要看看圖書館有什麼德文書，謝謝！

B館員：不客氣，如果有什麼問題，歡迎再來找我們。

Unit 2.3 Library Spaces

2.3.1 Location of Stack Areas

Situation: Student A wants to see what books in the German language are available in the library. So he goes to a librarian for help.

Student A: Hi, I'm new to Love River University and I'm not familiar with the library. Are there any German books in the library collection?

Librarian B: Sure. You'll find our books in German in the Western Languages Stacks on the 5th floor. Books are arranged by their subjects rather than by language. Is there any particular book you're looking for? You may use our online catalog to see if it is in our collection. The online catalog provides you with the call number of the book you want. This makes it easier to locate the book in the stacks.

Student A: No, I'm not looking for any particular book. I just want to see what German books we have in the library. Thank you!

Librarian B: No problem! If you have any other questions, please feel free to ask.

Unit 2.3 空間配置

2.3.2 詢問行政辦公室
情境：A教授和期刊組組長有約，要討論核心期刊的事情，但是不知道期刊組辦公室在哪裡，因此到1樓服務台詢問館員。

A教授：您好，我是英文系新任的圖書委員，我10點鐘和期刊組B組長有約，請問期刊組辦公室怎麼走？
C館員：期刊組辦公室在3樓。請您往右轉，那裡有電梯可以搭到3樓，出了電梯之後，請左轉直走，就會看到標示。如果不清楚，電梯旁有平面圖可以參考。當然您也可以走樓梯，樓梯在電梯的右側。
A教授：謝謝您。
C館員：不客氣。

Unit 2.3 Library Spaces

2.3.2 Location of Library Offices

Situation: Professor A has an appointment with the Head of the Department of Serials to talk about the core journals project. However she doesn't know where the Department Head's office is located and asks a librarian at the Information Desk on the 1st floor of the library.

Professor A: Excuse me. I'm a new library committee member in the English Department and I have a 10 o'clock appointment with Ms. B, the Head of the Department of Serials. I'd like to know where her office is and how to get there.

Librarian C: Hi. Ms. B's office is on the 3rd floor. You can use the elevator if you turn right at this corner. When you arrive on the 3rd floor, please turn left and then go straight ahead. You'll see a sign there identifying the office. If you're not sure, there is a floor plan next to the elevator for you to consult. If you'd like to take the stairs, they are located to the right of the elevator.

Professor A: OK, thanks!

Librarian C: You're welcome!

chapter 3

第三章

借還圖書資料
Borrow or Return Library Materials

Library Service English

Unit 3.1　申辦借書證

3.1.1 學生借書
情境：A同學和B同學想要申請借書證到圖書館借書，他們到1樓服務台詢問館員要如何辦理。

A同學：我是愛河的學生，請問要怎麼樣才能借書？
C館員：直接用您的學生證就可以了。
A同學：那麼，如果是校友的話，可以借書嗎？
C館員：可以的。校友需要申請校友借書證，只要填好申請表，現場就可以辦。
B同學：我是其他學校的學生，我可不可以在這裡借書？
C館員：很抱歉，我們還沒有開放校外人士辦理借書證。不過，如果您是在學的學生，可以透過您就讀學校的圖書館，以館際合作的方式向我們借書。
B同學：好的，我知道了，謝謝。
C館員：不客氣。

chapter 3

Unit 3.1 Library Card Application

3.1.1 Student Borrowing Privileges

Situation: Student A and Student B want to apply for a library card in order to check out books from the library. They come to the Information Desk on the 1st floor to ask for a librarian's help.

Student A: Excuse me. I'm a student at Love River. How can I borrow books from the library?

Librarian C: Your student ID card is your library card. As long as your student ID card is valid, you can use it to borrow library books!

Student A: I see. Well, what about the alumni? Can they borrow books from the library?

Librarian C: Sure, as long as they apply for an alumni library card. The application can be processed here in person.

Student B: Well, I'm a student at another university. Can I borrow books from here?

Librarian C: I'm sorry, but at the present non-affiliated students are not able to apply for a library card. However, you may borrow books from this library via the interlibrary loan services provided by your library.

Student B: Okay, I see. Thanks!

Librarian C: You're welcome.

Unit 3.1　申辦借書證

3.1.2 教職員眷屬借書
情境：寒假期間，A教授的先生和孩子想要到圖書館借書，可是他們並沒有借書證，於是A教授打電話到圖書館詢問眷屬是否可以用她的證件借書。

B館員：愛河大學圖書館，您好。
A教授：嗨，您好，我是社工系的A老師，我有個問題想請教您，我的先生和孩子想要到我們圖書館借書，但是他們並不是學校的教職員或學生，可以直接拿我的證件到圖書館借書嗎？
B館員：A教授，您好。很抱歉，圖書館規定必須使用自己的證件才能借書，除非是教授透過申請手續，授權研究生代為借書，這種情況下研究生才可以持教授的證件來借書。
　　　　至於教職員眷屬，圖書館開放直系血親或配偶申請借書證，不過可以借的冊數比較少，您只要準備兩吋照片1張和工本費100元就可以申請了。圖書館網站上有申請表格及相關的規定，您可以先參考看看。您可以直接下載表格，填寫後送來圖書館，或者，您也可以直接到圖書館1樓的服務台填表申請。
A教授：喔，我知道了，來學校服務還不到一年，很多規則和服務都不熟悉，謝謝您的說明！
B館員：不客氣！如果以後有需要幫忙的事情，請不用客氣。
A教授：好的，謝謝，再見！
B館員：再見。

Unit 3.1 Library Card Application

3.1.2 Faculty, Staff, & Family Members Borrowing Privileges

Situation: During the winter break, the husband and children of Professor A want to borrow books from the library, but they don't have Love River library cards. Professor A calls the library to see if her family can use her library card.

Librarian B: Hello, this is Love River University Library. May I help you?

Professor A: Hello, this is A in the Social Work Department. I'm wondering if my husband and children can use my library card to check out books from the library. They are not affiliated with Love River U.

Librarian B: Hi, Professor A. I'm sorry, but your family cannot use your library card to borrow library materials. The library card is not transferable to another family member or individual. The only exception to this policy is your ability to have one of your graduate students act as a proxy borrower for you. However, your family members may obtain their own library cards by completing the application form and submitting a passport-sized photo and the service fee of 100 dollars. You may get detailed information and the application form on the library website. Once the application form is ready, you may bring it over to the library. Or, you may fill in the form at the Information Desk in the library.

Professor A: Oh, I see. Thank you for your explanation. This is my first year in Love River University and therefore, I'm not yet familiar with all of the library's services and rules.

Librarian B: No problem! If you have further inquiries, please feel free to contact us. We'll be happy to help you!

Professor A: Alright, Thank you! See you.

Librarian B: See you.

Unit 3.1　申辦借書證

3.1.3 退還保證金
情境：A校友畢業時申請了校友借書證，當時付了1,000元的保證金，由於他不久就要出國留學，幾年內不會需要校友借書證，因此打電話詢問如何退還校友借書證，並取回保證金。

B館員：愛河大學圖書館，您好！
A校友：請問一下，我是愛河大學的校友，如果我要退還校友借書證，拿回當初繳的保證金，有什麼樣的手續要辦？
B館員：您只要攜帶校友借書證到圖書館1樓流通台辦理就可以了，請問您是否還有書沒還？
A校友：是的，還有兩本。
B館員：那麼，麻煩您將借的書一同帶來，如果您借的書沒有全部歸還，圖書館是無法退給您保證金的。
A校友：我需要帶當初圖書館給我的保證金收據嗎？可能已經找不到了。
B館員：那倒是不用，您有校友借書證，就代表您已經繳了保證金。
A校友：請問我可以週末去圖書館辦理嗎？
B館員：可以的，只要在圖書館的開放時間內您都可以來辦理，我們週末也開放。
A校友：謝謝。
B館員：不客氣。

Unit 3.1 Library Card Application

3.1.3 Security Deposit Refund

Situation: Alumnus A applied for an Alumni Library Card with a deposit of 1,000 dollars after he graduated from Love River. He is now going to study abroad and will not be able to use the library card for the next few years. He calls the library to ask how he can cancel the library card and get his security deposit back.

Librarian B: Hello, Love River University Library. What can I do for you?

Alumnus A: Hello, this is A. I'm a Love River alumnus. I'd like to cancel my Alumni Library Card and get the security deposit back. What do I need to do?

Librarian B: Please bring your library card in person to the Circulation Desk on the 1st floor of the library. By the way, have you returned all of the books that you have checked out?

Alumnus A: No, not yet. I still have two of them with me.

Librarian B: Then please bring the books along. You must return them; otherwise, we cannot give you the refund.

Alumnus A: What about the receipt? Should I bring it with me? I probably can't find it.

Librarian B: No, you don't need it. Just return your library card. The fact that the Alumni Library Card was issued is proof that the security deposit was paid.

Alumnus A: May I take care of this on the weekend?

Librarian B: Sure, anytime the library is open. We are open on weekends.

Alumnus A: Thanks a lot!

Librarian B: No problem!

Unit 3.2 借還資料

3.2.1 辦理外借手續
情境：A同學抱了10本想要借的書到流通台。

A同學：麻煩一下，我要借這些書。請問我可以借多久？
B館員：您可以借4個禮拜，如果沒有人預約，還可以續借兩個禮拜。請給我您的證件。
A同學：好的，在這裡。
B館員：這些書3月21號到期。
A同學：謝謝。
B館員：不客氣。

Unit 3.2 Borrow or Return Library Materials

3.2.1 Borrow Library Materials
Situation: Student A walks up to the Circulation Desk with ten books to check out.

Student A: Excuse me. I'd like to check out these books. How long can I keep them?
Librarian B: OK. The loan period is 4 weeks. If no one places a hold on a checked out book, you may renew it for another 2 weeks. May I have your student ID card?
Student A: Sure, here it is.
Librarian B: Okay, they will be due on March 21st.
Student A: Thanks.
Librarian B: You're welcome.

Unit 3.2 借還資料

3.2.2 借閱冊數上限
情境：A同學最近因為寫報告，連續幾天到圖書館借書，這一天他又搬了10幾本書到流通台要辦借書手續。

A同學：麻煩一下，我要借這些書。
B館員：好的。……可是依照電腦的紀錄，您已經借了24本，因為大學部同學借書冊數的上限是30本，所以今天您只能再借6本。
A同學：可是我最近有3篇報告要趕，這些書都是我需要的，不能例外嗎？
B館員：很抱歉，這是圖書館的規定。
A同學：為什麼圖書館要規定借書冊數的上限呢？
B館員：我們圖書館的藏書並不像國外一些大型圖書館那麼多，為了顧及不同讀者的需求及權益，也考慮到公平性，所以才有這樣的規定。
A同學：那麼是不是可以考慮以後將大學部同學的上限提高到40冊？
B館員：我們會列入考慮，未來如果有更多同學有這樣的需求時，我們會考慮修訂借書冊數的上限。
A同學：好吧，那麼我今天只借這6本。其他我不借的書需要拿回書庫嗎？
B館員：不用，交給我就可以了。書借好了，您的書5月24日到期。
A同學：謝謝。
B館員：不客氣。

Unit 3.2 Borrow or Return Library Materials

3.2.2 Maximum Number of Checkouts

Situation: With a number of term papers to write Student A has recently been coming to the library to check out a number of library materials. Today he pulls another ten books from the library stacks to check out at the Circulation Desk.

Student A: Excuse me. I'd like to check out these books.
Librarian B: Okay, let me see. You have already checked out 24 books on your library account. Since the maximum is 30 checkouts for undergraduates you can borrow only 6 more items.
Student A: But, I need these 10 books because I have 3 term papers to finish up. Are there any exceptions to this?
Librarian B: I'm sorry. There are no exceptions. This is the policy.
Student A: Why does the library set a limit on the number of checkouts?
Librarian B: Well, our collection, unlike some libraries overseas, is not extensive enough to allow unlimited checkouts. In order to meet various needs of our patrons, as well as in the interest of fairness, the library found it necessary to establish this type of policy.
Student A: I see. Then, is it possible in the future to raise the maximum number to 40 items for the undergrads?
Librarian B: Sure, we will consider revising this policy if more undergraduates express this need as you have done.
Student A: Okay. Then I'll check out these 6 books today. Shall I put the other books back in the stacks?
Librarian B: No, you don't have to do that. Just leave them with me. Alright, all set. Here you are. They will be due on May 24th.
Student A: Thanks a lot.
Librarian B: Sure, you're welcome.

Unit 3.2 借還資料

3.2.3 郵寄還書
情境：A同學暑假回到台北家中，才發現忘了在回家前把即將到期的書歸還圖書館。如果拖到開學再還，一定會累積一大筆逾期罰款，因此打電話到圖書館詢問。

B館員：愛河大學圖書館，您好。
A同學：對不起，我想請問一下，可以用郵寄的方式還書嗎？我有3本書明天到期，因為我人已經回到台北的家，要到開學才會回學校，如果那時候再還書，一定要繳很多罰款。
B館員：可以的，您需要把書包好，以免在寄運的途中受損。另外，請記得收件人一定要註明是圖書館，以避免遞送時發生錯誤，我們接到後就會處理。
A同學：可是我要怎麼繳罰款？
B館員：您開學時再來繳就可以了，如果我們這幾天收到您寄來的書，您需要繳的金額應該不會太多。
A同學：謝謝，我會儘快寄來。
B館員：不客氣。

Unit 3.2 Borrow or Return Library Materials

3.2.3 Return Checkouts in the Mail

Situation: Student A forgot to return some library books that will be due soon before going back home to Taipei for summer break. If she returns the books after the new semester starts, a great deal of overdue fines will have accumulated. She calls the library and asks what to do about this situation.

Librarian B: Hello, this is Love River University Library. Can I help you?

Student A: Hello! I'm wondering if I can return books in the mail. I have 3 books due tomorrow, but I'm in Taipei right now and won't be returning to Love River U until the new semester starts. If I return the books at that time, I'll have to pay a lot in overdue fines.

Librarian B: Sure, you may return books in the mail. Please pack the books carefully in order to avoid damage during shipping. Also, please address the package to the library so that it will be delivered to us right away. We will take care of it once we receive the package.

Student A: But how do I pay the overdue fines?

Librarian B: You can pay them when you get back to school. The overdue fines won't be too much if we receive your package in the next few days.

Student A: Great! I'll send them over soon. Thanks!

Librarian B: You're welcome.

Unit 3.2 借還資料

3.2.4 誤將他館的書還到自己學校的圖書館
情境：圖書館工作人員在處理還書時，發現還書箱裡有市立圖書館的書，B館員打電話聯絡市立圖書館，市立圖書館A館員接聽電話。

A館員：市立圖書館，您好。
B館員：您好，這裡是愛河大學圖書館，我姓B。有一件事情要請教您，有一位讀者誤將向　貴館借的書投到我們的還書箱裡，請問　貴館通常怎麼處理這樣的問題？
A館員：您好，能不能請您告訴我那本書的書名和登錄號，讓我查一下是哪一位讀者借的書，我再聯絡他到　貴館把書拿回來。
B館員：好的，這本書的書名是 *The World Is Flat*，登錄號是W0958458。
A館員：謝謝。嗯，如果我連絡到那位讀者，要請他到　貴館的什麼地方拿回這本書呢？
B館員：嗯，請他到愛河大學圖書館1樓流通台，說明要拿市立圖書館的書，我們的服務人員就會把書交給他了。
A館員：好的，謝謝。
B館員：不客氣。

Unit 3.2 Borrow or Return Library Materials

3.2.4 Drop Books from Other Libraries in the Book Return by Mistake

Situation: A library staff finds a book from the City Library in the book drop while he is checking in books. Therefore, Librarian B gives a call to the City Library, where Librarian A picks up the phone.

Librarian A: Hello, City Library, how can I help you?

Librarian B: Hi, this is B from Love River University Library. I'm calling to let you know that we just found one of your library's books in our book drop. I'd like to make sure how you deal with this problem in your library.

Librarian A: Hi. Would you please tell me the title and the barcode of the book? Then I can find out who checked out this item and I'll contact the patron to have him or her fetch the book.

Librarian B: Sure. The title is *The World Is Flat*. The barcode is W0958458.

Librarian A: Thank you. OK, when I contact the patron, where in the Love River University Library should I tell the patron to go to pick up the book?

Librarian B: Please tell the patron to come to the Circulation Desk on the 1st floor of the library. The patron should inform our staff that he or she has come to collect a book from the City Library collection and we will give it back to the patron.

Librarian A: Great and thank you very much.

Librarian B: You're welcome.

Unit 3.2 借還資料

3.2.5 誤將自己學校圖書館的書還到他館
情境：A館員接到B大學圖書館流通館員打來的電話，說他們在還書箱中收到愛河大學圖書館的書，經查證後，A館員確定該書是C同學借出，於是打電話給C同學。

A館員：請問C同學在嗎？我是愛河大學圖書館的A館員。
C同學：是的，我就是。
A館員：是這樣的，剛才B大學圖書館打電話來，說是收到一本您向我們圖書館借的 *Kite Runner*，他們麻煩您找時間去把書拿回來。
C同學：啊，一定是我上次去還另外一本書的時候，不小心把這本書也放進他們的還書箱了，抱歉。請問我現在要怎麼辦？
A館員：您可以直接到B大學圖書館的流通台，告訴他們您是愛河大學的學生，來拿一本還錯的書，再告訴他們書名，他們就會把書拿給您。
C同學：可以請他們直接把書寄回來嗎？
A館員：很抱歉，B大學圖書館和我們目前都無法提供這樣的服務。您必須親自去取書。
C同學：好的，那我知道了，謝謝您。
A館員：不客氣。

Unit 3.2 Borrow or Return Library Materials

3.2.5 Return Library Checkouts to Other Libraries by Mistake

Situation: Librarian A receives a call from a circulation librarian at the B University Library, who explains that they found a Love River University Library book in their book drop. Librarian A checks the library system to find the borrower's account and then makes a call to Student C, the borrower.

Librarian A: Hello, may I talk to Mr. C? I'm calling from Love River University Library.
Student C: Yes, speaking.
Librarian A: Hi, this is A, a librarian at Love River University Library. I'm calling to let you know that you returned the book *Kite Runner* in the B University Library book drop. A librarian there called to let us know. You'll need to go there to pick up the book.
Student C: Oops, I'm sorry. It must have happened the day I returned an interlibrary loan book borrowed from that library. I guess I mistakenly dropped *Kite Runner*. What should I do about it?
Librarian A: Please go to B University Library and collect the book at the Circulation Desk by telling the library staff you are a student from Love River, and you've mistakenly returned a book, *Kite Runner*.
Student C: Is it possible to ask them to send the book back in the mail?
Librarian A: I'm sorry. Our library and the B University Library are not yet offering this service. You'll have to go fetch the book in person.
Student C: Alright, I see. Thanks!
Librarian A: You're welcome.

Unit 3.3 續借

情境：A教授想要續借他明天到期的書，打電話到圖書館詢問辦理方式。

B館員：喂，愛河大學圖書館，您好！
A教授：您好，我是英文系的A老師，我有10本書明天到期，我想續借。請問：我要把書全部帶到圖書館辦續借嗎？還是有其他的方式續借？
B館員：您好，您不必把書帶來圖書館續借，您可以直接在線上自行續借未到期的書。我可以告訴您怎麼做，您手邊有電腦可以上網嗎？
A教授：太好了，請稍等一下，我開一下瀏覽器。
B館員：好的，不急，您慢慢來。
A教授：好了，請問要怎麼做？
B館員：您先開啟圖書館的網站，在首頁右上方，您會看到一個「借閱查詢」的選項，請點選這個超連結。
A教授：好，現在出現要輸入帳號密碼的畫面。
B館員：是的。請您輸入您的愛河大學教職員證號，密碼的預設值是您的出生年月日共8碼，例如：20080509。
A教授：我輸入好了。
B館員：您在畫面上有沒有看到一個「目前已借出XX本」的選項？請點選這個超連結。
A教授：有，現在畫面出現的是我借書的清單。
B館員：好的，在這個畫面上方有一個續借的功能，您要先勾選您要續借的資料，然後再點選「續借選取館藏」，畫面就會出現這些書續借之後的到期日了。
A教授：好的，我已經續借好了。以後如果我要續借，必須要在書到期的幾天前才可以上網續借？
B館員：到期日前7天就可以辦續借。不過，如果資料有人預約，您就一定

Unit 3.3 Renew Checkouts

Situation: Professor A calls the library to ask how to renew his library checkouts due tomorrow.

Librarian B: Hello, this is Love River University Library. May I help you?

Professor A: Hello, this is A from the English Department. I have 10 books due tomorrow and I'd like to renew them. Should I bring all of them to the library or is there another way to renew them?

Librarian B: Hi, Professor A, you don't have to bring the books to the library. You may renew them online. I can tell you how to do it. Do you have access to the Internet from your current location?

Professor A: Oh, that's great. Yes, I do. Please hold on a second. I'll open the browser.

Librarian B: Okay, take your time.

Professor A: All set. I'm ready. So, what should I do?

Librarian B: Please go to the library website. On the upper right hand side of the screen, do you see an icon indicating "View Your Account"? Please click on it.

Professor A: Okay, now a small window pops up, asking me to log in with an ID and a password.

Librarian B: Good. Please type in your Love River faculty ID number as the ID and your date of birth like this 20080509 (year, month, day) as the default password.

Professor A: Okay, I'm done.

Librarian B: Great. Now, do you see a link saying "Items Currently Checked Out" on the menu? If you do, please click on it.

Professor A: Yes, it shows the list of books I have checked out.

Librarian B: Right. On the upper part of the window, you'll see a button

　　　　要依照到期日還書了。另外要提醒您，依規定只能續借兩次。
A教授：好的，我知道了，謝謝。
B館員：不客氣。

labelled "Renew." Please select the items that you want to renew and then click "Renew the Selected." It will show you the new due date.

Professor A: Alright, it works now. So, how long before the due date can I renew books online?

Librarian B: Well, you may renew checkouts 7 days before the due date. However, if someone else places a hold on a checked out item, you'll have to return the item by its due date. By the way, you may only renew books twice.

Professor A: I see. Thank you for your assistance.

Librarian B: You're welcome.

Unit 3.4 預約

3.4.1 線上預約
情境：A教授到愛河大學圖書館詢問如何預約外借中的書。

A教授：請問一下，我想要借*Gone With the Wind*這本書，但是電腦畫面上顯示03-12-2009，我要如何借到這本書？
B館員：這本書已經外借了，畫面上顯示的日期是這本書的到期日；您可以預約這本書，如果沒有人排在你前面預約的話，這本書還回來的時候，您就可以借了。
A教授：那我需要填什麼表格嗎？
B館員：不用的，您只要告訴我您的教職員證號，我馬上就可以幫您預約！
A教授：太好了！那我也可以打電話預約嗎？
B館員：當然可以，另外您也可以在線上進行預約。
（館員示範如何在電腦上操作預約）
A教授：謝謝！我還有個問題，請問我怎麼知道預約的書已經可以借了呢？
B館員：當您預約的書回來時，系統就會自動發信到您的電子信箱，通知您預約書已到，到時候您再帶教職員證到流通台辦理借書就可以了！不過要提醒您的是，您必須在通知信發出後5天內來取書，過了5天，我們就不再為您保留。到時候書可能回到書庫，或者由下一個預約者借出了。
A教授：好的，我了解了，真是謝謝您！
B館員：不客氣！

Unit 3.4 Place a Hold

3.4.1 Place a Hold Online

Situation: Professor A walks into the library and asks how to place a hold on library items.

Professor A: Excuse me. I'd like to borrow the book *Gone With the Wind*, which shows the date March 12th, 2009 in the library catalog. What should I do to check out this item?

Librarian B: This item is already checked out; the date in the catalog is when the book is due back. You may place a hold on it and if you're the first person then you'll get the book right after it's been returned.

Professor A: Then do I need to fill out a form?

Librarian B: No, please tell me your Love River ID number and I'll place a hold on this item for you.

Professor A: Great. May I also phone the library to place a hold?

Librarian B: Sure and in addition, you may also do it online. Let me show you.

(Librarian B demonstrates how to place a hold online.)

Professor A: Thanks. I have another question. How will I know when the item I have requested is available for me to pick up?

Librarian B: Oh, when we check in the item, the system will automatically send you an email message. When you receive the message, you may come to the Library Circulation Desk to check out the book. Please remember to bring your Love River ID card with you. Let me also remind you that you need to pick up the book within 5 days of receiving the notice. Otherwise the book will be reshelved to the stacks, or the next patron who place a hold on it will be able to check it out.

Professor A: I see, thanks a lot!

Librarian B: You're welcome.

Unit 3.4 預約

3.4.2 無法預約,疑難排除
情境:A教授在網路上預約不成功,打電話詢問愛河大學圖書館。

B館員:愛河大學圖書館流通台,您好!
A教授:您好,我是英文系B老師,我想在網路上預約一本書,可是都不成功,請問為什麼會這樣呢?
B館員:讓我幫你查一下。請問您的教職員證號是?
A教授:287426621,謝謝。
B館員:電腦紀錄上顯示您還有一本 *In Cold Blood* 逾期沒還。
A教授:讓我想想…啊!對了,那本書還放在研究室。那我知道了,只要是有逾期紀錄還沒處理的情況,我就不能上網預約了,對吧!?
B館員:是的,您必須歸還逾期圖書,並且繳清罰款後,才能在線上預約!
A教授:那我明白了,謝謝!我會趕快去還書!
B館員:不客氣!

Unit 3.4 Place a Hold

3.4.2 Problems with Online Reservation
Situation: Professor A makes a call to the library because he was unsuccessful in placing a hold online.

Librarian B: Hi, Love River University Library Circulation Desk. May I help you?
Professor A: Hello, this is A from the English Department. I'd like to place an online hold for a book in the library catalog, but I can't make it work. I'm wondering what's wrong.
Librarian B: Let me check. May I have your faculty ID number?
Professor A: Sure, it's 287426621. Thanks!
Librarian B: Well, it shows in the system that you have one book overdue. The title is *In Cold Blood*.
Professor A: Oh, yes, right, that book. I left it in my office. So, this means if I have overdue materials, the system will not allow me to place a hold online. Right?
Librarian B: That's correct. You'll have to return the overdue item and pay the fines before you can place a hold online.
Professor A: Okay, I see. I'll return the book as soon as I can. Thanks.
Librarian B: Sure, no problem!

Unit 3.5 催還

情境：A同學正在撰寫一篇研究論文，急需閱讀一本關於公共衛生方面的書。他查過館藏目錄，這本書正借出中，因此他來到圖書館，詢問館員是否可以知道是誰借的，他希望請借書的人將書借他看幾天。

A同學：請問一下，如果我想借的書被其他人借走了，而我急著要看這本書，我可不可以知道是那位老師或同學借的？我想請他借我看幾天，我看完馬上還他。

B館員：對不起，為了保障個人隱私，我們不能告訴您這本書是誰借的，圖書館也沒有權力要借書的人在到期日之前將書拿來還。不過圖書館有「預約催還」的政策，如果您上網去預約這本書，假使它的到期日超過14天以後，系統會將它的到期日提早到今天算起的第14天；如果它的到期日離現在不到14天，系統就不會催還。請問這本書的書名是什麼？我查一下它什麼時候到期。

A同學：*International Public Health: Diseases, Programs, Systems and Policies*。

B館員：請等我查一下……，這本書的到期日是5月23日，如果您今天上網去預約這本書，系統會將它的到期日提早到今天算起的第14天，也就是5月15日，如果他準時還書，您就可以提早看到書。

A同學：有沒有更快的方法可以看到這本書？

B館員：當然，我們可以試試看其他的圖書館有沒有這本書，您再等我查一下……，C大學和D大學圖書館都有這本書，不過C大學圖書館的也是借出中，如果向D大學圖書館借，您必須負擔每本200元的郵寄及服務費用。

A同學：好吧，那麼我還是上網預約，等我們學校的這一本吧，謝謝。

B館員：不客氣。

chapter 3

Unit 3.5 Recall Borrowed Materials

Situation: Student A is working on a research paper and desperately needs a book about public health. After searching the library catalog and learning that the book is already checked out, Student A comes to the library and asks the librarian about the patron who borrowed the book. He wants to ask the patron to let him use the book for a few days.

Student A: Excuse me. Could you do me a favor? I need a book badly, but it has been checked out. Can I find out who borrowed the book? I want to contact the borrower and ask him or her to let me use the book for a few days.

Librarian B: For privacy reasons I'm unable to tell you the borrower's identity. Also, the library doesn't have the right to ask the borrower to return the material before the due date. However, we do provide patrons with a way to request materials that have been checked out. If you place a recall on an item, the library system will notify the borrower to return the book 14 days before the due date. However, when the due date of the item is less than 14 days from the date the recall is placed, the due date will not be adjusted. What's the title of the book you want? Let me check the due date.

Student A: Sure, the title is *International Public Health: Diseases, Programs, Systems and Policies.*

Librarian B: Okay, just a moment please. This book is due on May 23rd. If you place a recall on it, the due date will be changed to 14 days from today, which would be May 15th. You'll be able to get the book then if the borrower returns it on time.

Student A: Is there any way to get the book faster?

Librarian B: Yes. We can see if this book is available in other libraries. It'll be just a moment while I check. Well, both the C University and the D University libraries have this book. However, the one in the C University Library is also currently checked out. You may get this book from the D University Library through interlibrary loan. However, this is a fee-based service. You'll need to pay 200 dollars for delivery and service fees.

Student A: Well, then I'll place a recall on our library's copy instead. Thanks.

Librarian B: Alright. You're welcome.

Unit 3.6 逾期

3.6.1 沒收到圖書館電子郵件通知
情境：A同學發現手邊借的3本書已經逾期，回想起來，自己並不曾接到圖書館寄發的通知，因此在還書時詢問館員。

A同學：請問為什麼我一直沒有收到圖書館寄的email？
B館員：您是用學校電算中心提供的email帳號？還是市面上的免費電子信箱？
A同學：我是用Yahoo的email帳號。
B館員：圖書館是以學校email帳號寄發通知，您如果不是使用學校提供的email帳號就有可能收不到圖書館的通知。因為如果您用的是像Yahoo、PChome、Hotmail這些免費email帳號，他們常會將圖書館送出的信件誤判為垃圾郵件，而送到「垃圾信件匣」。為了避免發生這樣的情形，建議您養成習慣，時常上圖書館網站查詢自己的借閱狀況，看看是不是有快到期的書，以免會有逾期罰款。
A同學：原來是這樣，那麼我這次是不是可以不用繳罰款？下次我會特別注意。
B館員：很抱歉，圖書館是以書的到期日，而不是讀者有沒有收到通知來作為計算罰款的依據，一來因為收不到圖書館email的原因很多，二來記得還書日期是借書人的責任，圖書館的通知只是提醒的作用，所以我們沒有辦法取消您的逾期罰款。
A同學：好吧，那麼我要還這3本書，請問罰款是多少？
B館員：讓我查一下，……，3本書逾期3天，1本1天罰款5元，3本3天一共是45元。
A同學：這裡是50元。
B館員：好的，找您5元，這是您的收據。

chapter 3

Unit 3.6 Overdues

3.6.1 Library Notices via Email Not Received

Situation: Student A discovers that she has 3 overdue books. She can't recall receiving any library notices reminding her of the due dates for these three books. When she returns the overdue books to the library she asks a librarian why she didn't receive any reminders.

Student A: Excuse me. I'm wondering why I didn't receive any library notices in my email.

Librarian B: Well, do you use our university email service or a free commercial one?

Student A: I use Yahoo.

Librarian B: Library notices are sent via the university email service. If you don't use the Love River email service, problems may occur. When you use free commercial email services such as Yahoo, PChome or Hotmail, library email messages might be spammed. To avoid the problem of not receiving library notices, I highly recommend that you check your circulation records from your library account. That way you can determine the due dates of your checkouts and avoid overdue fines.

Student A: I see. I'll do that next time. But, may I have these overdue fines waived? I'll pay more attention next time.

Librarian B: I'm really sorry about this. However, the overdue fines are charged based on the due dates regardless of whether the patron has received a library notice. There are various reasons for patrons not receiving emails. Besides, library notices are sent as a courtesy to our patrons; it is the patron's responsibility to return the library materials on time. Therefore, your overdue

A同學：謝謝。
B館員：不客氣。

fines can't be waived. I'm sorry!

Student A: That's OK. So, how much do I owe for these 3 books?

Librarian B: Wait one moment and I'll check. You have 3 overdue books. Each will be charged 5 dollars per day and they are now 3 days overdue. Therefore, your overdue fines total 45 dollars.

Student A: Alright. Here's 50 dollars.

Librarian B: Here is your change, 5 dollars, and your receipt.

Student A: Thank you.

Librarian B: You're welcome.

Unit 3.6 逾期

3.6.2 逾期處理費
情境：A同學有5本書逾期了，到愛河大學圖書館詢問相關問題。

A同學：您好，我借的這5本書逾期了，請問會有罰款嗎？
B館員：讓我先幫您還書，請您稍等一下。紀錄上顯示您的書逾期1天，沒有罰款。
A同學：可是我的書已經逾期了，不是嗎？
B館員：因為系統設有3天的寬限期，所以您這次逾期的書不需要繳罰款。
A同學：喔……！也就是說如果我超過3天就會有罰款囉？
B館員：是的，不但有罰款，而且罰款金額會回溯至逾期的第1天，例如您的書是1月1日到期，您到1月4日才拿來還，1本書的罰款1天是5元，逾期3天，那就是15元。
A同學：那我知道了，謝謝！
B館員：不客氣。

Unit 3.6 Overdues

3.6.2 Library Overdue Fines

Situation: Student A has 5 overdue books. He raises some questions regarding the overdue policy while he is in the Love River University Library.

Student A: Excuse me. I have 5 overdue books. Here they are. Will I have to pay any overdue fines?

Librarian B: Well, let me check them in for you first. Please wait one moment. The system shows that these books are overdue by one day, so there is no overdue fine.

Student A: Great! But they are overdue, aren't they?

Librarian B: Yes, they are. But there is a 3-day grace period, so you do not have any overdue fines this time.

Student A: OK, in other words, it means that there will be overdue fines if I return books after the 3-day grace period?

Librarian B: Exactly. The overdue fines start accumulating the day after the due date. For example, if the material you checked out is due on January 1st, and you return it on January 4th, you'll be charged 15 dollars because the fine is 5 dollars per day per item and it was returned 3 days late.

Student A: Oh, I see. Thanks!

Librarian B: Sure, no problem!

Unit 3.7 遺失、損壞圖書資料

3.7.1 遺失圖書
情境：A同學遺失了一本向圖書館借的書，她來到流通台詢問該怎麼辦。

A同學：請問如果把圖書館的書弄丟了，要怎麼辦？
B館員：根據圖書館管理辦法的規定，您可以購買原書的同版本或較新版本，另外加上賠償處理費，親自來圖書館辦理就可以。如果這本書已經絕版，市面上買不到了，您必須依照原書的定價賠償，再加上賠償處理費。當然，如果這本書已經逾期，逾期處理費也是要付的。請問您遺失的是哪一本書？
A同學：是 *Drama and Theatre Arts*。
B館員：讓我查一下您的借書紀錄，……*Drama and Theatre Arts*，作者是 R.A. Banks 和 Pauline Marson，1998年8月出版的。
A同學：應該是吧。
B館員：這本書的定價是美金85元，以現在的匯率計算，大約是3,000元台幣。您要不要去書店或上亞馬遜網路書店（Amazon.com）看看可不可以買到這本書？
A同學：好貴喲，請問賠二手書可以嗎？
B館員：一定要狀況良好，而且內頁沒有劃線或筆跡的二手書才可以。
A同學：請問賠償處理費怎麼算？
B館員：每件資料200元。
A同學：好的，我現在去試試看能不能買到書，那麼逾期罰款還會累積嗎？
B館員：不會，既然您已經告訴我們書已經遺失，逾期處理費只會計算到今天，請放心。不過您要盡快處理書籍遺失賠償的部分，否則會影響您日後借書的權益。
A同學：好的，我會先去一般書店和網路書店找找看，謝謝。
B館員：不客氣。

chapter 3

Unit 3.7 Lost or Damaged Library Materials

3.7.1 Deal with Lost Books
Situation: Student A loses a book that she borrowed from the library. She comes to the Circulation Desk to ask what to do about this situation.

Student A: Excuse me. I have a question for you. What should I do if I have lost a library book?
Librarian B: Well, according to the library's policy you may buy an exact copy of the same title or a newer edition, return it in person to the library and then pay the replacement processing fee. If the title is out of print and completely unavailable, you'll have to pay the list price of the title and an additional replacement processing fee. In addition, if the checkout is already overdue, you must pay the overdue fines as well. May I ask which book you lost?
Student A: Sure, the title is *Drama and Theatre Arts*.
Librarian B: Just a second please. Let me take a look at your circulation record. Ok. This book, *Drama and Theatre Arts*, was written by R. A. Banks and Pauline Marson and published in August 1998. Right?
Student A: Yes, I think so.
Librarian B: Well, the list price of this book is 85 US dollars. Based on the current exchange rate, it will cost around 3,000 dollars. Why don't you check with a bookstore or online with Amazon.com to see if you can purchase this book?
Student A: Wow, it's really expensive. How about a used book? Is that acceptable?
Librarian B: Well, it must be in great condition. No highlighting or note-

taking marks inside the book.

Student A: Alright. Then what about the replacement processing fee? How much is that?

Librarian B: It is 200 dollars per item.

Student A: Well, I'll try to see if I can get this book. However, will the overdue fines keep accumulating?

Librarian B: No, overdue fines stop accumulating once you have reported the book as lost. Don't worry about the overdue fines. But, you have to take care of the replacement as soon as possible. Otherwise, your borrowing privileges might be suspended.

Student AC: Okay, I see. I'll check with both traditional and online bookstores for an acceptable replacment. Thank you!

Librarian B: You're welcome.

Unit 3.7 遺失、損壞圖書資料

3.7.2 找到遺失的圖書
情境：A同學在家裡整理房間時發現一本很久以前向圖書館借的書，因為當初一直找不到，已經賠了書款，他心想既然書已經找到，不知道是不是可以把書還給圖書館，拿回當初賠的書款，因此來到圖書館流通台。

A同學：請問一下，如果已經賠了書款，後來才找到了那本書，圖書館是不是可以退回我原先賠的錢？
B館員：很抱歉，可能沒有辦法。您當初賠的錢已經繳到學校財務部門，所有手續都已經完成。
A同學：可是我如果把這本書還給你們，你們就可以省了再買這本書的錢和時間。
B館員：這個我們了解，可是這是另外一回事。如果您願意，我們歡迎您將這本書捐給圖書館，畢竟這本書已經經過我們圖書館編目處理，很快就可以上架，讓其他讀者使用。當然既然您已經賠了書款，這本書是屬於您的，您有權決定是不是要捐出來，但是很抱歉，一旦書款繳到財務部門，是沒有辦法拿回來的。
A同學：好吧，那我還是留著這本書好了。
B館員：謝謝您。

Unit 3.7 Lost or Damaged Library Materials

3.7.2 Lost Books Found

Situation: While cleaning his room, Student A finds a book that he checked out from the library a long time ago. He was unable to find it at the time and therefore he had already paid the replacement fee. He asks a librarian at the Circulation Desk if it is possible to return this book and get the replacement fee refunded.

Student A: Excuse me. I have a question about the replacement fee policy. If I find the book that I thought I'd lost after I'd already paid the replacement fee, is it possible to get the money back?

Librarian B: I'm sorry, but I'm afraid not. The replacement fee has already been sent to the University Treasurer's Office, and all the procedures are completed.

Student A: But, if I return the book, the library could save money and time by not processing a new copy of it.

Librarian B: We understand, but that's another issue. If you'd like you may return this book as a donation. After all, this book is cataloged and ready for use; we would be able to shelve it immediately. However, since you have already paid the replacement fee, this book belongs to you now. You have the right to decide whether to donate it. I'm really sorry about the refund. Once your payment has been transferred to the Treasurer's Office, it is not possible to get a refund.

Student A: Well, then I'll keep the book for myself.
Librarian B: Alright. Thank you!

Unit 3.7 遺失、損壞圖書資料

3.7.3 損壞及污染資料
情境：A同學一邊喝咖啡，一邊看他從圖書館借來的書，不小心將咖啡灑在書上，他到流通台詢問該怎麼辦。

A同學：請問一下，我不小心把這本書弄髒了，這樣可以直接歸還嗎？
B館員：可以讓我看看嗎？這本書有好幾頁都沾到咖啡，未來會影響讀者閱讀，也會有保存上的問題，很抱歉，您需要賠償一本相同的書。
A同學：請問要怎麼賠？
B館員：根據圖書館管理辦法的規定，如果您可以買到一本相同的書，或者是這本書較新的版本，就可以直接賠書，另外再付賠償處理費就可以了。但是如果這本書已經絕版、買不到，就需要按定價賠償書款，並且另外付賠償處理費。
A同學：請問這本書的定價是多少？
B館員：通常封底或版權頁上會有，……，這本書的定價是台幣850元。
A同學：請問賠償處理費怎麼算？
B館員：每件資料200元。
A同學：這本書後天就到期了，如果我在後天之前買不到書怎麼辦？
B館員：沒關係，因為您在書到期前就來告訴我們書遺失了，所以我們會在系統中註明目前是「賠書中」，您就不必付逾期處理費。
A同學：如果我賠了書，這本受損的書就是我的了嗎？
B館員：當然，您現在就可以將污損的書帶回去。
A同學：好吧，我試試看能不能買到這本書，謝謝。
B館員：不客氣。

Unit 3.7 Lost or Damaged Library Materials

3.7.3 Deal with Damaged Books
Situation: Student A drinks coffee while he is reading a book borrowed from the library. Unfortunately, he spills some coffee on the book. He goes to the Library Circulation Desk to ask a librarian what he should do.

Student A: Excuse me. Due to my carelessness, this book was slightly damaged by a coffee-spill. May I return the book in this condition?

Librarian B: May I take a look at it please? Well, I see stains on several pages, and that will make it difficult for future patrons to read them. There is also the preservation issue. You'll need to replace it with a new copy. Sorry!

Student A: How do I go about replacing the book?

Librarian B: According to the library's policy, you may buy an exact copy or a newer edition of this title, and then pay the replacement processing fee. If the title is out of print then you'll pay the list price and also pay the processing fee.

Student A: Then, can you tell me the list price of this book?

Librarian B: Usually this information is available on the copyright page or on the back cover of the book. For example, this book costs 850 dollars.

Student A: OK. How much is the replacement processing fee?

Librarian B: It is 200 dollars per item.

Student A: This book will be due the day after tomorrow. What if I can't get a copy from a bookstore by then?

Librarian B: Don't worry about the due date. We will change the status to "Replacement" because you reported it before the due date. So,

chapter 3

there will be no overdue fines in this case.

Student A: Well, if I get a replacement copy to compensate for the damaged book, may I have the damaged one back?

Librarian B: Of course, you may have the book now.

Student A: Alright, I'll see if I can purchase a copy from a bookstore. Thanks!

Librarian B: Sure, you're welcome.

Unit 3.7 遺失、損壞圖書資料

3.7.4 賠書

情境：A同學在書店買到他遺失的*When Is a Planet Not a Planet?: the Story of Pluto*，因此拿到圖書館流通台辦理賠書手續。

A同學：對不起，請問一下，幾天前我來詢問過關於賠書的事，因為我已經在書店買到先前這本我遺失的書，不知道接下來要怎麼辦？

B館員：是的，麻煩您先給我您的學號。

A同學：219810078。

B館員：謝謝，您遺失的是2007年版的*When Is a Planet Not a Planet?: the Story of Pluto*，現在您買的這本也是2007年版的，沒問題，賠書的部分這樣就可以了。您另外還需要付資料的賠償處理費200元及逾期處理費20元，因為當初您告訴我們書遺失時，那本書已經逾期4天了，所以一共是220元。

A同學：好的，這裡是220元。

B館員：這是您的收據。

A同學：謝謝。

B館員：不客氣。

Unit 3.7 Lost or Damaged Library Materials

3.7.4 Replace Lost or Damaged Books

Situation: Student A buys a copy of the book, *When Is a Planet Not a Planet?: the Story of Pluto*, which is the one he lost from the Love River University Library collection. Then, he takes the book to the Library Circulation Desk to take care of the replacement process.

Student A: Excuse me. A couple of days ago I reported a book lost and then I bought a replacement copy in a bookstore. What should I do next?

Librarian B: Alright. May I have your Love River ID number?

Student A: Sure, it's 219810078.

Librarian B: OK, thanks! The book you have here is the same edition as the one you reported lost, *When Is a Planet Not a Planet?: the Story of Pluto*, 2007 edition. It's not a problem to substitute this new copy for the lost one, but you'll still have to pay the processing charge of 200 dollars for this item. Plus, there is an overdue fine of 20 dollars because you reported the loss after the book was already 4 days overdue. Therefore, your total payment is 220 dollars.

Student A: Alright. Here it is, 220 dollars.

Librarian B: Thank you! This is your receipt.

Student A: OK, thanks!

Librarian B: You're welcome.

Unit 3.7 遺失、損壞圖書資料

3.7.5 賠書款

情境：A教授遺失了向圖書館借的2001年出版的第1版 *Writing for Visual Media*，由於這本書2006年又出了第2版，她在實體書店和網路書店都買不到第1版，而第2版的價格比第1版高出許多，A教授認為不如直接賠償書款，因此她到流通台洽詢賠償書款的事。

A教授：請問一下，我買不到遺失的書，要直接賠錢，應該怎麼辦？
B館員：好的，麻煩您先給我您的教職員證號。
A教授：294360079。
B館員：您遺失的是Focal Press在2001年出版的*Writing for Visual Media*嗎？
A教授：是的。
B館員：它的定價是台幣1,334元。
A教授：除了書款，我還需要付其他費用嗎？
B館員：您還需要付賠書處理費200元，連同書款，一共是1,534元，您的書沒有逾期，所以不用付罰款。
A教授：這裡是2,000元。
B館員：謝謝，我還要找您466元，這是您賠書款的收據。
A教授：謝謝。
B館員：謝謝。

Unit 3.7 Lost or Damaged Library Materials

3.7.5 Replacement Bill

Situation: Professor A loses the book *Writing for Visual Media*, which was a first edition published in 2001. Since the most current edition is the second one published in 2006, she was unable to obtain a copy of the first edition from a local bookstore or from an online bookstore. However, the cost of the second edition is much more expensive than the first edition. Professor A prefers to pay the replacement fee and asks the librarian at the Circulation Desk about the procedure.

Professor A: Excuse me. I have a question. I can't get a new copy of the book I lost. I'd like to pay the replacement fee instead. What should I do?
Librarian B: Well, may I have your Love River ID number?
Professor A: Alright, it's 294360079.
Librarian B: According to your patron record, the book you lost is *Writing for Visual Media* published by Focal Press in 2001. Is this correct?
Professor A: Yes.
Librarian B: Okay, then the price of this book is 1,334 dollars.
Professor A: Is this the only charge I pay? Are there any other fees?
Librarian B: Well, besides the replacement fee, you must pay the processing charge of 200 dollars. The total is 1,534 dollars. Since it wasn't overdue, you have no overdue fines to pay. That's all.
Professor A: Okay, Here is 2,000 dollars.
Librarian B: Thank you. Just a second please. I'll give you change 466 dollars, and the receipt.
Professor A: Thank you!
Librarian B: Sure, thank you!

Unit 3.7 遺失、損壞圖書資料

3.7.6 遺失視聽資料
情境：A教授借了一片DVD在課堂上播放，下課時他忘了將DVD從電腦中取出，再回到教室時，那片DVD已經不見了，他到媒體資源中心詢問要怎麼辦。

A教授：嗨，我是通識教育中心的A老師，我想請問一下，我把向媒體資源中心借的DVD弄丟了，現在要怎麼辦？
B館員：很抱歉，如果將資料遺失了，您是需要賠償的。
A教授：即使DVD是因為教學使用而遺失也要賠償嗎？
B館員：是的，很抱歉，對圖書館而言，我們很難分辨老師借用資料的目的是教學用，還是休閒用，因此對教學或休閒使用，我們是一樣的處理原則。
A教授：那麼可以幫我查一下需要賠多少錢嗎？
B館員：好的，讓我查一下。這片DVD是公播版，價錢上比家用版貴。它的定價是4,500元，另外需要加收200元賠償處理費，所以一共是4,700元。
A教授：哇，真的很貴，圖書館為什麼一定要購買公播版呢？
B館員：因為學校是教育單位，老師在課堂上使用視聽資料的機率很高，圖書館購買公播版DVD，老師可以很放心地在教室播放而不會觸犯法律。
A教授：好吧，看來我只有賠償了。
B館員：日後如果您要讓同學觀看某一片DVD，另外一個做法是，您可以將那一片DVD設為課程指定參考資料，要求同學自己來媒體資源中心觀看，或者幾個同學借用團體欣賞室一起看，這樣或許可以減少將DVD借出圖書館而造成損壞或遺失的機會。
A教授：謝謝您的建議，全班一起觀看可以大家一起討論，不同做法各有

chapter 3

Unit 3.7 Lost or Damaged Library Materials

3.7.6 Lost Media Materials
Situation: Professor A checks out a DVD from the library for his class. He forgets to take the DVD with him after the class and when he returns to the classroom the DVD is gone. He comes to the Media Resources Center to report the loss and to ask what to do about it.

Professor A: Hi, I'm Professor A from the General Education Center. I lost a DVD borrowed from the Media Resources Center and would like to know what I should do about it.
Librarian B: Well, I'm sorry. Then you have to replace the lost item.
Professor A: Even though I used it for instructional purposes?
Librarian B: Yes. I'm sorry! It is difficult for the library to know whether the instructor checks out the audio-visual materials for instructional purposes or for personal leisure. Therefore, we set the same circulation policy no matter what the circumstances are.
Professor A: Alright, then what is the replacement fee?
Librarian B: Okay, one moment please. The DVD you lost had public performance rights. So the price is much higher than for DVDs licensed for home use. This one costs 4,500 dollars. In addition, there is a processing fee of 200 dollars. The total amount you need to pay is 4,700 dollars.
Professor A: Wow, that's really expensive! Why does the library must purchase DVDs with public performance rights?
Librarian B: Universities are educational institutions. It is very likely that an instructor will be using audio-visual materials in a public space, such as a classroom. We do not want to violate copyright law, so it is preferable that we have purchased public performance

　　　　利弊，我下次一定會小心使用。
B館員：您說得也是，這是您賠償費用的收據。
A教授：謝謝。那麼圖書館還會再買一片相同的DVD嗎？我以後上課可能還會需要。
B館員：會的，我們會試試看能不能買到。這樣就可以了，謝謝您。
A教授：謝謝。

rights for the materials.

Professor A: Alright. It looks like my only option is to replace the lost DVD with a new copy.

Librarian B: Well, in the future if you still want your students to watch a film, you may request the DVD as part of your course reserves. That way students can watch the film individually or as a small group in the Media Resources Center. This should reduce the chances of the DVD getting damaged or lost.

Professor A: Thank you for your suggestion! But I had planned for a group discussion after watching the film together in class. However, different approaches may have interesting results. I'll be more careful the next time that I play a DVD in a class.

Librarian B: Yes, that is a good idea. This is the receipt for your replacement and processing fees.

Professor A: Thanks! By the way, will you purchase another copy of the DVD I lost? I might need it for another class in the future.

Librarian B: We will try our best to get a copy of the title. Thank you!

Professor A: Thanks!

Unit 3.8 宣稱已還書

情境：A同學收到2本書的逾期通知，可是她印象中書已經還了，因此到流通台詢問。

A同學：請問，有兩本書我已經還了，為什麼還是收到逾期通知？
B館員：您可以給我您的學號嗎？
A同學：109810001
B館員：麻煩您等一下，……紀錄中的確顯示您還有兩本書沒還，而且都已經過期了。
A同學：可是我都已經還了。
B館員：請問您是親自還的嗎？
A同學：是的。
B館員：您是什麼時候還的？
A同學：上個禮拜三或禮拜四。
B館員：發生這種情形可能有幾個原因，在圖書館方面，有可能是我們的疏忽，雖然很少發生，但是工作人員還是有可能沒有徹底完成歸還的動作，我們會在書架上仔細尋找，當然您也可以自己去書庫中找找看，如果找到書，歸還後我們會以email通知您。如果在書架上找不到書，很抱歉，我們就沒有辦法為您清除借書紀錄。
A同學：可是我記得真的還了，那該怎麼辦呢？
B館員：我們希望您能回去再仔細找一找，有可能您記錯了，書並沒有歸還，還在您家中，或者您還錯了書，而沒有察覺。這些情形在圖書館也常發生。很抱歉的是，我們必須以電腦系統中的紀錄為準，在沒有看到書的情況下，我們不能清除您的借書紀錄。
A同學：那麼圖書館工作人員可以先幫我找找看嗎？
B館員：好的，麻煩您填一下「已還書處理紀錄表」，不論找到或找不

Unit 3.8 Claim a Return

Situation: Student A receives a library notice indicating she has 2 overdue books remaining on her account. She believes that she has already returned the books. Therefore, she comes to the Library Circulation Desk and asks a librarian about the situation.

Student A: Excuse me. I have a question about an overdue notice I received. 2 books that I think I have already returned are listed on the notice.
Librarian B: May I have your Love River University ID number?
Student A: Sure, it is 109810001.
Librarian B: One moment please. On your account, it does show that you have 2 books overdue and not yet returned.
Student A: But I have already returned them.
Librarian B: Did you do it in person?
Student A: Yes.
Librarian B: When was this?
Student A: Sometime last Wednesday or Thursday.
Librarian B: Well. This happens. One possibility is that we did not scan the barcode due to an oversight, although this seldom happens. We will search for the books in the stacks. And, you may also check to see if they are on the shelf. Once they are found, we will send you an email notice. If they are not found, we cannot remove the two items from your check-out list. Sorry about this!
Student A: But I remember that I did return them already. What can I do?
Librarian B: Would you please check your place again? This kind of situation happens quite often. Library patrons claim they have returned the library items, but they eventually find them at

借還圖書資料 Borrow or Return Library Materials

　　　　　到，一個禮拜內我們都會通知您。
A同學：如果真的找不到呢？
B館員：依規定就要賠書了。
A同學：好吧，我回去再找找看，謝謝！
B館員：不客氣。

home or they have instead returned other items. That is why we cannot remove the items from your account. We are sorry. We must first ensure that the items claimed as returned are indeed in the library before we can remove the lost charge from your library account.

Student A: OK, can you search for the two books in the library stacks?

Librarian B: Sure! First please fill in this "Claim a Return" form. Whether or not they are found, we will definitely send you a notice in a week.

Student A: What if they are not found?

Librarian B: According to the library's policy, you'll be charged with replacement and processing fees for the 2 books.

Student A: Oh, well, then I'll go back and search my place again. Thanks!

Librarian B: You're welcome.

第四章

chapter 4

取得圖書館找不到的資料
Access Materials Not Available in Local Library

Library
Service
English

Unit 4.1 館際合作／文獻傳遞

4.1.1 國內費用及時限
情境：A同學寫期末報告需要參考一本書裡面的內容,但是愛河大學圖書館沒有這本書,他到流通台詢問館員要如何借到這本書。

A同學：您好,我想找一本書,可是圖書館裡沒有,有什麼辦法可以借到這本書嗎?

B館員：您方便給我書名嗎?

A同學：*A History of Violence*。

B館員：好的,請等我確認一下,……我們圖書館的確沒有這本書。我先幫您查聯合目錄,麻煩您稍等一下。

A同學：好的。

B館員：嗯,高雄B大學跟台南C大學都有這本書。

A同學：那可以請他們把書寄過來嗎?

B館員：可以,但是您必須付手續費及郵資。

A同學：請問手續費加郵資大約是多少錢?

B館員：大約150-200元。

A同學：那寄回去也要我再付一次費用嗎?另外,書是寄到我家嗎?

B館員：除了這筆費用,您不必再付費;書會寄到圖書館,我們會用email或電話通知您來取書。

A同學：我需要先付錢嗎?

B館員：不用,等我們通知您來取書的時候再付錢就可以。

A同學：大概多久可以收到書?

B館員：通常是3-5天,有些學校可能要5-7天。

A同學：那麼我可以借多久呢?

B館員：那要看各個大學圖書館的規定,一般來講是3個禮拜。順便提醒您一下,您可以到「全國文獻傳遞系統」申請一個帳號,以後就可

chapter 4

Unit 4.1 Interlibrary Loan & Document Delivery Services

4.1.1 Services for Domestic Libraries

Situation: Student A needs a book for her final paper. However, Love River University Library does not have a copy of this title. Student A approaches the Circulation Desk and asks a library staff member how she can obtain the book.

Student A: Excuse me. I need a book which is not available in our library. What can I do to get this book?

Librarian B: May I have the book title, please?

Student A: Sure, it's *A History of Violence*.

Librarian B: Alright, let me see, one moment please. You're right. We don't have this title. I'll check the union catalog and see which library has a copy of this book.

Student A: Okay.

Librarian B: Well, B University in Kaohsiung and C University in Tainan have this book.

Student A: May I ask one of them to send the book over here?

Librarian B: Of course, but you'll have to pay the service fee and postage.

Student A: How much is it?

Librarian B: It'll cost approximately a total of 150 to 200 dollars.

Student A: What about the postage for returning the book? Do I pay for it? By the way, is the book delivered to my address?

Librarian B: No, you'll have no other payment. The book will be delivered to our library and you'll receive an email notice or a phone call to inform you that the book is available for pickup in the library.

Student A: Do I pay the service fee and postage now?

Librarian B: No. Please pay it when you come in here to pick up the book.

取得圖書館找不到的資料 Access Materials Not Available in Local Library

　　　　　以自己申請了！
A同學：真的嗎？申請程序會不會很複雜呀？
B館員：不會的，跟申請email一樣簡單！如果您有時間，我可以馬上教您用自己的帳號申請！
A同學：好啊！
B館員：您先到愛河圖書館的首頁，右上角的地方有個「館際合作」，點選後可以看到申請辦法的第2點有「全國文獻傳遞系統」超連結，再點選進去可以看到「登入」畫面，在「申請帳號」這個地方填妥您的資料，之後等我們審核通過，大約需要一、兩天，收到email通知後，您就可以自己使用了！
A同學：太好了，真是謝謝您！
B館員：不客氣！

Student A: How long does it take to get the book?

Librarian B: Usually 3 to 5 days. But in some cases, it can take as long as 5 to 7 days.

Student A: What is the loan period?

Librarian B: It depends on which library you borrow the book from. Generally, the loan period is 3 weeks. By the way, you can go into the "National Document Delivery System" to create your own account so that you can send the request yourself the next time.

Student A: Really? Is it complicated to make a request?

Librarian B: Not at all! It is as easy as applying for an email account. If you have time, I can show you right now.

Student A: That'd be great.

Librarian B: On the Love River University Library website, you'll see the link to "Interlibrary Loan" in the upper right hand corner of the page; Click on it. Now you'll see the link for "National Document Delivery System" as the second entry under "How to Apply." When you click on this link the "To Get an Account" option will appear on the page. Select the "Log In" option and then you can fill in the information required on the form. It takes about one or two days to activate your account. You'll receive an email notice when it is activated.

Student A: Great. This is easy. Thanks for your time.

Librarian B: You're welcome.

Unit 4.1　館際合作／文獻傳遞

4.1.2 國外費用及時限
情境：外文系A教授因為研究需要一篇德文文章，因此請C助理打電話詢問愛河圖書館如何取得這篇文章。

C助理：喂，您好，我是外文系A教授的助理，A教授想要一篇國外德文期刊的文章，她已經有「全國文獻傳遞系統」的帳號，她請我向圖書館詢問，這篇文章是否可以直接線上申請？

B館員：可以的，只要A教授在「全國文獻傳遞系統」上填妥期刊名稱、卷期、出版年月等資料，我們就可以幫老師送出申請件。

C助理：大概需要多久的時間？

B館員：要看申請資料的類型決定，一般文獻複印大約是10-14天，至於比較不容易取得的資料像是微縮片，則需要1個月至半年不等。

C助理：費用呢？會不會很貴？

B館員：這要看提供服務的圖書館而定，以我過去處理申請件的經驗，費用從450元到2,400元都有。

C助理：順便問一下，如果是借書，費用也是一樣嗎？還有，碩博士論文也可以借嗎？

B館員：國外借書每本至少要900元，另外還需要加上寄回圖書資料的航空掛號郵資。至於碩博士論文，英國地區每本3,000元，美加地區碩博士論文，每本2,000元，其他地區依該單位的定價收費，當然這些國外資料的費用會依照匯率不定期調整。

C助理：那就麻煩您先幫A教授處理這篇文章。

B館員：好的，沒有問題。

C助理：如果有其他問題，我再向您請教，謝謝。

B館員：不客氣。

Unit 4.1 Interlibrary Loan & Document Delivery Services

4.1.2 Services from Overseas Libraries

Situation: Professor A in the Foreign Languages Department needs an article in the German language for her research project. She asks her graduate assistant to call the Love River University Library and find out how to get the full-text of the article.

Graduate Assistant C: Hello! This is C, Professor A's graduate assistant in the Foreign Languages Department. She needs the full-text of an article in German. Professor A already has a user account with the National Document Delivery System. We'd like to know if it is possible to get the article through this system.

Librarian B: Sure! As long as Professor A logs into the system, fills in the bibliographic information correctly, and submits the request form, we will be able to process her request.

Graduate Assistant C: How long will it take to get the document?

Librarian B: It depends on the material type. It takes about 10 to 14 days for article photocopies. For material such as microforms, which are more difficult to obtain, it may take a month or even as long as 6 months.

Graduate Assistant C: What about the service fee? Is it expensive?

Librarian B: It depends on which library holds the journal article. Based on my experience, the cost is about 450 dollars per copy and sometimes it can be as much as 2,400 dollars.

Graduate Assistant C: By the way, is it the same cost for borrowing books? Are theses or dissertations available through interlibrary loan?

Librarian B: It costs at least 900 dollars to borrow books from overseas, in addition to the postage for registered airmail. As for theses or dissertations, it will cost 3,000 dollars per title from the UK, and 2,000 dollars per title from Canada or USA. Service fees for items from libraries in other countries will vary. Of course, the cost also depends on the foreign exchange rates.

Graduate Assistant C: I see. Would you please process Professor A's request?

Librarian B: Sure, no problem!

Graduate Assistant C: Thank you! I might come back with other questions.

Librarian B: You're always welcome.

Unit 4.1 館際合作／文獻傳遞

4.1.3 到他館借書
情境：A同學寫研究報告需要一本書，愛河圖書館沒有，可是C大學圖書館有，因此A同學到流通台詢問要如何借閱。

A同學：您好，我想要向C大學圖書館借一本愛河圖書館沒有的書，雖然我有NDDS的帳號，可是我不想花錢，請問我可以自己到C大學圖書館借書嗎？

B館員：可以的，您只要拿「全國館合借書證」，就可以到C大學和大部分的大學圖書館借書了，而且是免費的。

A同學：那我現在可以借館合借書證嗎？

B館員：可以。請給我您的學生證。好了，這張「全國館合借書證」的到期日是1月3號。提醒您，您要先到C大學還清所借的書，然後再來這裡歸還這張「全國館合借書證」。

A同學：請問C大學圖書館的書一次可以借幾本？可以借多久？

B館員：5本，借期是3週。

A同學：好的，我知道了，謝謝！

B館員：不客氣。

Unit 4.1 Interlibrary Loan & Document Delivery Services

4.1.3 Walk in and Borrow Books from Other Libraries

Situation: Student A needs a book for his research paper. He does not find the book in Love River University Library, but determines that it is available at C University Library. Student A visits the Library Circulation Desk and asks how to obtain the book.

Student A: Hi, I'd like to borrow a book from C University Library. It is not available in Love River. Although I have an NDDS account, I want to save money. Is it possible for me to visit C University Library and check out books there?

Librarian B: Yes, you may obtain a reciprocal borrowing card here and use it at most of the university libraries in Taiwan, including C University. And, there is no cost for it!

Student A: May I get a reciprocal borrowing card now?

Librarian B: Sure, please give me your Love River ID Card. OK, you're all set now. This card is due on January 3rd. Don't forget to return all of the C University books you borrow before returning this card back here.

Student A: How many items can I borrow from C University and for how long?

Librarian B: You may borrow up to 5 items and the loan period is 3 weeks.

Student A: Alright, I see. Thank you!

Librarian B: Glad to help!

Unit 4.2 尚未上架的資料

4.2.1 一般讀者詢問

情境：A同學在愛河圖書館的線上目錄上找到一本書，它的館藏狀態是「已登收」，A同學想要看這本書，於是他到愛河圖書館流通台詢問。

A同學：請問一下，我剛剛在電腦上查到一本書，它顯示「已登收」，請問這是什麼意思？
B館員：您方便給我書名嗎？
A同學：好的，是 *Patriotism*。
B館員：您可以拼給我聽嗎？
A同學：好的，是 P-a-t-r-i-o-t-i-s-m。
B館員：謝謝。嗯，這本書正在點收中，表示這本書已經買進圖書館，但是我們還沒有完成編目手續。
A同學：那就是不在書架上囉？難怪我剛剛找不到！
B館員：是的，您急著要看這本書嗎？
A同學：是的，很急迫，因為過兩個星期就要發表期末專題報告，我需要參考這本書的資料。
B館員：好的，您可以填這張「緊急編目單」。
A同學：我填完可以馬上拿到書嗎？
B館員：5本圖書資料以內，緊急編目處理的時間是以5個工作天為原則，所以您應該5天內就可以拿到書。我們會依您填的聯絡資料通知您來取書。
A同學：太好了，謝謝您！
B館員：不客氣，其實您也可以由圖書館網頁下載表格，直接在線上申請。
A同學：真的嗎？我下次會試試看，謝謝了！
B館員：不客氣。

chapter 4

Unit 4.2 Materials Not Available on Shelves

4.2.1 Inquiry from Library Patrons

Situation: Student A finds a book in Love River University Library's online catalog, with the status of "Order Received." He wants to read it, so he goes to the Library Circulation Desk and asks a librarian about borrowing it.

Student A: Excuse me. I just found this book in WebPAC and it shows "Order Received." What does that mean?

Librarian B: May I have the book title?

Student A: Sure, it is *Patriotism*.

Librarian B: Would you please spell it out for me?

Student A: Of course. P-a-t-r-i-o-t-i-s-m.

Librarian B: Thanks. Well, the book was just received in the library and it has not yet been cataloged.

Student A: So, it means the book is not on shelf? No wonder I did not find it there.

Librarian B: You're right. Are you in a hurry to read this book?

Student A: Yes, I need it right away. I'll be presenting my final project in 2 weeks and I need this book as a reference for my project.

Librarian B: I see. If you'd like, you may fill in this "Rush Cataloging Reguest Form."

Student A: Will I get the book after completing the form?

Librarian B: Well, it usually takes 5 working days to complete 5 items in process. I think you'll have the book in less than 5 days. Once it is ready for checkout, we will contact you to come and pick it up.

Student A: Great, thanks!

Librarian B: You're welcome. In fact, you may download the form on the library website and send your request online.
Student A: Is that right? I'll try it next time. Thanks!
Librarian B: You're welcome.

Unit 4.2　尚未上架的資料

4.2.2 介購者詢問
情境：A老師在線上查詢他之前推薦的一本書，發現館藏狀態是「One Copy Under Consideration」，他不明白是什麼意思，打電話到愛河圖書館詢問。

A老師：哈囉，您好，我是環工系A老師。
B館員：嗨，您好。
A老師：我想請問一下，上學期我薦購了一本書，我查了一下館藏目錄，上面寫的是「One Copy Under Consideration」，請問這是什麼意思？
B館員：「One Copy Under Consideration」表示這本書正在採購中，您方便給我書名讓我再查一下嗎？
A老師：書名是*Biological Species Concept*。
B館員：謝謝，請您稍等一下，是的，這本書圖書館已經送出訂單，但是已經過了一學期，書還沒有到館，有可能書已經絕版，或者我們的代理商還沒訂到，我需要詢問一下代理商，A老師，我可以等一下再打電話給您嗎？
A老師：好的，我的分機是5308。
B館員：謝謝您。
（B館員詢問代理商後，撥電話給A老師。）
A老師：喂？
B館員：嗨，我是愛河圖書館的B館員，請問A教授在嗎？
A老師：嗨，我就是。
B館員：經過我詢問代理商，這本書正在再版中，應該兩、三個禮拜內就會出版。
A老師：那麼書什麼時候會來？
B館員：出版後大約兩週就會寄到圖書館，到館後我們會緊急編目，大約5

Unit 4.2 Materials Not Available on Shelves

4.2.2 Inquiry from a Patron Requesting Library Purchase
Situation: Professor A searches the library catalog for a book he recommended for library purchase and finds it with the status of "One Copy Under Consideration." He does not understand what this means, so he calls Love River University Library to ask.

Professor A: Hello, this is A from the Department of Environmental Engineering.
Librarian B: Hi, what can I do for you?
Professor A: Yes, well, last semester I recommended a book for library purchase. I just checked the library catalog and it shows the message "One Copy Under Consideration." What does this mean?
Librarian B: It means that the book is still on order. If you don't mind, may I have the title just to double check?
Professor A: Sure, it is *Biological Species Concept*.
Librarian B: Thank you. Just a second please. Yes, this book is on order. However, since it has been a semester, it may be out of print or likely the vendor hasn't found the book for us. I'll contact the vendor to see what the situation is. May I call you afterwards?
Professor A: Sure, my extension number is 5308.
Librarian B: Thank you.
(Librarian B calls Professor A after she has spoken with the vendor.)
Professor A: Hello!
Librarian B: Hello, this is B from the library. May I talk to Professor A, please?
Professor A: Yes, speaking.

　　　　　個工作天後我們就會通知您來圖書館借書。
A老師：好的，我知道了，謝謝。
B館員：不客氣。

Librarian B: In talking with the vendor, I learned that a second edition of the book is being prepared. It is supposed to be published within 2 to 3 weeks.

Professor A: So when do you think the library will receive the book?

Librarian B: I think we will receive it 2 weeks after it has been published. Once the book is received, we will rush the cataloging, which might take 5 working days. We will contact you when it is available for checkout.

Professor A: Good. I see. Thanks!

Librarian B: Sure, no problem!

Unit 4.2　尚未上架的資料

4.2.3 過期期刊送裝訂

情境：暑假期間，平面設計系的A同學要找2007年5月的*Journal of Art and Design Education*，可是在圖書館館藏目錄上看到這本期刊目前的狀態是「裝訂中」，因為他不知道圖書館裝訂期刊的作業時間需要多久，於是，他用IMS（Instant Message Service）詢問館員。

Guest2540：Hi, 我想請問一下，我查館藏目錄，2007年5月v. 26 no. 2的 *Journal of Art and Design Education*現在的狀態是裝訂中，不知道什麼時候才會上架？

B館員：嗯，我們送裝訂的期刊大約都是在快要開學的時候才會裝訂好送回來，開學前一定會整理好上架。

Guest2540：有沒有可能請裝訂廠商把已經裝訂好的部分先送回來圖書館？

B館員：這個我不清楚，您可以等一下嗎？讓我問一下負責期刊的館員。

Guest2540：好的，麻煩您。

（館員詢問後，回到電腦前）

B館員：Hi, 我問好了，的確可以請廠商把已經裝訂好的期刊先送回來。

Guest2540：能不能麻煩查一下*Journal of Art and Design Education*, v. 26 no. 2這一期是不是已經裝訂好了？如果還沒裝訂好，可不可以請他們優先裝訂這一期？

B館員：通常裝訂廠商的作業程序，是同一種語文的期刊整批作業，我們可以請他們先裝訂英文期刊，不過因為是整批作業，所以時間上無法預估。另外，裝訂好的期刊回到圖書館後，我們還需要編目才能上架，因此會需要一些時間。我們可以先幫您詢問英文期刊是否已經裝訂好，再和您連絡，您願意留一下email或電話嗎？

Unit 4.2 Materials Not Available on Shelves

4.2.3 Back Issues Sent To Be Bound

Situation: It is during summer break. Student A, a graphic design major, needs an issue of the *Journal of Art and Design Education* published in May 2007. He searches the library catalog, which shows the status as "At the Bindery." He has no idea how long it will take to have the bound issues available in the library. Therefore, he asks a librarian through IMS, the Instant Messaging Service.

Guest2540: Hi, I'm looking for the *Journal of Art and Design Education*, v. 26 no. 2. It shows "At the Bindery" in WebPAC. I'm wondering when it will be available on the shelf.

Librarian B: Well, usually the bound serial volumes aren't received until a couple of weeks before the new semester starts. The library will definitely shelve the bound volumes before school starts.

Guest2540: Is it possible to have the finished bound volumes sent back to the library earlier than that?

Librarian B: Well, I'm not sure. I'll need to check with the Serials Librarian before I can answer this question. Please hold on a second.

Guest2540: Sure, thanks!

(Librarian B returns after she has consulted with her colleague.)

Librarian B: Hi, I'm back. We can ask the bindery to send back the finished bound volumes now.

Guest2540: Is it possible to check if the *Journal of Art and Design Education* v. 26 no. 2 is already bound? If it's not, is it possible to ask them to do this first?

Librarian B: Well, they usually bind the serial volumes in groups by

Guest2540：麻煩您了！我的email是daveice@yahoo.com 謝謝！
B館員：不客氣，我們會再和您連絡。

chapter 4

language. We can ask them to bind the serials in English first, but it is difficult at this time to estimate how long it will take to complete the binding. Plus, these bound volumes must be cataloged after we receive them. Therefore, it will take some time before they are ready to shelve. We will check with the bindery to see if the English journal titles have been bound and then we will contact you. Do you mind leaving your email or phone no. for me?

Guest2540: No problem at all. My email is daveice@yahoo.com Thanks!

Librarian B: You're welcome. You'll be hearing from us.

Unit 4.3 推薦訂購

情境：A同學在網路書店看到一本想看的書，發現愛河圖書館沒有這本書，於是她到愛河圖書館詢問。

A同學：您好，昨天我在網路書店上看見一本書，書名是 A Home at the World's End，我查了一下愛河圖書館的目錄，沒有這本書，請問是不是可以請圖書館買這本書？

B館員：請您稍等，我查一下，……是的，我們的確沒有這本書。您要推薦這本書嗎？我可以馬上幫您把這本書輸入圖書資料推薦系統。

A同學：好的，麻煩您。我也可以在線上自己推薦嗎？

B館員：當然，只要是愛河大學的教職員工及學生，都可以在線上推薦圖書或多媒體資料。

A同學：所有推薦的資料都會訂購？

B館員：您所推薦的圖書資料必須符合圖書館館藏發展政策，我們會根據館藏發展政策決定是否採購，再回覆給您。

A同學：如果圖書館決定買的話，書多久會買進來？

B館員：不一定，通常中文書比較快，外文書比較慢。如果您短時間內需要這本書，可以透過館際合作申請借書。

A同學：不用了，我只是想看看裡面的一、兩個章節，不過還是謝謝您。

B館員：不客氣。

A同學：可以再請教一個問題嗎？推薦者是不是可以第一個借到這本書？

B館員：是的，推薦者有優先借閱權，圖書資料採購到館處理完畢後，我們會用email或電話通知您來借閱。

A同學：太好了！謝謝！

B館員：不客氣。

Unit 4.3 Library Purchase Recommendations

Situation: Student A sees a book in an online bookstore, but it is not available in Love River University Library. She visits the library and approaches a staff member.

Student A: Hi, I have a question. I found the book *A Home at the World's End* in an online bookstore yesterday. Then I searched our library catalog and found that it was not available here. Is it possible for the library to purchase this book?

Librarian B: Just a moment please, let me check first. Well, you're right. We don't have this book in our holdings. Would you like me to suggest that the library purchase it? I can enter the book information into our recommendation system right now.

Student A: Yes, please. But can I do it by myself online?

Librarian B: Sure, as long as you're affiliated with Love River University, you may suggest a purchase of both books and multimedia materials.

Student A: Will everything suggested be purchased by the library?

Librarian B: Well, it must meet the criteria of the Library Collection Development Policy. We will let you know if your recommendation will be purchased.

Student A: If it is selected, how soon will the item be purchased and received in the library?

Librarian B: It depends. Generally speaking, it is faster to get books in Chinese than in foreign languages. If you need this book more quickly, you may request it through interlibrary loan.

Student A: That's alright. I just want to read one or two chapters in it. Thank you anyway.

Librarian B: No problem!

Student A: I have one more question. Is the person who makes the purchase recommendation the one who gets to check it out first?
Librarian B: Yes, he or she has priority to check out the item once it is ready. We will inform you with an email notice or by phone.
Student A: That's great. Thanks!
Librarian B: You're welcome.

Unit 4.4　尋書

情境：A同學做報告需要參考一本書，他查過愛河圖書館館藏目錄，確定館藏狀態是「在館內」，但是在書架上卻找不到這本書，於是到服務台詢問。

A同學：您好，我在書架上找不到 *The Global Environment* 這本書，可是它的狀態是在館內，請問怎麼會這樣？
B館員：好的，請稍等，讓我查一下……，這本書的確是在館內，有可能是某位讀者正在圖書館裡閱讀這本書，或者是書在歸架時放錯了地方，所以您在書架上找不到。您可以填寫這張尋書單，我們會幫您找這本書。
A同學：請問通常填完多久以後可以拿到書？
B館員：尋書作業大約需要15個工作天，原則上我們會到書架上尋找3次，如果3次都找不到，就會用email或電話通知您尋書的結果。
A同學：15天喔！好像有點久，如果在4月1日前沒有找到，我就不需要了！
B館員：好的，您可以在尋書單上註明。
A同學：那麼除了剛剛說的那種情形，還有什麼狀況下會找不到書呢？
B館員：最常見的就是其他人翻閱過這本書後自行歸架，但沒有把書放回原來的位置，或是有人把書藏起來，免得被別人借出去；通常我們會先在「待上架書區」找，看看是不是書才還回來，還沒來得及上架。這幾種情況都是可能的。如果還是找不到，我們會評估是否立刻採購複本。
A同學：原來是這樣，我已經填好尋書單，就麻煩你們了，謝謝。
B館員：不客氣。

chapter 4

Unit 4.4 Search Service for Missing Books

Situation: Student A needs a book as a resource for his paper. He couldn't find it on the shelf even though it showed up as "Available" in the library catalog. He then goes to the Library Information Desk and asks a library staff member.

Student A: Hi, excuse me, I could not find the book *The Global Environment* on the shelf, but in the library catalog the status showed up as "Available." Why is that?

Librarian B: Well, just a second please. Let me check. You're right. It should be available in the library. This may be because somebody is using it here in the library or because it has been misshelved. If you want, you may fill in this "Missing Book Search Request Form" and we will search for the book for you.

Student A: How long does it usually take to find the book?

Librarian B: We will search for the missing item a maximum of 3 times during a 15-day period. If we still cannot find it we will send you an email notice or give you a call.

Student A: 15 days? That's a little bit too long. I won't need the book if it is not found by April 1st.

Librarian B: Alright. You should make a note of that on the request form.

Student A: By the way, in addition to what you just mentioned, are there any other reasons why the item might be missing?

Librarian B: Of course! Actually, the most common situations are that somebody took the book from the shelf but did not put it back in the correct place or that the book was hidden on purpose to keep it from being checked out. Usually, we will search the "Waiting To Be Shelved" area first to see if the book has just been returned to the library and not yet reshelved. These are

the likeliest possibilities based on our experience. We will also decide whether it is necessary to promptly purchase an additional copy if we cannot find it after searching.

Student A: I see. Here is the completed request form. Thank you for your help!

Librarian B: You're welcome.

第五章
chapter 5

線上借閱服務
Online Services

Library Service English

Unit 5.1　查看個人借閱狀況

5.1.1 忘記密碼

情境1：A同學因為忘記自己向圖書館借了哪些書，以及這些書什麼時候到期，於是以IMS向館員詢問。

Guest1658：您好，我想請問一下我向圖書館借了哪些書，還有什麼時候到期？

B館員：您好，關於這個問題，因為IMS上面都是guest的身份，我們無法在這裡確認您是否為本人，所以很抱歉無法直接回答這樣的問題。不過，您可以在線上查看您的借閱狀況。

Guest1658：好的。請問要怎麼看？

B館員：請您現在連線到圖書館的首頁，畫面右方有個快速連結「借閱紀錄」，請點選這個項目。

Guest1658：好，我看到了，這裡要輸入借書證號碼和密碼，但是我不知道我的密碼是什麼。

B館員：密碼的預設值是您的出生年月日共8碼，例如：20080507，請您試一下。

Guest1658：好的，等一下。

Guest1658：可以，我看到我的紀錄了，謝謝。

B館員：不客氣。

Guest1658：881：)　（註：881 = bye bye）

B館員：881。

chapter 5

Unit 5.1 View Personal Library Account

5.1.1 Forget Password

Situation: Student A forgets what she has checked out from the library and the book due dates. So, she uses IMS to ask the librarian.

Guest1658: Hi, I'd like to determine what books I have checked out and their due dates. Is it possible to get this information from you right now?

Librarian B: Hi, well, your inquiry represents a personal privacy situation. It is inappropriate to answer your questions on IMS because we can not confirm your real identification through this guest ID. However, there is an alternative that will allow you to get this information. You can access your library account online and view your current list of checked out items there.

Guest1658: Oh, I see. However, I don't know how to view my library account. Can you tell me more about it?

Librarian B: Sure! First you need to access the library website. You'll find a short-cut list on the right hand side of the screen. You should see "View Your Library Account" on this list. Please click on it.

Guest1658: Yes, I see this, but it asks for a library ID number and PIN. I don't know what to type in for my PIN.

Librarian B: The default is your birth year and date. 8 numbers in the format like 20080507. Please try it out!

Guest1658: OK. Just a second.

Guest1658: Great! I see my record. Thanks!

Librarian B: Sure!

Guest1658: Bye :)

Librarian B: Bye

Unit 5.1　查看個人借閱狀況

5.1.2 借閱紀錄異常
情境2：A教授因為無法登入系統讀取自己的借閱紀錄，打電話到圖書館詢問館員。

A教授：您好，我是財金系的A老師，請問一下系統是不是故障？因為我要上線看我的借閱紀錄，可是卻無法進入系統。
B館員：請問您帳號密碼有沒有輸錯？英文大小寫會有差別。
A教授：我確定我沒有輸錯。
B館員：請問您是什麼時候發現這個情況的？
A教授：今天早上大概7點多。
B館員：喔，那個時候系統當機，因為昨天晚上跳電，不斷電系統的電力有限，我們8點上班後發現這個問題，就趕緊重新開機，目前運作正常。您應該可以順利使用系統看您的借閱紀錄了。
A教授：喔，原來是這樣。謝謝！
B館員：不客氣。
A教授：Bye bye！
B館員：再見。

chapter 5

Unit 5.1 View Personal Library Account

5.1.2 Cannot Access Personal Account
Situation: Professor A is unable to log into his library account, so he calls a librarian for help.

Professor A: Hello, this is A from the Department of Finance. I'm wondering if the library system is functioning properly because I can't log into my library account to view my checkout record.
Librarian B: Hi, Professor A. Are you sure that you typed your library ID and password correctly? They are case sensitive.
Professor A: I'm sure. No typos.
Librarian B: Well, when did you try to log into the system?
Professor A: Sometime around 7:00 this morning.
Librarian B: Oh, I see. Let me explain. Because of a sudden power outage last night, the UPS system went down eventually. We did not discover the problem until 8:00 this morning when we came to the office so the library system was down all night. This system has been restarted and is fully functional now. You can now log into your library account without a problem.
Professor A: Oh, I see. Thanks for your explanation!
Librarian B: You're welcome.
Professor A: Bye bye!
Librarian B: Bye bye!

Unit 5.1　查看個人借閱狀況

5.1.3 更改個人資料
情境3：A同學因為搬家加上email被駭客盜用，打電話到圖書館流通台更新連絡資料。

A同學：您好，我是經濟系的學生，因為最近搬家，而且以前用的email被盜用，我想要更新聯絡資料。您可以幫我更新嗎？
B館員：很抱歉，麻煩您自行上網更新，因為除非您親自來圖書館，出示證件確定是本人，我們才能直接在系統上修改您的資料，否則，就必須請您自行登入借閱紀錄更新個人資料。
A同學：我沒有用過這個功能，您可以告訴我要怎麼做嗎？
B館員：請問您現在手邊有電腦可以上網嗎？
A同學：有，可是我還沒開機。您可以等一下嗎？
B館員：當然可以，或者您要等一下再打來也可以。
A同學：好，我等一下再撥，謝謝！
B館員：不客氣。
（過了一會兒，圖書館電話又響起。）
B館員：喂，愛河圖書館，您好！
A同學：您好，我是經濟系的學生，剛剛打過電話來詢問更新個人聯絡資料的事情。
B館員：是的，您的電腦可以上網了嗎？
A同學：可以了。
B館員：好的，請先上圖書館網頁，在首頁右上方有個「借閱紀錄查詢」的選項，請點選這個功能。
A同學：好，這個功能我用過。修改個人資料也在這裡面啊？！
B館員：是的，您進去系統，上方有個「個人資料」選項，要更新您的聯絡資料，就是點這個選項。
A同學：好的，我知道了，謝謝！

chapter 5

Unit 5.1 View Personal Library Account

5.1.3 Update Personal Information
Situation: Student A calls the Circulation Desk to update his contact information since he recently moved and his email account has been hacked.

Student A: Hello, I'm a student majoring in Economics. I'm wondering if you would update my contact information because I've just moved to a new place and my email account has been hacked.
Librarian B: I'm sorry, but I'm afraid that you must do this yourself on the web. However, if you come to the library in person and show your identification card we are allowed to update your information directly in the system. Otherwise, you must log into your library account to update your personal information.
Student A: I've never used this function before. Would you please tell me how to do it?
Librarian B: Are you at a computer with Internet access?
Student A: Yes. But I haven't turned it on. Would you please hold on for a second?
Librarian B: Sure, or you may call back later when you're ready.
Student A: Alright, then I'll call back in a litte while. Thanks.
Librarian B: Don't mention it.
(A short while later the phone rings again.)
Librarian B: Hello, this is Love River Library. May I help you?
Student A: Yes. I'm a student majoring in Economics. I called a few minutes ago and asked a question about updating my personal contact information.
Librarian B: Yes. So can you access the Internet now?
Student A: Yes. It is ready.

B館員：不客氣。
A同學：Bye！
B館員：再見！

Librarian B: Great. Now please access the library website. On the upper right hand side of the site, you'll find a service called "Check your Library Account." Please click on it.

Student A: OK. I've used this function before. Updating personal information is also through this page?

Librarian B: Yes. Once you get into the system, you'll see the menu "Personal Information" at the top of the page. Click on it if you'd like to update your contact information.

Student A: Alright. I've got it. Thanks a lot.

Librarian B: Not at all.

Student A: Bye!

Librarian B: Bye!

Unit 5.2 線上續借或預約

5.2.1 如何續借及預約

情境：A同學因為報告還沒寫完，需要續借一些書，另外還想借幾本書，但其中有些書已經被別人借走了。因為不知道要怎麼辦，所以上線用IMS向館員詢問。

Guest1436：Hi，我想請問一下，如果要續借書，我一定要到圖書館辦理嗎？

B館員：不一定，您可以在線上辦續借。不過，如果您借的書已經有人預約，您就得歸還。要續借的話，您可以到圖書館的首頁，畫面右上方有個快速連結「借閱紀錄」，輸入借書證號碼和密碼，也就是學號和生日共8碼，例如：19850413。進入系統後，您會看到借書的狀況，然後勾選您要續借的書，點選「續借選取館藏」就可以了。如果是有人預約的書，就無法續借，您必須在到期日之前歸還。

Guest1436：喔，我知道了。因為我要借的書被別人借走，您可以幫我預約嗎？

B館員：可以。請告訴我書名或作者。

Guest1436：*Media Literacy : a Reader*, edited by Donaldo Macedo & Shirley R. Steinberg（註：由WebPAC書目資料貼上）

B館員：OK，請告訴我您的證號

Guest1436：278953201

B館員：好，請稍等一下。…

B館員：OK了，預約成功了。下次您可以自己在線上預約。

Gguest1436：真的嗎？怎麼做？

B館員：先在館藏目錄上查到您要的書之後，如果書被外借了，您在畫面上方會看到一個「預約」的按鈕，點選之後，輸入你的借書證證號和密碼，查核身份正確後，就預約成功了。

Guest1436：這麼簡單，好，我以後會試試看。謝謝！

Unit 5.2 Renew or Place a Hold Online

5.2.1 Steps for Online Renewals and Reservation

Situation: Student A would like to renew some books because she hasn't finished her papers. In addition, she'd also like to check out a number of books, several of which have already been checked out. She is asking a librarian through IMS because she doesn't know what procedures to follow.

Guest1436: Hi, excuse me. Do I have to come to the Library if I'd like to renew books?

Librarian B: Not necessarily. You can do it online. However, if any of your checkouts have been placed on hold by someone else, you must return the item. Please go to the library website to renew your checkouts. On the upper right hand side of the site, you'll see a shortcut called "Check Your Library Account." Type in your Love River ID number and your PIN. Your PIN is your birth year and date in 8 digits such as 19850413. Once you log into your account, you can determine the status of your current checkouts. Just select the items you want to renew and click on "Renew the Selected" and it's all set. You won't be able to renew an item if someone else has placed a hold on it. In that case you must return the item by the due date.

Guest1436: OK, I see. Since what I need is currently checked out, could you do me a favor and place a hold on it for me?

Librarian B: Certainly. Please tell me the book title or the author.

Guest1436: The title is *Media Literacy: a Reader*, edited by Donaldo Macedo & Shirley R. Steinberg.

Librarian B: OK, now may I have your Love River ID number?

Guest1436: 278953201.

B館員：不客氣。
Guest1436：881
B館員：881

chapter 5

Librarian B: Please wait a second.

Librarian B: OK, now it is on your reservation list. You can place a hold online by yourself next time.

Guest1436: Really? How?

Librarian B: Look up the book you want in the library catalog. If it is currently checked out, click on the button "Request" at the top of the page and it will ask you to enter your Love River ID number and PIN. Once it is authenticated, your request will be processed successfully.

Guest1436: This is easy. OK, I'll give it a try. Thank you.

Librarian B: You're welcome.

Gguest1436: Bye.

Librarian B: Bye.

Unit 5.2 線上續借或預約

5.2.2 無法續借及預約
情境：A同學想要在線上預約他想借的書，可是無論他怎麼試，都無法順利預約。於是打電話到圖書館，順便幫他同學詢問線上續借無法執行的原因。

A學生：喂，您好，我剛剛想要用網路預約要借的書，可是都不成功。請問該怎麼辦？

B館員：您方便告訴我您要預約的書名嗎？

A學生：可以啊，書名是 *Learning to Think Things Through*。

B館員：好的，請稍等一下，我查查看。

A學生：好，謝謝。

B館員：這本書現在外借中，您應該可以預約。如果圖書是「在館內」的狀態，就不能預約。您可以告訴我您的證號嗎？我需要看一下您的讀者紀錄，才知道問題在哪裡。

A學生：好的，我的學號是263412215。

B館員：請稍等一下，……。我知道您無法預約的原因了，那是因為您已經預約了10筆資料，這是圖書館開放學生預約的上限。所以，如果您很想預約這本書，您必須先取消一筆您已經預約的資料。

A學生：喔，原來如此，我知道了。我還有一個問題。

B館員：請說。

A學生：昨天，有一位朋友說他要在線上續借圖書，可是也不成功。為什麼會這樣？

B館員：嗯，如果他有逾期處理費沒繳或是需要賠書，就不能續借。另一個可能是，如果那本書已經逾期，也不能續借。再不然，就是那本書已經有人預約了。到目前為止，線上續借會有問題幾乎都是因為以上3種原因。麻煩您轉告您的同學，請他看看他的借閱紀錄

Unit 5.2 Renew or Place a Hold Online

5.2.2 Problems with Online Renewals and Reservations
Situation: Student A has a difficult time reserving books online no matter how hard he tries. He calls the library for help and also asks about his classmate's inability to renew books online.

Student A: Hello. My name is A. I had problems when I tried to reserve a library book online. Can you help me with this?
Librarian B: Would you please tell me the book title?
Student A: Sure. It is called *Learning to Think Things Through*.
Librarian B: Alright, hold on please. Let me check it for you.
Student A: OK, thank you.
Librarian B: This book has been checked out, so you should be able to place a hold on it. It's only when the status of library materials shows as "Available" that a hold request is not allowed. Well, I'll have to take a look at your library account in order to figure out the problem. May I have your Love River ID number?
Student A: Sure, it is 263412215.
Librarian B: Just a moment, please. Okay, I know why you couldn't place a hold. It's because you've already reserved 10 items, which is the maximum number of items students are allowed to reserve. If you do want to place a hold on the book you just mentioned, you have to cancel one reserved item from your list.
Student A: No wonder. OK, I see. Now, I have one more question.
Librarian B: Yes, what is it?
Student A: I want to ask why my friend was unable to renew some books online yesterday.

　　　　　是不是有以上3種情況。如果不是以上3種狀況的話，再請他本人
　　　　　來圖書館1樓流通台處理。
A學生：好，我知道了。謝謝，Bye bye！
B館員：不客氣，Bye bye！

Librarian B: Well, he isn't allowed to renew checkouts if he has overdue fines or replacement fees. Another possibility is if the item he wanted to renew was overdue then it is not eligible for online renewal. Or, maybe the book has been reserved by someone else. So far, these three scenarios are the most common issues that impact online rewewals. Ask your friend if his situation matches one of these situations. If not, please ask him to consult with us at the Circulation Desk on the 1st floor in the library.

Student A: Ok, I got it. Thank you. Bye bye.

Librarian B: You're welcome. Bye bye.

Unit 5.3 研究小間申請

情境：A同學在2樓看到圖書館的研究小間，覺得如果能夠在裡面安靜地念書、打報告，應該不錯，因此到圖書館1樓服務台詢問使用的權限。

A同學：您好，我剛剛在2樓看到有一間一間的研究小間，請問可以自由使用嗎？還是需要預約登記？

B館員：請問您是本校的研究生嗎？目前因為研究小間數量很少，我們只開放給本校研究生登記使用。

A同學：太好了，我是歷史研究所的學生，請問一次可以借用多久？

B館員：每次預約登記可以使用兩個月。使用期滿，如果有人預約，就不能繼續使用，必須讓給下一位預約者。

A同學：請問，我要在哪裡預約？

B館員：您可以直接在圖書館網站上預約，預約的時候您就可以看到研究小間的預約及使用狀況。您要不要現在上網看看？

A同學：好呀。

B館員：進了圖書館網站後，在「線上服務」這個選項中，有一個「研究小間」的項目，看起來目前只剩下一間無人使用，您可以申請使用這一間。如果，您屬意其他的研究小間，也可以看一下它的使用截止日，然後點選預約申請，填入您的資料，這樣就預約成功了。要提醒您的是，使用研究小間一定要遵守使用規則，這些規則，我們都張貼在研究小間的門上，也公布在圖書館網頁上。

A同學：好的，我知道了。我可以現在申請這間空的嗎？

B館員：當然可以，請您在表格上輸入您的資料。

A同學：好，謝謝！我還有一個問題。

B館員：好的，請說。

Unit 5.3 Request a Study Carrel

Situation: Student A sees the Study Carrels on the 2nd floor of the library and thinks it would be great if she could use a carrel to study in and work on her papers. Therefore, she inquires about getting access to a carrel when she goes to the Information Desk on the 1st floor.

Student A: Excuse me. I saw some Study Carrels on the 2nd floor and I want to ask if they are available for walk-in use or if it is necessary to reserve one in advance.

Librarian B: Are you a graduate student here? Since there are only a few carrels in the library, right now only graduate students of this university are allowed to reserve a carrel.

Student A: Great. I'm a graduate student in the Department of History. So, how long is the allotted time for carrel assignments?

Librarian B: Two months. When this time is up and the carrel has been reserved by someone else, it will be assigned to the next user.

Student A: Okay, where should I go to request the reservation?

Librarian B: You may make a reservation online from our library website, where you can also check the availability. Would you like to check it out now?

Student A: Good idea.

Librarian B: When you're on the library website, you'll see "Study Carrels" under the menu of "Online Service." As you can see here, currently there is only one carrel available and you may request it now. If you prefer another one you may check its due date. Then, click on the reservation link here and type in the personal information requested on the form. Then your reservation will be complete. Please remember that you must follow the policy posted on the

A同學：如果有人預約了，可是都沒有來使用，那麼，那間研究小間會開放其他人預約嗎？
B館員：會的，只要預約成功的人在收到使用通知之後一個星期內都沒來使用，我們就會開放給下一位預約者。而且，那位預約而沒來用的同學一學期內也無法再預約研究小間，所以如果您臨時決定不需要使用研究小間，記得要上網取消預約，或者打電話告訴我們一聲。
A同學：好的，我知道了，謝謝！
B館員：不客氣。

door of the study carrel, which you may also find on the library webpage.

Student A: No problem. I've got it. So may I request the available one now?

Librarian B: Certainly. Please fill in the online registration form.

Student A: Alright. Thanks. Well, I have another question.

Librarian B: Yes, please.

Student A: If someone doesn't show up to use the carrel he or she reserved, will it become available for others to reserve?

Librarian B: Yes. As long as the person doesn't show up within one week after we send out the notice of approval, we will open the carrel to the next person. Furthermore, an individual who does not come to use the carrel after making the reservation will have his or her right to make another carrel reservation suspended for one semester. Therefore, should you decide not to use the study carrel as planned please be sure to cancel your reservation online or contact us by phone.

Student A: OK, I see. Thank you very much.

Librarian B: Sure, it's my pleasure.

第六章
chapter 6

查詢館藏資源
Search Library Collection & Resources

Library
Service
English

Unit 6.1　以資料性質區分

6.1.1 館藏圖書資料
6.1.1.1 以圖書類別詢問館藏樓層
情境：A同學想要到圖書館找有關學華語的書，因此在服務台詢問館員。

A同學：您好，請問圖書館有關學華語的書放在哪裡？
B館員：這一類的中文書放在4樓，西文書則是放在5樓。您有沒有特別要找哪一本書？可以先用館藏目錄查出索書號。
A同學：我沒有特別要找什麼書，只是想要隨便看看。可以告訴我大概放在什麼地方嗎？
B館員：好的，請您稍等一下，我確認一下分類號。這一類的中文書，您可以到4樓802.6或是802.86的書架上看看。如果是西方語文，您可以到5樓，495.18的書架上看看。
A同學：好的，謝謝您。
B館員：不客氣。

Unit 6.1 Search by Material Types

6.1.1 Library Materials
6.1.1.1 Location of Specific Subjects in Collection
Situation: Student A goes to the library to find books about learning the Chinese language. He asks a librarian at the Information Desk.

Student A: Excuse me, would you please tell me where I can find books for learning the Chinese language?
Librarian B: Sure, you'll find books in Chinese on the 4th floor, while those in Western languages are shelved on the 5th floor. Is there a specific title you're trying to find? If that's the case then you can search the library catalog for its call number.
Student A: No, I'm just looking around. Can you give me an idea of where to look for them?
Librarian B: Sure. Wait a moment, please. Let me confirm the classification number for you first. Alright, you may find them by the classification numbers of 802.6 or 802.86 on the 4th floor. And the number 495.18 is for publications in Western languages on the 5th floor.
Student A: Great and thank you very much.
Librarian B: Not at all.

Unit 6.1 以資料性質區分

6.1.1 館藏圖書資料
6.1.1.2 尋找多媒體資料
情境：Professor A想要到圖書館借視聽資料作為課程輔助教材，可是不熟悉圖書館的媒體資源要怎麼找，因此到圖書館流通台詢問館員。

A教授：您好，我是英文系的A老師，我想要借圖書館的多媒體資料到課堂上播放，可是我這學期才來愛河大學，不熟悉圖書館的視聽資料怎麼找，方便幫我介紹一下嗎？
B館員：嗨，您好。我們的多媒體資料集中在2樓的媒體資源中心，資料可以透過館藏目錄查到。如果您要直接到架上看，資料是按照媒體類型排列的，例如，DVD、VCD、CD、錄音帶、錄影帶。在同一種類型之下，再依照東方或西方語文分類，依照索書號，您就可以找到資料了。
A教授：好，我知道了，謝謝。
B館員：不客氣。

Unit 6.1 Search by Material Types

6.1.1 Library Materials
6.1.1.2 Search Multimedia Resources
Situation: Professor A would like to check out audiovisual materials from the library as supplemental teaching materials. He goes to the Library Circulation Desk to ask a librarian for help since he is unfamiliar with how to search for multimedia materials.

Professor A: Hi, I'm A from the English Department. I'd like to check out some multimedia materials for my class, but I'm new at Love River U and don't know how to search for audiovisual materials in the library. Would you mind giving me a brief overview?

Librarian B: Not at all. Our multimedia collection is mainly located in the Media Resources Center on the 2nd floor. You may find the materials by searching in the library catalog. If you'd like to browse the shelves, materials are arranged by their media types such as DVD, VCD, CD, audio cassette and video cassette. Under each media type, materials are organized by language such as oriental or western languages. You can find what you want by the call numbers.

Professor A: Alright, I see. Thank you very much.
Librarian B: You're welcome.

Unit 6.1　以資料性質區分

6.1.1 館藏圖書資料
6.1.1.3 排架方式
情境：　A同學是大學部新生，他不知道圖書館書架上的書要如何找起，
　　　　到1樓服務台請館員幫忙。

A同學：嗨，您好。我在館藏目錄上找到*Global Sourcing Logistics*這本書，
　　　　我查到的號碼是658.7 C711。請問，可以告訴我要怎麼找到這本
　　　　書嗎？
B館員：您好！好的，這是英文書，我們先到5樓西方語文書庫。如果以後
　　　　您要找其他語文的書，可以看電梯旁的樓層位置圖。
A同學：喔，好的。
（B館員和A同學一起到5樓）。
B館員：請往這邊走，您可以先看書架側邊，側邊標示牌上會標示出索書
　　　　號的範圍，愛河圖書館西方語文圖書是採用杜威分類法，貼在書
　　　　脊上的這個標籤我們叫它書標，書標上面第一排的號碼就是杜威
　　　　分類號，同一類的書會集中在一起。圖書館排書的方式是從左到
　　　　右，從上到下，依分類號由小而大排列。找到658.7之後，再看書
　　　　標上的第二排號碼，這個叫做作者號，依照英文字母從A排到Z，
　　　　相同作者，同一主題的書就會集中在一起。您看，您要找的書在
　　　　這裡。
A同學：喔，太好了。謝謝，以後我知道怎麼找書了。
B館員：不客氣！

chapter 6

Unit 6.1 Search by Material Types

6.1.1 Library Materials
6.1.1.3 Arrangement of Library Materials
Situation: Student A is a college freshman. He doesn't know how to locate a book he wants. Therefore, he goes to the Information Desk on the 1st floor and asks for a librarian's help.

Student A: Hi, I found a book *Global Sourcing Logistics* in WebPAC and the call number is 658.7 C711. Would you please tell me how and where to find it?

Librarian B: No problem. This is an English book. Let's go to the Western Lanuguages Stacks on the 5th floor. Next time if you need books in other languages, you may take a look at the floor plans beside the elevators on each floor.

Student A: Oh, OK.

(Librarian B accompanies Student A to the 5th floor.)

Librarian B: This way, please. You'll see tags showing the range of call numbers on each side of the book shelves. At Love River, we utilize the Dewey Decimal Classification system for books in Western languages. Look, the label pasted on the book spine is called the call number label, on which the first row of numbers is the Dewey Decimal Classification number. Books of the same subject are shelved together using this system. We shelve books on the basis of the classification number from small to large numbers, from left to right and from top to bottom on the bookshelves. After you find the number 658.7, you should look at the number on the second row of the label, which is called the Cutter number or author number and arranged in alphabetical order A to Z. In this way, books by the same author and with the same topic will be gathered together.

查詢館藏資源 Search Library Collection & Resources

Look, here it is. This is the book you want.
Student A: Oh, great. Thank you. Now I understand how to locate books.
Librarian B: Good for you and you're welcome.

Unit 6.1 以資料性質區分

6.1.2 查詢期刊文獻
情境：A教授想要找一篇發表在*Second Language Research*第15卷第1期的論文。但不知道圖書館有沒有這一期的期刊，打電話詢問館員。

A教授：喂，您好，請問圖書館有沒有*Second Language Research*這份期刊？
B館員：您好，請稍等一下，我查一下。… 我們有訂購這本期刊，請問您要的是哪一卷哪一期？
A教授：第15卷第1期。
B館員：嗯，我們圖書館有這一期，放在3樓的裝訂期刊區，是按照期刊名稱的第一個字母排列。
A教授：太好了，謝謝您！
B館員：不客氣。
A教授：再見！
B館員：再見！

chapter 6

Unit 6.1 Search by Material Types

6.1.2 Find Journal Articles

Situation: Professor A is looking for an article published in the journal *Second Language Research*, volume 15, issue 1. He is calling a librarian because he doesn't know if the issue is available in the library.

Professor A: Hello. This is A. I'm wondering if journal issues of *Second Language Research* are available in our library.
Librarian B: Hi, please hold on a second. Let me check. Yes, we have this title. So, which volume and issue would you like?
Professor A: Volume 15, issue 1.
Librarian B: Yes, we do have this issue in the Bound Periodicals Area on the 3rd floor. The volumes are in alphabetical order according to the initial letter of the journal title.
Professor A: That's great. Thank you very much.
Librarian B: Not at all.
Professor A: Bye bye.
Librarian B: Bye bye.

Unit 6.1 以資料性質區分

6.1.3 查詢新聞資料
情境：A同學要準備一場演講，需要蒐集報紙的報導，他不知道圖書館報紙收藏的情況，因此到圖書館詢問館員。

A同學：請問圖書館有沒有2003年7月4日的*New York Times*？
B館員：抱歉，因為圖書館空間不足，我們只保留最近一年的報紙。不過，我們有訂購Lexis-Nexis電子資料庫，您可以用這個工具查查看。請稍等一下，我幫您查一下。有，您可以在Lexis-Nexis找到2003年7月4日的全文報導，不過，沒有圖，只有文字，這樣可以嗎？
A同學：沒關係，只要有報導內容就可以了，謝謝。
B館員：不客氣。

Unit 6.1 Search by Material Types

6.1.3 Find Newspaper Articles

Situation: Student A is preparing for a public speech and needs to collect some newspaper articles as references. He doesn't know anything about the newspaper collection in the library. Therefore, he goes to a librarian for help.

Student A: Excuse me. I'm wondering if I can find the *New York Times* for July 4th, 2003 in the library.

Librarian B: I'm sorry. We keep newspapers in print for one year only due to the library's space limitations. However, we do subscribe to an electronic database called Lexis-Nexis. You may try this tool. Please hold on a second. Let me check it for you. Yes, you may access the fulltext of the *New York Times* for July 4th, 2003 in Lexis-Nexis. However, only the text is available, no graphics. Is this okay with you?

Student A: Sure, text only is good enough. Thanks.

Librarian B: You're welcome.

Unit 6.1　以資料性質區分

6.1.4 查詢學位論文
情境：A同學想要看愛河大學研究生的畢業論文，可是不知道要怎麼找，到參考諮詢台詢問館員。

A同學：您好，我想要找愛河大學國際關係研究所去年畢業的研究生碩士論文，請問要怎麼找？
B館員：在我們學校，只要是2000年以後研究生的碩博士論文都是存放在「愛河大學學位論文系統」，網址是http://etd.loveriver.edu.tw，您可以到這裡下載電子全文。如果您要找的是2000年以前的論文，我們還沒有收錄在系統裡，要請您到4樓碩博士論文區，那裡的論文是依照學院和系所名稱排列的。
A同學：好的，我知道了。那麼請問要怎麼上「愛河大學學位論文系統」的網頁？
B館員：請您先到愛河圖書館網站，在畫面右上方，有個快速連結選項：「愛河大學學位論文系統」。點選這裡，就可以查了，而且可以下載全文。
A同學：好的，謝謝！我還有另外一個問題，除了電子全文之外，研究生是不是規定要把他們的紙本論文交給圖書館保存？
B館員：是的。
A同學：那麼，如果是去年的碩博士論文，請問圖書館會在什麼時候上架？
B館員：通常研究生繳交論文的時候都在學期末，我們會集中在暑假期間建檔編目，新學期開學前一個月會把論文整理好上架。
A同學：那麼，如果是其他學校的論文，圖書館會蒐集嗎？還是，我們可以透過愛河論文系統查到？
B館員：其他學校的碩博士論文，不容易完整蒐集到紙本論文，放在圖書

chapter 6

Unit 6.1 Search by Material Types

6.1.4 Find Theses and Dissertations
Situation: Student A would like to read the theses and dissertations written by Love River University graduate students, but he has no idea how to find them. Therefore, he goes to the Reference Desk to ask a librarian.

Student A: Excuse me. Can you tell me how to find last year's master theses from the Graduate School of International Relations at Love River University?
Librarian B: All of the Love River theses and dissertations from the year 2000 forward are available in the "Love River Electronic Theses and Dissertations System," which you'll find at this url: http://etd.loveriver.edu.tw. You can download the electronic fulltext from this sytem. If you'd like to get those completed before 2000, you must go to the Theses and Dissertations Area on the 4th floor because we haven't digitized them into the system yet. They are arranged alphabetically by college or school and then by department.
Student A: OK, I got it. Then how can I access the website of "Love River Electronic Theses and Dissertations System"?
Librarian B: Log onto the Love River Library website first. You'll see a shortcut link called "Love River Electronic Theses and Dissertations System" on the upper right hand side of the site. Click on this and you may start to search and download the theses.
Student A: OK, thanks. Another question, in addition to the electronic fulltext, are graduate students required to submit their theses in print to the library for its collection?
Librarian B: Yes, they are.
Student A: Then when will the library put last year's theses on the shelf?

館裡。我們通常都是到「全國碩博士論文系統」查詢，有些研究生會開放論文電子全文下載，有些不開放，這時候就必須利用館際合作的方式取得。其實很多大學也有建置和「愛河大學學位論文系統」一樣的碩博士論文全文系統，我們已經匯整好，放在圖書館網站上的「碩博士論文」專區，點選「國內大學」，就可以看到各校的論文系統超連結。各校都個別設定全文開放的權限限制，不過，這是尋找其他大學碩博士論文比較方便的方式。

A同學：喔，聽起來有點複雜，我需要自己試試看。
B館員：聽起來是有點複雜，但是實際上去做，你會發現沒有那麼困難。
A同學：好的，謝謝！
B館員：不客氣。

Librarian B: Graduate students usually hand in their theses or dissertations at the end of the semester. We collect and start to catalog them during the summer break. Theses and dissertations are available on the shelf a month before the new semester starts.

Student A: Are theses and dissertations from other universities available in our library? Or can we search for them in the "Love River Electronic Theses and Dissertations System"?

Librarian B: It's not easy to collect theses or dissertations from other universities. In general, we would try to search for those in the "National Theses and Dissertations System." Some graduate students agree to have their works available open access to the public while others do not. In this latter case, you have to request it through interlibrary loan. In fact, many universities have developed similar electronic theses and dissertations systems like the "Love River Electronic Theses and Dissertations System." We have already collected most of the links to these services on a webpage, available from the library website, called "Theses and Dissertations." Just click on "Colleges and Universities in Taiwan" and you'll see the link to each university's system. Each college or university has set its own limitations for open access. This is a more convenient way to search for theses from other universities.

Student A: Oh, it sounds a bit complicated. I need to try it out for myself.

Librarian B: It does. But you'll find that it is not as hard as you think when you give it a try.

Student A: Alright. Thanks.

Librarian B: It's my pleasure.

Unit 6.1 以資料性質區分

6.1.5 查詢研究報告

情境： A同學要寫一篇報告，老師規定一定要用學術性的資料作為參考文獻。他在網路上找的資料，老師看過都說不可以，所以他到圖書館詢問館員。

A同學：請問一下，要怎麼樣才能找到學術性的資料？

B館員：要找學術性資料，最方便的方法是利用圖書館訂購的電子資料庫來找。

A同學：我在網路上找到的資料都不算是學術性資料嗎？

B館員：您在網路上有可能找到學術性的資料，可是未必都能夠看到全文內容。網路上找到的資料，像部落格的文章，就不能算是學術性的資料，那只是個人的創作書寫。一般來說，學術性資料都會出版或發表在一些學會出版品或是有名的出版社期刊上，必須訂閱才能取得。但近年來，有些期刊透過網路，免費提供大眾取用全文，這種期刊叫做open access journals。

A同學：那麼，要怎麼找這些開放取用的學術論文呢？

B館員：在圖書館網站上，我們已經整理出來了，放在「電子期刊」這個項目之下，在這裡您會看到有Open Access Journals的網頁，上面會有說明。另外，如果您不是要找特定的期刊，其實可以用我們網頁上的「期刊論文入口網站」（Academic Articles Search Gateway），這裡整合了所有圖書館訂購的，還有網路上開放取用的電子期刊。您只要輸入關鍵字，入口網站就會幫您找出相關文章。您先查查看，如果需要幫忙的話，不用客氣，再來找我們。

A同學：好的，謝謝。

B館員：不用客氣。

chapter 6

Unit 6.1 Search by Material Types

6.1.5 Find Research Papers

Situation: Student A is writing a paper for which his professor has stipulated that only academic or scholarly resources are allowed as references. All of the resources that he finds on the web are rejected by the professor. Therefore, he turns to a librarian for help.

Student A: Excuse me, how can I find scholarly materials?
Librarian B: The best way to search for them is to use the electronic databases that the library subscribes to.
Student A: Doesn't the stuff on the Internet count as scholarly material?
Librarian B: You can find scholarly materials on the Internet, but fulltext is not necessarily accessible. Moreover, formats like the blog are not usually considered scholarly writing. Rather, blog entries represent more personal entries than academic writing. In general, scholarly materials are published by academic institutes or in journals by prestigious publishers, which contents are accessible by subscription only. But in recent years, there are some scholarly journals making their contents freely available to the public on the internet. They are called open access journals.
Student A: Then where can I find these open access scholarly articles?
Librarian B: You'll find a collection of Open Access Journals on the library website under the category of "Electronic Journals," where you'll see a brief description of "Open Access Journals." On the other hand, if you're not looking for a particular journal, you can use "Academic Articles Search Gateway," which is also available on the library website. This is a federeated search engine, which integrates resources subscribed to by our library and the free Open

Access Journals. Just type in your keywords and the Gateway will retrieve the relevant articles for you. Why don't you give it a try? And if you need any help, please feel free to come back to us.

Student A: OK. Thank you very much.

Librarian B: Don't mention it.

Unit 6.1 以資料性質區分

6.1.6 考古題
情境：A同學是大二的學生，他聽說圖書館有考古題可以供學生參考，期末考快到了，但他在圖書館的網站上仍然找不到任何考古題的資料，於是打電話到圖書館詢問。

A同學：喂，您好，我是歷史系二年級的學生，請問一下，圖書館有沒有蒐集各系期中或期末考的考古題？
B館員：您好，很抱歉，圖書館並沒有蒐集考古題，您可以問問看學務處的學習輔導中心。幾年前，圖書館已經把考古題的題庫系統移轉給學習輔導中心了。其實，這個訊息，我們一直放在圖書館網站上的「常問問題集」裡面，您可以再上網看看。
A同學：是這樣子嗎？可是我朋友告訴我他們學校的圖書館有考古題。
B館員：每個學校圖書館對於類似考古題的資料有不同的處理原則，我們學校是交給學習輔導中心。很抱歉，造成您的困擾。
A同學：沒關係，謝謝您的說明，那麼我再到學習輔導中心的網站上去看看，謝謝！
B館員：不客氣。

Unit 6.1 Search by Material Types

6.1.6 Old Exam Questions
Situation: Student A is a sophomore. He has heard there are copies of old exam questions available in the library for students. The final exam is approaching and he is still having difficulty finding these resources on the library website. He calls the library.

Student A: Hello, I'm a sophomore in the Department of History. I have heard there are copies of old midterm and final exam questions from each department in our library.
Librarian B: Well, I'm sorry, but we don't have these exam questions. You may contact the University Learning Center in the Office of Student Affairs. A couple of years ago we transferred the database of old exam questions and papers to the University Learning Center. In fact, we have added this information to the FAQ on the library website. You can check it out there.
Student A: Is it? But my friends told me they do have old exam questions at their university libraries.
Librarian B: Each university library has its own policy for dealing with this kind of resource. At Love River University, the database of old exam questions is managed by the University Learning Center. I'm sorry if that causes you any inconvenience.
Student A: That's fine. Thanks for your explanation and I'll take a look at the Univeristy Learning Center's website. Thank you.
Librarian B: You're welcome.

Unit 6.2 以工具類型區分

6.2.1 館藏目錄
6.2.1.1 以作者為檢索點
情境：A同學想要找Umberto Eco的書，可是不知道要如何開始，到服務台詢問館員。

A同學：您好，請問我們圖書館有沒有Umberto Eco的書？
B館員：您好，Umberto Eco這麼有名的作者，我們應該有他的作品，等我查查看。有的，共36筆資料。您要找哪一種語文的書？
A同學：我要看英文的，就是這一本*History of Beauty*。
B館員：好的，這本書在館內，索書號是111.85 E19，在5樓西方語文區。
A同學：您可以教我怎麼查嗎？下次我可以自己查。
B館員：當然可以，像這樣，我操作給您看，用我們的館藏目錄，選擇作者這個欄位，輸入作者的名字，記得要先輸入姓氏，例如：Eco, Umberto，這樣就可以找到他的作品。
A同學：謝謝。
B館員：不客氣。

Unit 6.2 Library Research Tools

6.2.1 Library Catalog

6.2.1.1 Search by Author

Situation: Student A is asking a librarian at the Service Desk how to find Umberto Eco's books in the library.

Student A: Hi, I'd like to know if Umberto Eco's books are available in our library holdings.

Librarian B: Hi, Umberto Eco is such a famous writer. I'm sure we must have his titles in our collection. Just a minute, let me check. Yes, there are 36 results. In what language are you looking for his works?

Student A: In English. Yes, this one, *History of Beauty*.

Librarian B: OK, this shows the status of the book as available. The call number is 111.85 E19, which is located in the Western Languages Stacks on the 5th floor.

Student A: Would you mind showing me again how to search so that I can check it by myself next time?

Librarian B: Sure! Like this, let me show you. Click on the library catalog, choose author field, and type in the author's name. Be sure to type the author's last name first. For example, Eco, Umberto, and then his books in our holdings will be displayed in the search results.

Student A: Thank you.

Librarian B: You're welcome.

Unit 6.2 以工具類型區分

6.2.1 館藏目錄
6.2.1.2 以主題為檢索點
情境：A同學想要找有關台灣旅遊的書，但找不到適合的書，到服務台詢問館員。

A同學：您好，我剛剛用目錄都找不到介紹台灣旅遊景點的英文書，您可以告訴我要怎麼找嗎？
B館員：請問您是用什麼方法找的？
A同學：我用書名查，然後輸入taiwan and guidebook。
B館員：嗯，我建議您用關鍵字，這樣可找到比較多相關的資料。您可以輸入：taiwan and travel，然後把出版日期限制在2006到2008，這樣可以找到比較新的旅遊書。
A同學：好，我現在就去試試看，謝謝！
B館員：不客氣，祝您好運！

Unit 6.2 Library Research Tools

6.2.1 Library Catalog
6.2.1.2 Search by Subject
Situation: Student A is looking for books about traveling in Taiwan, but she has difficulty finding what she wants. She then goes to the Information Desk to ask a librarian for help.

Student A: Hi, I cannot find any books in English on tourist attractions in Taiwan in the online catalog. Can you show me how to search?
Librarian B: Do you mind showing me the way you did the search?
Student A: Sure, I chose the title search and typed in "taiwan and guidebook."
Librarian B: Well, I would suggest you search by keyword. You can find more information this way; for instance, you can type Taiwan and travel and then, for the most recent publications, limit the publication year to 2006 through 2008.
Student A: OK, I'll give it a try right away. Thank you very much.
Librarian B: You're welcome. Good luck!

Unit 6.2 以工具類型區分

6.2.2 聯合目錄

情境：A同學要找Alain De Botton的書*The Art of Travel*，愛河圖書館沒有這本書，她想知道附近有哪一個圖書館可以借到這本書，可是不知道要怎麼查，到服務台詢問館員。

A同學：您好，我要找一本書，可是我們圖書館沒有。有沒有什麼辦法可以查到附近哪個圖書館有這本書？

B館員：嗯，有的。請您看一下這個畫面，圖書館網站上有一個「查詢圖書」的網頁，這裡有一個「查看他館館藏」，點選這個超連結，就可以查詢台灣所有圖書館的館藏，您可以限定區域，這樣就可以將範圍縮小在愛河大學鄰近的區域了。您要現在在這裡查？還是要自己到WebPAC查詢台查呢？

A同學：麻煩您幫我查一下，好嗎？

B館員：好，請您告訴我書名。

A同學：*The Art of Travel*，作者是Alain De Botton。

B館員：好的，請稍等一下。哈瑪星大學和蓮湖學院圖書館都有這本書。

A同學：那，我可以到這兩個圖書館借書嗎？

B館員：可以。不過，您需要到流通台借一張「館際合作借書證」，再用這張借書證到他們圖書館借書。

A同學：好的，謝謝您。

B館員：不用客氣。

Unit 6.2 Library Research Tools

6.2.2 Union Catalog

Situation: Student A is looking for a book called *The Art of Travel* written by Alain De Botton, which is not available in Love River University Library. She wonders from which library in the neighborhood she can borrow the book. She has no idea how to find this information, so she asks a librarian at the Information Desk.

Student A: Hello, I'm looking for a book which is not available in our library. Is it possible to get this book from any other library nearby?

Librarian B: Yes, please take a look here. We have a service called "Search Books" on our library website. Under this heading, you'll find a link for "Online Catalogs of Other Libraries." Click on it and you'll find links to the online catalogs of all the libraries in Taiwan. You may narrow your search results to the area within the neighborhood of Lover River University. Do you want to search it right now or later on your own at our WebPAC stations?

Student A: Would you please look it up for me?

Librarian B: Sure, please tell me the title again.

Student A: The title is *The Art of Travel*, and the author is Alain De Botton.

Librarian B: Alright, please wait a moment. It shows the book is available at Hamasei University and at Lotus Lake College.

Student A: Can I check out books from these two universities then?

Librarian B: Yes, but to do this you need to check out a reciprocal borrowing card at our Circulation Desk. Then use this card to check out books from either one of these libraries.

Student A: OK! Thank you!
Librarian B: You're welcome.

Unit 6.2 以工具類型區分

6.2.3 電子資料庫
情境：A教授想要找有關德國當代文學的資料，而且她要找的是以德文撰寫的文獻，但是她不清楚圖書館有什麼工具或資源可以利用，直接到圖書館詢問館員。

A教授：您好，我想要找有關德國當代文學的資料，如果我要找以德文撰寫的文獻，有什麼資料庫可以用？

B館員：您好，目前圖書館並沒有訂購德文資料庫，不過，美國Modern Language Association的MLA International Bibliography這個資料庫收集了英文以及其他歐洲語文的書目資料，您可以查查看。

A教授：嗯，我用過MLA International Bibliography，我以為它只有收集英文文獻。

B館員：雖然這裡收錄的資料以英文的文獻居多，可是我們的確可以在這裡找到其他的外文資料，只要您輸入關鍵字之後，再設定一下語言類型，在畫面下方有個Language的欄位請選擇German，這樣系統就會過濾出只有德文的文獻資料了。

A教授：好的，我知道了，那麼我再試試看，謝謝。

B館員：不客氣，如果還有什麼問題，您可以直接打電話過來問。

Unit 6.2 Library Research Tools

6.2.3 Electronic Databases

Situation: Professor A wants to search for information and articles about German contemporary literature written in German, but she has no knowledge of the resources available in the library. Therefore, she goes directly to a librarian.

Professor A: Excuse me. I'd like to search for some information or articles about German contemporary literature in German. Which databases should I use?

Librarian B: Hi. Well, we don't have any specific German databases available. However, you may try the MLA International Bibliography, provided by the Modern Language Association in the U.S. The coverage includes bibliographic information in English as well as in European languages.

Professor A: Oh, I've used this before, but I thought it provided information in English only.

Librarian B: Well, in fact it does offer more information in English, but we can still find information in other foreign languages too. When you type in your keywords, remember to limit your search by language to German. Then the system will retrieve articles in the German language.

Professor A: Alright, I got it. I'll try it later. Thank you.

Librarian B: You're welcome. If you have further questions, please feel free to give us a call.

Unit 6.2 以工具類型區分

6.2.4 電子期刊

情境：A同學是機械系教授的研究助理，教授給他一張書目，請他把資料找齊，其中有幾篇文章，A同學在電子資料庫中找不到全文，而且，有時候會碰到無法順利開啟電子全文的情形，所以到圖書館詢問館員。

A同學：您好，我想要找幾篇文章，可是在電子資料庫裡面找不到全文，請問，有什麼辦法可以找到嗎？

B館員：您有用館藏目錄查查看圖書館是不是有那本期刊雜誌或是論文集嗎？

A同學：沒有。

B館員：您方不方便讓我看一下您要找的文章的書目資料？

A同學：好啊，在這裡。

B館員：謝謝，請您稍等一下，我幫您查一下。比如這一篇文章，是發表在 *International Journal of Engineering Mechanics* 的第18卷第4期。您可以用館藏目錄，在書刊名的地方輸入 *International Journal of Engineering Mechanics*，查詢之後的結果，您看，我們有訂電子版和紙本期刊。您可以點選這個電子版，然後展開它的卷期，這樣就找到這篇文章的全文了。您要我把這篇全文先email給您嗎？還是您有帶隨身碟可以下載存檔？

A同學：太厲害了，您能幫我存到我的隨身碟嗎？

B館員：沒問題，存好了。

A同學：真的很謝謝您。那麼，其他文章也是用這樣的方法找嗎？

B館員：對啊，您試試看，如果還有問題，請不用客氣，再來找我們。

A同學：對了，有時候我用電子資料庫查到全文，卻沒有辦法下載，就是

Unit 6.2 Library Research Tools

6.2.4 E-Journals

Situation: Student A is a graduate assistant of a professor in the Mechanical Engineering Department. He is given a bibliography and needs to get all of the articles on the list. He couldn't find the fulltext of some articles in the electronic databases and some electronic fulltexts could not be opened successfully. Therefore, he comes to ask a librarian in the library for help.

Student A: Hi, I'm looking for some articles, for which the fulltext is not available in the electronic databases. What can I do?
Librarian B: Have you tried our library catalog to see if the journal or proceedings is in our library holdings?
Student A: Nope.
Librarian B: May I take a look at the bibliographic information?
Student A: Sure, here it is!
Librarian B: OK, thanks. Let me check for you. Just one moment please. Look at this one. It is published in the *International Journal of Engineering Mechanics*, volume 18, issue 4. You just type the journal title in the title field here in the library catalog. The search results show that we have the journal in electronic format as well as in print. Now when you click on the electronic version and the specific volume and issue, you'll find the article fulltext. Do you want me to email you this fulltext file or would you prefer downloading it to your USB?
Student A: Terrific! Would you please save the file to my USB?
Librarian B: No problem. Here it is!
Student A: Thanks a lot. So, I could try this same strategy for the other

　　　　　　雖然全文的軟體一直跑，可是等了很久之後，全文還是沒辦法顯
　　　　　　示。請問這要怎麼解決？
B館員：這個問題可能有兩種原因，一個原因和網路速度有關，網路速度如
　　　　果太慢，再加上如果PDF或其他全文影像檔很大的話，下載速度變
　　　　得很慢，就會造成這種情況。另一個原因可能是軟體的問題，這種
　　　　全文閱讀軟體大部分都是免費軟體或是試用版，如果軟體的版本和
　　　　全文的格式不相容或是試用期滿，也會造成這種狀況。所以，您可
　　　　以檢查看看是什麼問題。如果是網路速度的問題，那麼，您就得避
　　　　開網路尖峰時間。軟體的問題比較容易解決，只要更新或是重新申
　　　　請試用就好了。
A同學：好的，我知道了，我再試試看。謝謝！
B館員：不客氣！

articles?

Librarian B: Yes, you can. Why not give it a try? If you have further questions, you're welcome to contact us.

Student A: By the way, I have problems downloading fulltext files from some electronic databases. The reader software to open the file keeps running, but after waiting for a long time the message "Can't Display" appears. What can I do about this?

Librarian B: Well. There are two possibilities. It may be because of the internet speed. If the fulltext PDF file or other image format is too large, this will slow down the speed of the download and may cause the problem. The other reason may be a problem with the reader software. Most of the reader software is freeware or trial version. If the format of the electronic fulltext is not compatible with the version of the reader software or the trial period expires, the problem with downloading will also happen. Now you'll be able to figure out the problem. If this is because of the internet speed, you might want to try avoiding the busiest hours. If it is the software problem, then it's an easy fix. You just need to upgrade the version or re-download the free trials.

Student A: OK, I see. I'll try this later. Thank you.

Librarian B: You're welcome.

Unit 6.2 以工具類型區分

6.2.5 電子書

情境：A同學是愛河網路大學的學生，老師規定寫報告除了使用期刊文獻，也要利用圖書。因為他實在不方便到圖書館去借書，而住處附近的圖書館並沒有合適的專業圖書，於是用IMS詢問圖書館館員。

Guest1671：Hi，我是愛河網路大學的學生，想請問一下，圖書館是否提供圖書宅配的服務？
B館員：您好，很抱歉，我們尚未開放這樣的服務。嗯，您有沒有試過圖書館的電子書，看看有沒有您要找的書？
Guest1671：電子書？可以告訴我要怎麼找嗎？
B館員：當然可以。在圖書館網站，畫面上方有個Resources的選項，其中有個「Electronic Books」，這裡將圖書館蒐集和訂購的電子書依照出版商或代理商及收錄主題的特色排序。有些是開放性的資源，有些則需要校外連線設定，輸入您的學號和密碼之後，才可以使用。這個功能，您使用過嗎？
Guest1671：這個我知道，查電子資料庫的時候設定過了。
B館員：那麼，您就先查查看電子書，如果有問題，再上線或email來詢問。
Guest1671：嗯，請問這些電子書是專業學術性的？還是一般休閒閱讀的書？
B館員：都有，不過，專業和學術性的居多。
Guest1671：可以列印嗎？
B館員：可以，但是只能一頁一頁列印，大部分的電子書系統不會有一次就能印出整本的設計。

chapter 6

Unit 6.2 Library Research Tools

6.2.5 E-Books

Situation: Student A is a distance ed learner at Love River University. He has an assignment to work on and the professor requires journal articles and monographs as references for the paper. It is inconvenient for him to visit Love River Library and he cannot find appropriate materials in the libraries in his neighborhood. Therefore, he seeks help via IMS from a librarian at Love River Library.

Guest1671: Hi, I'm a distance ed student at Love River. I'm wondering if the library provides home delivery service.

Librarian B: Hello, I'm sorry but we are not providing that service yet. However, have you ever tried our e-book collection?

Guest1671: E-books? Would you tell me how to find this collection?

Librarian B: Sure. At the top of the library website, you'll see a menu for Resources, under which there is a category called "Electronic Books." We arrange the e-book collection by the publisher or vendor and the subject. Some of them are available open access and some require authentication by typing in your Love River ID no. and PIN. Have you used this remote access service before?

Guest1671: Yes, it is required when I access electronic databases.

Librarian B: Right. Now you can try a search of the e-book collection and if you have further questions, you may ping me again or send your question via email.

Guest1671: Alright. BTW, are these ebooks professional materials or of general interest?

Librarian B: Both, but more for professional and academic use than of

Guest1671:好的,了解,謝謝。
B館員:不客氣。

general interest.

Guest1671: May I print out the contents?

Librarian B: Of course, but only page by page. Most of the vendors don't allow printing out the entire book with just one click.

Guest1671: Alright. I see. Thanks.

Librarian B: You're welcome.

Unit 6.2 以工具類型區分

6.2.6 專利文獻
情境：研發處的A助理想要知道有關專利的資訊，可是不知道從何查起，直接打電話問館員。

A助理：您好，我是研發處的A助理，最近我負責整理全校教職員申請到專利的相關資料，不知道有哪些工具可以查詢專利紀錄？
B館員：請問您要查的是台灣的，還是國外的專利？
A助理：台灣和國外的都要。
B館員：嗯，如果是台灣的，您可以用經濟部智慧財產局的「專利資料檢索」；如果要查美國的專利，可以用美國專利商標局的「專利全圖文資料庫」（Patent Full-Text and Full-Page Image Databases）；世界性的，就可以用WIPO世界智慧財產權組織的網站。這些機構以及專利資料庫的網址，都可以在圖書館的網頁上找到。
A助理：請問在圖書館網站的什麼地方？
B館員：在網站上方有一個「主題資源」的選項，裡面有關於專利查詢的詳細說明，您可以參考看看。如果還需要幫忙，請您再打電話來或是親自來圖書館。
A助理：好，我先上圖書館網頁看看，謝謝您！
B館員：不客氣。
A助理：bye bye。
B館員：再見。

chapter 6

Unit 6.2 Library Research Tools

6.2.6 Patent Information

Situation: Assistant A from the Research and Development Office wants to learn how to search for patent information. She calls the library for help.

Assistant A: Hello, this is A from the R&D office. I'm working on a project to gather information about our faculty and staff members who are receiving patents. I don't know how to find this kind of information.

Librarian B: Do you want patents registered in Taiwan or internationally?

Assistant A: Both.

Librarian B: Hmm, to find patent information in Taiwan, you can try "Taiwan Patent Search" provided by the Intellectual Property Office. If you need patent information from the United States, please try "Patent Full-Text and Full-Page Image Databases" from the United States Patent and Trademark office. To find world patent information, you can use the WIPO patent search from the WIPO website. You can find links to all of the patent search databases I just mentioned listed on the library website.

Assistant A: Where on the library website?

Librarian B: At the top of the website, there is a menu called "Subject Guides," under which detailed information about patent searching and databases is provided. It is a good reference tool. If you need further help, you're welcome to call back or come to the library for more information.

Assistant A: OK. I'll take a look at it first. Thank you.

Librarian B: You're welcome.

Assistant A: Bye bye.

Librarian B: Bye.

Unit 6.2 以工具類型區分

6.2.7 網際網路

情境：A同學利用網路上的搜尋引擎Lingo查資料，想要找有關發生在非洲的種族大屠殺的資料，可是查到的網頁資料有數萬筆，她因為不知道要怎麼選擇資料，也不知道要如何將如此龐大的資料量縮小範圍，於是直接到參考諮詢台詢問館員。

A同學：您好，請問一下，如果我在網路上找到的資料太多，要怎麼把資料縮小範圍？

B館員：嗨，您好。您可以試著將主題縮小，也就是再加上幾個關鍵字，記得要仔細閱讀搜尋引擎的輔助說明，看看要使用什麼符號表示and, or, not 來作為您的搜尋策略，或是，要下什麼指令可以指定語言別、網站類型或國家。請問，您用什麼搜尋引擎？

A同學：我用Lingo。

B館員：好的，那麼，您可以將加號放在關鍵字前面，表示這個字一定要在網頁裡面出現。如果你要找的是台灣教育機構網站的網頁資料，你可以輸入site:.edu.tw。事實上，這些方法都可以在搜尋引擎首頁的輔助說明裡面找到。

A同學：如果我要侷限在學術性的資料，我是不是要把網址限制在.edu這樣的網站？

B館員：不一定，因為有些學會或出版社出版的文章，會有部分開放在網路上，他們的網址，可能是.org或.com。有比較方便的做法，例如：Google或Yahoo這兩大搜尋引擎，他們都有設立學術性資料的獨立網站，例如：Google Scholar或Yahoo Academia，只要在這種網站裡面找到的資料，都會是學術性的書刊資料，不過，如果要讀取全文，還是要透過它所提供的連結到資料庫或電子期刊才能取得，並非全部的資料都開放全文。

Unit 6.2 Library Research Tools

6.2.7 Internet Resources

Situation: Student A searches for information about genocide in Africa using Lingo, an internet search engine. The search results in thousands of pages. She doesn't know how to select information from the results or how to limit her search to narrow down the huge number of results. She goes to the Reference Desk for help.

Student A: Hi, excuse me. I have a question. What should I do to narrow down the huge search results from this search on the Internet?

Librarian B: Well, try to narrow down your topic by adding more keywords. One thing to remember is to read the search engine help screen carefully. You can learn about what symbols to use for a Boolean search strategy, such as AND, OR, NOT, as well as how to limit by language or known websites or country. By the way, which search engine do you use?

Student A: Lingo.

Librarian B: Alright. Then you may try putting a plus sign in front of your keyword. This means that the keyword must appear in the web pages. If you want your information specifically from the educational institutions in Taiwan, you can type in the word site colon dot edu dot tw. In fact, these strategies are available from the "search help" section on the top page of the search engine.

Student A: If I want to limit my search to scholarly information, I would set the websites to dot edu, wouldn't I?

Librarian B: Not necessarily. Some articles published by academic societies or publishers may be freely accessible on the web, and their website domain names are likely to be dot org or dot com.

A同學：那麼，這些搜尋引擎和電子資料庫有什麼不一樣？
B館員：電子資料庫需要付費訂購才能使用，而搜尋引擎則只要可以上網就可以查詢。所以，相對來說，其實是電子資料庫的功能和介面比較完整而可靠。而且，使用網路上的資料時需要警覺和存疑，而且必須要評估及查證。從電子資料庫裡面找到的資料，是可以讓你比較放心而且信賴的。
A同學：好的，我瞭解了，謝謝您花那麼多時間為我講解！
B館員：不客氣。

chapter 6

There is a better way to search for scholarly information. For instance, Google and Yahoo provide search engines, such as Google Scholar and Yahoo Academia, which retrieve scholarly information. All of your results will be scholarly bibliographic information, but not all of them provide fulltext. To access the full contents, you still need to link to the corresponding electronic databases or e-journals subscribed to by the library.

Student A: Then, what's the difference between these search engines and electronic databases?

Librarian B: Well, we need to pay an annual subscription fee to access electronic databases. While it is free to use search engines such as Google Scholar, as long as you have Internet access, the search functions and interface design of fee-based electronic databases provide a more thorough and reliable experience. Plus, it is important to remain vigilant and skeptical when you use information from the Internet; you must take care to evaluate and verify it. On the other hand, the results that you retrieve from the electronic databases are more trustworthy than those from the Internet.

Student A: Oh, I see. Thank you for your time and help.

Librarian B: Sure, you're welcome.

Unit 6.3 校外連線使用

情境：新年假期圖書館不開放，A同學想要趁著長假利用圖書館的電子資源，蒐集資料，準備撰寫碩士論文所需要的文獻分析。她打電話到圖書館，詢問館員有沒有什麼辦法可以使用這些資源。

A同學：您好，因為後天開始圖書館要閉館一個禮拜，我需要找資料寫我的畢業論文，請問圖書館網站上的電子資源可以開放在圖書館以外的地方查詢嗎？

B館員：可以的，您只要在校內都可以使用。如果是在校園以外的地方，只要設定校外連線，由系統確認身分正確之後也是可以使用的。請問，您是愛河大學的學生嗎？

A同學：是的。請問要怎麼設定？

B館員：您現在手邊有電腦可以上網嗎？

A同學：有啊，我現在的畫面就是在圖書館的首頁。

B館員：太好了，請您看一下畫面上方有一個叫做「電子資源」的選項，請點選這個項目，您就會看到「遠端使用說明」的網頁，照著裡面的步驟去設定代理伺服器，最後輸入您的學號以及密碼，身分確認成功之後，就可以用了。

A同學：好的，我看到了。謝謝！

B館員：不客氣。

Unit 6.3 Remote Access

Situation: The library will be closed for the New Year holidays. Student A wants to do some research for her thesis. She plans to use library electronic databases to work on a literature review during the holidays. She calls the library to ask if she can access these electronic resources when the library is closed.

Student A: Hello, I have learned that the library will be closed for a week in 2 days, but I need to do some research for my thesis. I'm wondering if the electronic resources on the library website are accessible from outside the library.

Librarian B: Sure. You can access them from anywhere on campus as long as you can get online. If you're off campus, you can also access the resources as long as you configure the proxy settings and enter your username and PIN correctly. Are you a student at Love River University?

Student A: Yes, I am. How do I configure the proxy settings?

Librarian B: Are you at a computer with Internet access right now?

Student A: Yes. And I'm currently on the library website.

Librarian B: Great. Now at the top of the website, you'll see a link called "Electronic Resources." Please click on it and then you'll see "Setup for Remote Access." Just follow the instructions step by step and you'll successfully configure the proxy settings. At the end, it will ask you to enter your Love River ID number and PIN. Once you're authenticated as a valid user, it will allow you to access these resources.

Student A: OK. I got it. Thanks.

Librarian B: You're welcome.

chapter 7
第七章

使用媒體資源中心
Use of Library Media Resources Center

Library Service English

Unit 7.1　不得攜入提袋、背包、食物及飲料

情境：A同學由咖啡輕食區出來，打算到媒體資源中心看影片。

B館員：對不起，麻煩您將背包及飲料放在外面的儲物櫃。
A同學：為什麼不能帶背包和飲料進去？我咖啡還沒喝完，而且是放在有蓋子的杯子裡。
B館員：因為這裡有很多管線、設備及視聽資料，食物碎屑和飲料會引來蟑螂、螞蟻，甚至老鼠，這些昆蟲和動物對設備和資料可能造成損害。而且大部份的視聽資料體積比較小，為了資料安全，也麻煩您不要將背包和提袋帶進來。
A同學：原來是這樣，謝謝。
B館員：謝謝您的配合。

Unit 7.1 Bags, Food and Drinks Are Not Allowed in the Center

Situation: Student A just came out of the Café and is heading for the Media Center to watch videos.

Librarian B: Excuse me. Please leave your backpack and drink in the locker outside the Center.
Student A: Why can't I take my backpack and drink with me? I haven't finished my coffee yet and the cup has a lid on it.
Librarian B: You can't take the drink in because there are lots of wires, equipment and audio-visual materials in the Center. Food crumbs and drink will attract cockroaches, ants and even mice. These insects and animals will cause damage to our equipment and materials. For security purposes, since most of the audio-visual materials are small-sized, backpacks and bags are not allowed in the Center.
Student A: I see. Thank you.
Librarian B: Thank you for your cooperation.

Unit 7.2 視聽資料借用

情境：A教授挑好3片DVD，到流通台準備辦理借出手續。

A教授：請問這些DVD可以借多久？
B館員：您是要教學用？還是一般借用？
A教授：這一片我想在課堂上播放，其他兩片是要自己看。
B館員：教學用資料可以長期借閱，借期是一個月，一般借閱只能借3天。
A教授：好的。
B館員：您上課要用的這片DVD10月21日到期，另外兩片9月24日到期。
A教授：謝謝。
B館員：不客氣。

Unit 7.2 Borrow Media Materials

Situation: Professor A picks out 3 DVDs and wants to check them out at the Circulation Desk.

Professor A: Excuse me. For how long can I borrow these DVDs?
Librarian B: Are they for teaching purposes or just for general viewing?
Professor A: I would like to show this DVD in my class, but the other two will just be for leisure viewing.
Librarian B: If it's for teaching purposes the materials can be borrowed for a longer period, which is a month. If it's not, the loan period is 3 days.
Professor A: OK.
Librarian B: The one you want to show in your class will be due on October 21st. The due date for the other two DVDs is September 24th.
Professor A: Thank you.
Librarian B: You're welcome.

Unit 7.3 預約小團體欣賞室

情境：A同學和3位同學來到媒體資源中心，想要借小團體欣賞室，一起看「*蜘蛛人II*」。

A同學：請問現在可以借小團體欣賞室嗎？
B館員：抱歉，所有的小團體欣賞室都有人用，您要不要預約其他時間？
A同學：真是太不巧了，請問我可以約後天下午兩點嗎？
B館員：可以的，請問還是您們四位嗎？
A同學：是的。
B館員：以後您可以上網預約，從媒體資源中心網頁上您可以看到小團體欣賞室的預約情況，這樣就不會白跑一趟了。
A同學：謝謝您告訴我。
B館員：不過請您特別注意，如果預約時間過了10分鐘，您們還沒有來，我們就不再為您們保留，這時候如果臨時有人要用，就會讓他們使用。
A同學：好的，我們會記得準時來。
B館員：謝謝。

Unit 7.3 Reserve Small-Group Viewing Room

Situation: Student A comes to the Media Resources Center with 3 of his classmates. They want to borrow *Spiderman II* and watch it together in the Small-Group Viewing Room.

Student A: Excuse me. Can we use the Small-Group Viewing Room now?
Librarian B: I'm sorry. All of the Small-Group Viewing Rooms are currently being used. Do you want to reserve one for another time?
Student A: Too bad. Can we reserve one for the day after tomorrow at 2:00 p.m.?
Librarian B: Sure. Is this still for the four of you?
Student A: Yes.
Librarian B: Next time you might want to make a reservation online. From our webpage you can see what times the rooms are available. That way you don't waste a trip.
Student A: Thank you for letting me know.
Librarian B: I would like to remind you that if you don't show up within 10 minutes after the reserved time, the room will no longer be held for you. We will let other people use it if they request it.
Student A: OK. We will be on time.
Librarian B: Thank you.

Unit 7.4 設備故障

情境：A同學因為觀看DVD時聽不到聲音，到媒體資源中心服務台請求協助。

A同學：抱歉，不知道為什麼這片DVD只看得到影像，聽不到聲音。
B館員：您有沒有檢查一下耳機插座是不是鬆了？
A同學：我看過了，沒有鬆。
B館員：請問您的座位是幾號？
A同學：15號。
B館員：也許是耳機有問題，等一下我會請工作人員過去檢查，麻煩您改用8號座位。
A同學：好的，謝謝。
B館員：不客氣。

Unit 7.4 Facilities Out of Order

Situation: Student A can't hear the sound track while watching a DVD in the Media Resources Center. She goes to the Service Desk for help.

Student A: Excuse me. I don't know why there were only pictures without sound when I was watching this DVD.
Librarian B: Did you check the headset plug to see if it was loose?
Student A: Yes, I did. It wasn't loose.
Librarian B: What was your seat number?
Student A: No. 15.
Librarian B: It might be a problem with the headset. I'll ask someone to check it out later. Would you please use Seat No. 8 instead?
Student A: Sure, thanks.
Librarian B: You're welcome.

Unit 7.5 資料轉錄

情境：A教授希望上課時播放一段*Roman Empire*電影錄影帶，可是教室裡沒有錄放影機，只有DVD放映機，因此他詢問媒體資源中心館員是否可以代為轉錄成DVD。

A教授：嗨，您好！我查過圖書館的目錄，媒體資源中心只有*Roman Empire*錄影帶，沒有DVD，我想要在課堂上放一小段，可是教室裡沒有錄放影機，不知道媒體資源中心可不可以幫我轉錄成DVD？

B館員：很抱歉，因為轉錄視聽資料違反著作權法，我們沒辦法提供這樣的服務。

A教授：即使是公播版的錄影帶也不能轉錄嗎？

B館員：是的，真的很抱歉，不過您可以請學生自己來媒體資源中心觀賞。

C教授：謝謝，我會請學生來看。

B館員：不客氣。

Unit 7.5 Media Materials Conversion

Situation: Professor A wants to show a clip of the video *Roman Empire* to his class. The classroom does not have a tape player, but there is a DVD player. He asks the librarian in the Media Resources Center if she can make a DVD copy for him.

Professor A: Hi. I have checked the library catalog. *Roman Empire* is not available on DVD in the library, only on VHS tape. Since I want to show a clip of the movie to my students and there is only a DVD player in the classroom, can you make a DVD copy for me?

Librarian B: I'm sorry. We don't provide that kind of service because it is against the copyright law to make a copy.

Professor A: Even though it includes the public performance rights?

Librarian B: No, I'm sorry, we can't make a copy. You can always ask your students to come to the Center and watch the tape here.

Professor A: Thank you. I'll do that.

Librarian B: You're welcome.

Unit 7.6 校外使用隨選視訊系統

情境：愛河大學圖書館的隨選視訊系統提供非常多影片、教材及學校活動紀錄，深受師生喜愛。A同學在媒體資源中心隨選視訊系統上看了一期「空中英語教室」，明天就是週末了，她很想知道回家以後是不是可以繼續看其他期的內容，於是到服務台詢問館員。

A同學：請問媒體資源中心隨選視訊系統上的影片，在家裡可以看嗎？
B館員：可以的，我們的隨選視訊系統是校園版的，就像您在家利用圖書館訂的電子資料庫一樣，只要上圖書館網頁，在隨選視訊系統網頁輸入帳號密碼就可以了。
A同學：那麼，畫面的品質也和在圖書館看一樣嗎？
B館員：一般來說應該是相同的，但也需要看您電腦螢幕的解析度和家裡ADSL的網路頻寬是不是足夠。還有，請記得不要同時開好幾個網站，那樣會讓影片播放的速度變慢。
A同學：好的，謝謝您。

chapter 7

Unit 7.6 Remote Access to Video-On-Demand

Situation: The VOD system at Love River University Library contains a large number of videos, teaching materials and school event archives. They are very popular among faculty and students. Student A viewed one issue of Studio Classroom on VOD in the Media Resources Center. Tomorrow is the weekend. She wants to know whether she can view other issues from home. Therefore, she asks a librarian at the Service Desk.

Student A: Excuse me. I'm wondering if I can watch Studio Classroom on Video-On-Demand from home.

Librarian B: Certainly you can. Like the databases subscribed to by the library, our VOD system can be accessed from anywhere on or off campus. You just go to the library website and key in your username and password on the VOD webpage to view it.

Student A: Will it have the same visual quality as when I view it at the library?

Librarian B: Generally speaking, it should be the same, but it also depends on the resolution of your computer screen and the ADSL bandwidth at your home. Also, please remember not to connect to too many websites at the same time. That will cause the video speed to slow down.

Student A: OK. Thank you.

第八章

chapter 8

使用館內硬體設備（電腦、電話、影印機、印表機、掃瞄器……）
Use of Library Facilities
(PCs, Phones, Photocopiers, Printers, Scanners, etc.)

Library Service English

Unit 8.1 無線上網

8.1.1 登入帳號密碼

情境：A同學第一次帶他的手提電腦到圖書館，開機後發現當他要使用圖書館資源時，螢幕上就跳出要他輸入帳號密碼的視窗，他輸入自己平常校外連線認證用的帳號密碼，但無法進入，因此到服務台詢問。

A同學：對不起，請問一下，我在討論區使用手提電腦，為什麼我輸入平常校外連線認證用的帳號密碼，卻一直沒辦法進入？

B館員：您是第一次在校內使用手提電腦嗎？

A同學：是的。

B館員：是這樣的，為了保障校內的資訊安全，學校必須對所有使用網路的非校內電腦進行認證，您一定要用學校提供的email帳號和密碼通過認證，沒有帳號密碼的人就不能進入學校的任何資訊系統。預設的帳號是您的學號，密碼是您身分證字號的後4碼，這裡要求您輸入的就是這組帳號密碼。

A同學：那麼我能不能更改帳號及密碼呢？

B館員：帳號是不能改的，但是您可以更改密碼。您需要修改的應該是學校email的密碼，因為使用手提電腦進入學校系統，需要以這一組帳號密碼來通過驗證。

A同學：那麼要怎麼修改我的密碼呢？

B館員：您需要先以學校預設的帳號密碼進入個人網路信箱，點選上方的「設定」功能，再進入「變更密碼」的功能就可以了。

A同學：好的，謝謝。

B館員：不客氣。

Unit 8.1 Wireless Internet Access

8.1.1 Log in

Situation: It is the first time for Student A to bring his laptop to the library. When he turns on the computer and tries to use the electronic resources, a window pops up asking him to key in his username and password. After keying in the login information he normally uses, Student A still can't get access. He goes to the Service Desk for help.

Student A: Excuse me. I have a question. I was trying to use my laptop in the discussion area, but I couldn't get a connection with the login information I normally use. Why is this?

Librarian B: Is this the first time you have used your laptop on campus?

Student A: Yes.

Librarian B: That's why. In order to protect information security on campus, the university needs to authenticate all the internet computers which are not owned by the university. For this reason you have to use the email address and PIN provided by the university. No one can access any University Information System without this PIN. The default username is your student number and the default password is the last four digits of your personal ID number. These are the username and password required of you.

Student A: Can I change the PIN?

Librarian B: You may change the password, but not the username. What you might want to change is the password for your University Webmail because whenever you want to access the University Information System through a laptop, this PIN is always required for authentication.

Student A: Then how can I change my password?

Librarian B: First you need to log into the University Webmail with your default PIN provided by the university. Click on the "Preferences Option" key at the top of the screen to select the "Change Password" function.

Student A: I see. Thank you.

Librarian B: You're welcome.

Unit 8.1 無線上網

8.1.2 訊號接收不良
情境：A同學在書庫區的閱覽座位使用手提電腦上網,試了好多次,都無法連上,她到服務台詢問原因。

A同學：請問一下,為什麼我的手提電腦在4樓書庫區一直沒辦法連上網?
B館員：連不上無線網路的原因,通常是因為您坐的位置正好處於訊號死角,或和無線寬頻數據機(AP)之間有書架或柱子,因為訊號傳送的路線被擋住了,妨礙了訊號的收送,所以沒有辦法連上。您要不要換個離書架及柱子較遠、四周空間大些的座位試試看?
A同學：好的。
B館員：如果還是不能連上,麻煩再告訴我們。
A同學：好的,謝謝。
B館員：不客氣。

Unit 8.1 Wireless Internet Access

8.1.2 Poor Connection Quality
Situation: Student A has tried many times to access the Internet with her laptop in the Book Stacks, but fails. She goes to the Service Desk to ask why this happens.

Student A: Excuse me. Why can't I access the Internet from the Book Stacks on the 4th floor?
Librarian B: If you can't access the Internet, it's usually because you're sitting in an area which is not reachable by the AP's signal or there are bookshelves or structural poles between you and the AP. Since the route for the signal to travel is blocked, the Internet is not accessible. I suggest that you move to a more spacious area where the poles or bookshelves are farther away and try again.
Student A: OK.
Librarian B: If you still can't access the Internet, please let us know.
Student A: Yes, I'll. Thank you.
Librarian B: You're welcome.

Unit 8.2 卡式或投幣式影印

情境：A同學在參考資料區的一本書上找到他需要的圖片，由於參考資料區的書不能外借，他決定將圖片影印下來，但不知道那裡有影印機，因此到服務台詢問。

A同學：請問我想要影印一張圖片，那裡有影印機？
B館員：圖書館每層樓都有影印室，固定在洗手間對面。
A同學：影印機是卡式的，還是投幣式的？
B館員：兩種都有，如果您要用儲值卡，可以直接在影印室購買，影印室裡也有加值機，儲值卡裡的錢不夠了，您可以自己加值。
A同學：如果我要掃瞄呢？
B館員：地下1樓數位區有掃瞄器，您可以把書拿下去掃瞄以後存在您的隨身碟上，您也可以用儲值卡把掃瞄的圖列印出來。
A同學：謝謝。
B館員：不過要提醒您，不論是影印或掃瞄資料，請務必遵守著作權法的規定，在合法的範圍內，或符合合理使用原則的情形下複製及利用資料。
A同學：我會的，謝謝您。
B館員：不客氣。

Unit 8.2 Photocopy Services

Situation: Student A finds a picture he needs from a book in the Reference Collection Area. Since the books in the Reference Collection cannot be checked out, he decides to make a copy of the picture. He doesn't know where the copier is located, so he goes to the Service Desk to ask for directions.

Student A: Excuse me. I want to make a copy of a picture. Would you mind telling me where there is a copier?
Librarian B: There is a Photocopy Room on every floor, located right across from the restroom.
Student A: Are they card-operated or coin copiers?
Librarian B: We have both. If you want to use the prepaid card, you can buy it in the Photocopy Room. There is also a deposit machine for the prepaid card. If there is not enough money on your card, you can make a deposit yourself.
Student A: What if I want to scan the picture?
Librarian B: There are scanners in the Digital Area on the ground floor. You can take the book there to scan it and save the scanned copy on your USB. Or you can print out the scanned copy with your prepaid card.
Student A: Thank you.
Librarian B: I would like to remind you about something. When you photocopy or scan materials, please do obey the copyright law. Only copy and use the materials within the legal limit or follow the fair use doctrine.
Student A: I will. Thanks.
Librarian B: You're welcome.

Unit 8.3 使用電腦

8.3.1 無法使用IMS

情境：A同學在圖書館資訊檢索區想和朋友線上對談，發現電腦裡並沒有安裝MSN、Yahoo! Messenger等即時通訊軟體，他到服務台詢問原因。

A同學：請問資訊檢索區的電腦為什麼不提供MSN或Yahoo! Messenger的功能？
B館員：多數人使用MSN這類即時通訊軟體的目的是聊天，資訊檢索區電腦數目有限，而這裡的電腦主要是供大家查資料或做作業用的，因此不提供這類軟體。如果您要使用IMS的功能，可以到地下1樓的數位區，那裡的電腦安裝有即時通訊軟體。
A同學：哦，我知道了，謝謝。
B館員：不客氣。

Unit 8.3 Use of PCs

8.3.1 Instant Message Service Not Available
Situation: Student A wants to chat with his friend online in the Information Access Area of the library, but he discovers that neither MSN nor Yahoo! Messenger is installed. He goes to the Service Desk to ask about it.

Student A: Why doesn't the library install MSN or Yahoo! Messenger on the computers in the Information Access Area?
Librarian B: Most people use IMS to chat. Since we have only a limited number of computers in the Information Access Area, they are reserved for people who need to find information or to do assignments. Therefore no IMS software is provided. If you need to use IMS, you can go to the Digital Area on the ground floor. The computers there are installed with IMS software.
Student A: I see. Thank you.
Librarian B: You're welcome.

Unit 8.3 使用電腦

8.3.2 特殊軟體需求

情境：A同學是視覺藝術系的同學，她的期末報告需要製作紀錄片，她希望知道圖書館有沒有比較專門的軟硬體可以用，因此打電話來詢問。

B館員：喂，愛河大學圖書館，您好！
A同學：嗨，您好，我是愛河大學的學生，請問圖書館有沒有高解析度的掃瞄器，或者圖書館的電腦有沒有安裝像是Photoshop或Premiere Pro5之類的專業影像處理、影片剪輯軟體？我需要掃瞄一些圖片，並且剪輯影音檔。
B館員：有的，您可以到地下1樓的多媒體電腦區，那裡有專業的多媒體電腦和高解析度的掃瞄器，多媒體電腦區的電腦都安裝有專業多媒體編輯軟體。不過您可能需要先上網預約。
A同學：是在圖書館網頁上預約嗎？
B館員：是的。
A同學：謝謝。
B館員：不客氣。

Unit 8.3 Use of PCs

8.3.2 Specific Software Needs

Situation: Student A is a student in the Department of Visual Arts. She needs to make a documentary video for her final project. She wants to know if there is any special software and hardware available in the library that she could use. So, she calls the library to find out.

Librarian B: Love River Library. May I help you?

Student A: Yes. I'm a student at Love River University. I'm wondering if the library has any high resolution scanner or professional image processing or editing software, like Photoshop or Premiere Pro5 installed. I need to scan some pictures and edit some audio and video files.

Librarian B: Yes, we do. You'll want to go to the Multimedia Studio on the ground floor. They have professional multimedia computers and high resolution scanners. All of the computers there have professional multimedia editing software installed. You'll need to make an online reservation first.

Student A: Do I reserve the computer through the library webpage?

Librarian B: Yes.

Student A: Thank you.

Librarian B: You're welcome.

Unit 8.3 使用電腦

8.3.3 無法將資料存在電腦中
情境：A同學由網路上抓了一些要用的資料，卻發現沒辦法存在電腦上，他覺得不解，因此到服務台詢問館員。

A同學：對不起，我想請問一下，為什麼我沒有辦法把在網路上找到的資料存在電腦裡？

B館員：請問您是用那一區的電腦？

A同學：就是那邊標示「館藏查詢區」的電腦。

B館員：是這樣的，為了管理上的考量，圖書館各樓層的「館藏查詢區」電腦是採用系統集中管理。在這些電腦上，您沒有辦法由硬碟中存取資料，必須將資料存在自己帶來的隨身碟上。「館藏查詢區」的電腦主要用途是提供大家查詢圖書館有那些資料，如果您在查詢之外，還需要存取資料時，建議您用1樓「資訊檢索區」或地下1樓「數位區」的電腦，這些電腦上使用的限制比較少。

A同學：那我現在找到的資料該怎麼辦？你們有隨身碟可以借我儲存嗎？

B館員：很抱歉，圖書館沒有辦法提供這方面的服務。

A同學：好吧，我只好自認倒楣了。

B館員：對不起，希望您能諒解。

Unit 8.3 Use of PCs

8.3.3 Problems with Saving Files on Library PCs

Situation: Student A has downloaded some useful information from the Internet, but can't save it on the computer. He is puzzled and goes to the Service Desk to ask a librarian why this is.

Student A: Excuse me. I would like to know why I can't save the information I downloaded from the Internet to the computer.
Librarian B: In which area were you using the computer?
Student A: The area with the sign "Online Catalog."
Librarian B: I see. In order to better manage the workstations, WebPAC stations on each floor are centrally controlled by the system. On those computers you can neither save nor retrieve information to or from the hard disk. You have to save the file on your own USB instead. The main function of those WebPAC stations is for users to search the library's collection. If you also want to save or retrieve information, I suggest you use the computers in the Information Access Area on the 1st floor or the Digital Area on the ground floor. There are fewer restrictions on those computers.
Student A: Then what should I do about the materials I have already downloaded? Does the library have a USB I can borrow?
Librarian B: I'm sorry. We do not provide that service.
Student A: OK. I guess I'm just not very lucky today.
Librarian B: I'm sorry. Thank you for your understanding.

第九章
chapter 9

教師服務
Faculty Services

Library Service English

Unit 9.1 教師指定參考資料

情境：學期即將結束，圖書館發出一封email給全校教師，調查下學期課程是否有圖書資料要列為教師指定參考資料。

主旨：指定參考資料推薦作業已經開始

親愛的老師，您好：

下學期的教師指定參考資料申請作業即將展開，請各位老師將本郵件所附的「指定參考資料申請表」填妥後寄至本館電子郵件信箱（abc@mail.loveriver.edu.tw）。本次的推薦截止日期為12月15日，請各位老師多加利用，謝謝。

以下是申請時需要注意的事項：
1、新進老師請於取得任教課表後一週內提出推薦，以便圖書館作業。
2、所開列圖書若已外借，本館將予以催還；若館內並無收藏，則以緊急採購處理；如為老師私人圖書，請送交流通台；如為影印資料，請授課老師自行裝訂後送交流通台。
3、學期中教師如需增列指定參考書，本館隨時受理。

若有疑問，歡迎洽詢圖書館A先生，分機3208，
Email: abc@mail.loveriver.edu.tw。

Unit 9.1 Course Reserves

Situation: It is going to be the end of the semester. A library email message is sent to all the faculty members and instructors to ask them if they will put any course reserves for the upcoming semester.

Topic: Submit Course Reserves for the New Semester

Dear Faculty Members,

It is time to submit your course reserves for the next semester. Please fill out the "Course Reserves Request Form" attached to this email and mail to the library (abc@mail.loveriver.edu.tw). The deadline for submission is December 15th. You're encouraged to do so by this date. Thank you.

When submitting the form, we would like to remind you of the followings:
1. For new faculty the form may be turned in within a week of when the course schedule is received from the Office of Academic Affairs.
2. The library will recall books that are checked out. If materials are not available in the library, you may submit requests for urgent purchases. For items from your personal collection, please send books or bound articles to the library's Circulation Desk.
3. If you need to put additional items on course reserves during the semester, we are happy to help.

Should you have further inquires, please feel free to contact Mr. A at campus extension 3208 or email: abc@mail.loveriver.edu.tw。

Sincerely yours,

Unit 9.2 委託代借

情境:C教授沒空到圖書館借書,因此將他的證件交給研究助理,委託他到圖書館代為借書。

A助理:您好,我是C教授的研究助理,他託我用他的證件來借書。
B館員:嗯,根據紀錄我們並沒有收到C教授委託代借的申請,請您稍等一下,我先和C教授連絡一下。請你告訴我他的分機號碼。
A助理:6514。
(B館員拿起電話撥給C教授。)
B館員:喂,請問是C教授嗎?我是愛河大學圖書館B館員。
C教授:您好,我就是。
B館員:您好,我想要確認一下您是否委託您的助理A先生用您的證件來幫您借書?
C教授:是的,因為我最近沒空上圖書館,所以請他去幫我借書。請問有什麼問題嗎?
B館員:嗯,是這樣的,讓我稍微解釋一下。圖書館的確有提供老師委託代理人借書的服務,不過,做法上並不是由教授將自己的證件直接交給代理人來圖書館借書,因為這樣並不能確認您是否真正授權,所以,為了確保是授權代理,您必須向圖書館申請委託代借,最多可以指定兩位代理人。委託代借有兩種形式:一種是「基本授權」,另一種是「完全授權」。您可以到圖書館網站下載申請表,或者,我可以直接將申請表email給您。
C教授:麻煩您直接email表格給我,另外,請問這兩種授權形式有什麼差別?
B館員:「基本授權」指的是,您的代理人只要告知我們您的教職員證號並出示他的證件確認身分,他所代為外借的書,就會出現在您的借閱紀錄中。不過,如果您有兩位代理人,這樣的做法無法顯示是哪一位代理人來幫您借的,而且代理人也無法幫您線上續借或

Unit 9.2 Proxy Borrower Request

Situation: Professor C is too busy to go to the library, so he gives his faculty ID card to Assistant A and asks him to borrow books for him.

Assistant A: Hi, I'm Professor C's assistant. Professor C gave me his faculty ID card and wants me to borrow books for him.
Librarian B: Hmm. We don't have a record of Professor C's proxy borrowing application here. Just a moment please, let me check with Professor C. Would you mind giving me his campus extension number?
Assistant A: 6514.
(Librarian B picks up the phone and dials Professor C's extension number.)
Librarian B: Hello. May I speak to Professor C? I'm B from Love River Library.
Professor C: Hi, this is Professor C speaking.
Librarian B: Hi, Professor C. I'm calling to verify that you sent Mr. A to borrow books for you with your faculty ID card.
Professor C: Yes. I have been very busy recently and haven't had time to get to the library, so I asked my assistant to borrow books for me. Is there a problem?
Librarian B: Yes. There are a few things I would like to explain to you. The library does provide the proxy borrowing service for faculty, but not by letting your assistant check out books with your faculty ID card. Since we cannot be sure that you have granted another person this right, you need to apply for proxy borrowing first. You can grant the right to up to two persons. There are two types of proxy borrowing. One is "Basic Proxy" and the other one is "Enhanced Proxy." You can download the

　　　　　預約。如果是「完全授權」，表示您授權給代理人的權限和您本人的相同，他們可以在線上讀取您的借閱紀錄，幫您辦理線上續借或者預約。這樣的完全授權，會由圖書館發給您一組專屬的帳號，由您轉告給您所授權的代理人使用。
C教授：好的，我知道了，之前我並不曉得圖書館的委託代借是這樣辦理的。那麼，這一次，能不能先通融一下，讓我的助理先用我的證件借書？
B館員：好的，不過，下不為例喔。請問您的email帳號是什麼？我等一下把申請表寄給您。
C教授：好的，謝謝。我的email是ccc@mail.loveriver.edu.tw。
B館員：不客氣，再見！
C教授：麻煩您了，再見！
（B館員放下電話，轉向A助理。）
B館員：抱歉，讓您久等了。請您給我C教授的證件，我先幫您辦理外借的手續。以後，就要依照規定辦理了！
A助理：好的，證件在這裡，謝謝您的協助。
B館員：不客氣。好了，這5本書是7月16日到期。
A助理：謝謝！
B館員：不客氣！

application form from the library website or I can just email you the form.
Professor C: Please email me the application form. What are the differences between these two types of proxy borrowing?
Librarian B: With "Basic Proxy," your deputy needs only to tell us your faculty number and show his own ID card to check out books for you. All of the books he checks out with proxy borrowing will be on your record. By doing this, if you have assigned proxy borrowing to two deputies, it is not clear which of the deputies has borrowed books for you. Also, your deputy can't renew books or place a hold online for you. With "Enhanced Proxy," your deputy has exactly the same rights as you do. That means he or she can view your borrowing record, renew books or place a hold online. If this is the type of proxy you apply for, the library will give you a PIN number. Your deputy can use this PIN to check out books for you.
Professor C: Good. Now I know. I didn't know about the proxy borrowing policy before. Can you make an exception this time and let my assistant check out books for me with my faculty ID card?
Librarian B: Yes, I can, but not the next time. Would you mind giving me your email address? This is so I can email you the application form later.
Professor C: Thank you. My email address is ccc@mail.loveriver.edu.tw.
Librarian B: You're welcome. Bye.
Professor C: Bye. Thank you for your help.
(Librarian B puts down the receiver and turns to Assistant A.)
Librarian B: I'm sorry to make you wait for so long. Would you please give me Professor C's ID card and I'll check out the books for you.

> Next time you'll have to follow the policy.

Assistant A: Yes. Here is the ID card. Thank you for your help.

Librarian B: You're welcome. Here are the books. These 5 books are due on July 16th.

Assistant A: Thank you.

Librarian B: You're welcome.

Unit 9.3 支援課程—安排圖書資源利用說明

情境：A教授開設一門大學部「英文研究寫作」以及研究所「研究方法」的課，課程中有文獻搜尋的單元，A教授想要請圖書館員到課堂上為學生介紹圖書館資源以及解說資料查詢的方法，於是打電話到圖書館預約時間。

D館員：喂，愛河圖書館讀者服務組，您好。
A教授：喂，您好，我是英文系的A教授，我想請館員到課堂上來為學生說明圖書館資源和找資料的方法，請問，我應該和誰連絡？
D館員：嗯，課程支援方面是由B小姐負責，她的分機是3126，請稍後，我幫您轉接。
A教授：好的，謝謝您。
D館員：不客氣。
（D館員將電話轉給B館員。）
B館員：喂，讀者服務組，您好。
A教授：嗨，您好，請問是B小姐嗎？我是英文系的A老師。
B館員：是的，我就是，A教授，有什麼需要我幫忙的地方嗎？
A教授：是這樣的，如果想請館員到我的課堂上為同學介紹圖書館資源和資料查詢的方法，我需要怎麼申請？
B館員：請問，您開的是什麼課？
A教授：有兩門課，一門是大三的「英文研究寫作」，一門是研究所一年級的「研究方法」。
B館員：好的，那麼您計畫什麼時候要安排這兩個單元？
A教授：大三的課是5月2日星期五上午10:00-12:00，研究所的是5月7日星期三下午2:00到4:00。
B館員：嗯，5月2日這一天沒有問題，不過，5月7日的這個時間，教育系

Unit 9.3 Library Instruction for a Class

Situation: Professor A is teaching "English Research Writing" to undergraduates and "Research Methods" to graduate students. Both courses include an information research unit. Professor A wants to ask a librarian to introduce library resources and explain how to do information research in both of the classes. She calls the library to make the arrangements.

Librarian D: Love River Library, Public Services Department. May I help you?

Professor A: Hi. I'm Professor A from the English Department. I would like to ask one of the librarians to introduce library resources and information research methods in my classes. Who should I contact about the details?

Librarian D: You'll want to talk with Ms. B. Her extension number is 3126. Please hold on for a moment. I'll transfer you.

Professor A: Thank you.

Librarian D: You're welcome.

(Librarian D forwards the call to Librarian B.)

Librarian B: Public Services Department. May I help you?

Professor A: Hi, is this Ms. B? I'm Professor A from the English Department.

Librarian B: Yes, I'm Ms. B. Hi, Professor A, what can I do for you?

Professor A: I would like to have a librarian come to my class to introduce library resources and information research methods to the students. How do I arrange for this?

Librarian B: May I know the title of your course?

Professor A: There are two courses. One is "English Research Writing" for junior students. The other one is "Research Methods" for first year graduate students.

教師服務 Faculty Services

　　　　　有一位老師前幾天已經和我們約好了，所以，很抱歉，我們因為人力不足，這個時段沒有辦法幫忙。不知道老師能不能夠改時間？
A教授：這樣的話，如果延後一週，5月14日，可以嗎？
B館員：這一天可以，沒有問題。那麼，請問這兩個班的學生人數分別有多少人？
A教授：大三這個班有32個人，研究所有15人。
B館員：這樣可以用圖書館6樓的資訊素養教室。那麼，能不能請您帶同學到圖書館來？資訊素養教室裡每人可以有一台電腦，同學實際上機練習，可以加深印象。
A教授：好啊，這樣很好。我會事先告訴他們，到時候就請他們直接到圖書館6樓資訊素養教室。
B館員：好的，到時候，我會在教室等您們。
A教授：麻煩您了，謝謝！
B館員：不客氣，如果在時間上或講解內容上有任何變動或臨時有什麼需要我配合的事情，請提早告訴我。
A教授：好的，謝謝！再見。
B館員：再見。

Librarian B: OK. When do you plan to have these 2 units?

Professor A: The one for the junior students is Friday, May 2nd, 10:00 a.m. to noon. The one for graduate students is Wednesday, May 7th, 2:00 to 4:00 p.m.

Librarian B: The one on May 2nd is fine, but not the one on May 7th. I've already scheduled a class for that date with an instructor from the Department of Education a couple of days ago. I'm sorry. It is impossible to send someone else for that period of time because there are not enough librarians. Could you make it another date?

Professor A: Is it OK if I change the date to a week later, that is, May 14th?

Librarian B: May 14th is fine with me. Would you mind telling me how many students are in each class?

Professor A: There are 32 students in the junior class and 15 students in the graduate class.

Librarian B: Then we can use the Training Room on the 6th floor. Could you bring the students to the library? There are enough computers for all of the students. They can practice on the computers and have a better learning experience.

Professor A: Good. I'll tell them beforehand, so they will go directly to the Training Room on the 6th floor of the library.

Librarian B: Great. I'll wait for you in the Training Room.

Professor A: Thank you for your help.

Librarian B: You're welcome. If there are any changes in the time or course contents, or if you want me to assist in any other aspect, please let me know as soon as possible.

Professor A: Yes, I will. Thank you. Bye bye.

Librarian B: Bye bye.

Unit 9.4 專案計畫用圖書資料送交圖書館

情境：材料工程系C教授申請到國科會研究計畫，除了設備外，也計畫買一些書，因為學校規定專案計畫用書，在計畫結案之後，要送到圖書館典藏，他的助理A打電話向館員詢問辦理方式。

B館員：採訪組，您好。
A助理：嗨，您好，我的名字是A，我是材料工程系C教授的助理，C教授正在執行今年的國科會計畫，我們計畫買一些書。據我了解計畫結案之後，這些書必須送到圖書館典藏，圖書館是不是有一些採購程序上的要求需要我們遵守及注意的？
B館員：是的，在計畫結案前兩個月您要核銷圖書經費時，請記得將清單明細、所有清單上的書及發票送來採訪組，必須經過我們點收無誤，您才能繼續完成核銷的手續。
A助理：點收之後我們可以將書拿回去嗎？計畫沒有結案前，我們都會需要這些書的。
B館員：當然，這個我們了解，完成驗收手續的書，您可以拿回去繼續用。在C教授的計畫結案後，麻煩您再把書和清單送來圖書館，我們會分類編目上架，開放給全校師生借閱。
A助理：那麼，我們需要的書，也要向圖書館申購，由圖書館來購買嗎？
B館員：不需要，你們可以自行購買，不過記得所有書和單據要保存好，以便核銷、結案。
A教授：好的，我知道了，謝謝。
B館員：不客氣。

chapter 9

Unit 9.4 Submit Books Acquired for Research Projects to the Library

Situation: Professor C from the Department of Material Engineering has received a research grant from the National Science Council. Besides equipment, he also plans to buy some books. According to university policy all books acquired for research projects should be turned into the library, to be added to the collection, at the end of the project. Professor C's assistant A calls the library to ask about the hand-in procedure.

Librarian B: Acquisitions Department. May I help you?

Assistant A: Hi, my name is A. I'm Professor C's assistant from the Department of Material Engineering. Professor C is in charge of this year's NSC project and plans to buy some books. As I understand it, the books bought for the project have to be given to the library at the completetion of the project. Are there any library requirements we need to follow or pay special attention to during the acquisition procedure?

Librarian B: Yes, there are. Two months before the project ends, when you want to complete the account verification process, please remember to send the acquisition list, all of the books on the list and the invoices to the library's Acquisitions Department. Once we are sure that everything is in order, you'll be able to continue with the account verification process.

Assistant A: Can we take the books back after you have finished checking them against the list and the grant specifications? We will still need the books before the project comes to an end.

Librarian B: Of course. We understand that. So yes, after we have finished this process, you may take them back. Please bring all of the books and the list back to the library after Professor C has

completed the project, so we can catalog and shelve them. Then the books will be available to all faculty and students.

Assistant A: Do we need to make a purchase request with the library so that the library will purchase the books for us?

Librarian B: No, you can purchase the books yourselves. Just remember to keep all of the books and the invoices. This is so you can later complete the account verification process and finish the project.

Assistant A: OK, I understand. Thank you.

Librarian B: You're welcome.

chapter 10
第十章

技術服務業務用語
Technical Services

Unit 10.1 索取目錄

情境：採訪館員以email向出版公司索取出版目錄。

A小姐，您好！

久聞　貴公司在法律、投資、會計及財產管理方面出版甚多專業圖書，本校自去年成立「不動產管理系」以來，圖書館一直努力徵集相關主題圖書，如蒙惠寄出版目錄及價目表，不勝感激。

（省略問候語及下款）

chapter 10

Unit 10.1 Request for Publisher Catalogs ✉

Situation: The Acquisitions Librarian writes an email to a publisher to request a catalog.

Dear Ms. A:

We are aware that your company has published many professional books on the subjects of law, investment, accounting and asset management. Since the Department of Real Estate Management at our university was just established last year, we have been working on collecting books in the related subject areas. Please send me your catalogs and price lists. Thank you.

Yours sincerely,

Unit 10.2 詢價、下訂及催貨

10.2.1 詢價

情境：圖書館計畫向曾有往來的國外書商採購一批西班牙文書籍，採訪館員以email和書商聯絡。

A先生，您好！

附上圖書清單一份，依照已往優惠折扣為定價的75折，請提供報價，並麻煩告知從下訂至圖書到館約需多少時間，謝謝。

（省略問候語及下款）

B小姐，您好！

謝謝您4月2日來信詢價，本公司報價請見附檔，其中所列為75折後的價格，目前都有庫存，預計海運寄送大約需要20個工作天。如有其他問題，請不吝指教。

（省略問候語及下款）

chapter 10

Unit 10.2 Price Quotes, Place and Claim an Order ✉

10.2.1 Quotation

Situation: The library plans to acquire some Spanish books from an overseas dealer from whom the library has ordered books before. The Acquisitions Librarian writes an email to ask about the details.

Dear Mr. A,

We would like to have price quotations for the attached list of titles. With our previous orders, we have accepted the discount terms of 25% off the publisher's price. Please also let us know the approximate time it will take for the books to arrive. Thank you.

Yours sincerely,

Dear Ms. B,

We are pleased to receive your email of April 2nd inquiring about the price of our books. Please see the attached quotations which include the 25% discount. All of the titles are in stock now. It will take approximately 20 working days via ocean freight for the books to arrive. Should there be any question, please feel free to contact us.

Yours sincerely,

Unit 10.2 詢價、下訂及催貨

10.2.2 下訂及確認訂單
情境:採訪館員下訂,並收到廠商回信。

A先生,您好!

謝謝您4月5日的報價,麻煩代為處理,並請在寄書時附上圖書清單、發票及匯款資料。

(省略問候語及下款)

B小姐,您好!

謝謝您4月9日寄來的訂單,我們兩天內就會出貨,訂單編號是08-328,希望 貴館能如期收到。

(省略問候語及下款)

Unit 10.2 Price Quotes, Place and Claim an Order ✉

10.2.2 Place and Confirm an Order

Situation: The Acquisitions Librarian places an order and receives a confirmation email from the dealer.

Dear Mr. A,

Thank you for your quotation of April 5th. We would like to place an order. When sending the books, please include the title list, the invoice and the bank account information needed for remittance.

Yours sincerely,

Dear Ms. B,

We are pleased to receive your order of April 9th. The items will be on our delivery schedule tomorrow. The Order Number is 08-328. Hope it arrives on time.

Yours sincerely,

Unit 10.2 詢價、下訂及催貨

10.2.3 催貨

情境：下訂至今已一個多月，圖書館並未收到訂購的圖書，採訪館員因此發email詢問國外廠商。

A 先生，您好！

根據您4月11日的來信，訂單編號08-328的36本西班牙文圖書20個工作天可以寄到本館，但是現在已經是5月底了，我們還沒有收到書，麻煩代為查詢我們至今還沒有收到書的原因，謝謝。

（省略問候語及下款）

B小姐，您好！

很抱歉，經我們查證，由於本公司同仁的疏忽，錯將訂單編號08-328的圖書寄至台北B大學圖書館，我們已立刻和該館聯繫，他們會盡快將書轉寄到　貴館，發生這樣的錯誤，我們真的很抱歉，日後我們一定會小心，不再發生類似錯誤。

（省略問候語及下款）

chapter 10

Unit 10.2 Price Quotes, Place and Claim an Order ✉

10.2.3 Claim an Order

Situation: It has been more than a month since the library placed the order, but no books have been received. The Acquisitions Librarian sends an email to the overseas publisher.

Dear Mr. A,

According to your email dated April 11th, Order No. 08-328 of 36 Spanish books would take 20 days to arrive. Now it is almost the end of May and we haven't received the books yet. Please let us know what causes the delay. Thank you.

Yours sincerely,

Dear Ms. B,

I have checked with my colleagues and regret to inform you that by mistake we shipped Order No. 08-328 to B University Library in Taipei instead of to your library. We have contacted the librarian at B University Library and have asked him to forward the package to you as soon as possible. We apologize for the mix-up and will be extra careful not to make similar mistakes in the future.

Yours sincerely,

A先生,您好!

謝謝您的回覆,我們已收到B大學圖書館轉寄來的圖書,希望日後　貴公司同仁能夠多加留意,不要再發生類似的情形。

(省略問候語及下款)

Dear Mr. A,

Thank you for your reply. We have received the package forwarded by B University Library. We hope that your colleagues will be more careful in the future and that similar mistakes won't happen again.

Yours sincerely,

Unit 10.2 詢價、下訂及催貨 ✉

10.2.4 詢價及決定不下訂
情境：圖書館計畫直接向國外書商採購一批英文書籍，採訪館員以 email和書商聯絡。

A先生，您好！

附上圖書清單一份，請提供報價，謝謝。

（省略問候語及下款）

B小姐，您好！

謝謝您來信詢價，本公司報價請見附檔。如有其他問題，請不吝指教。

（省略問候語及下款）

A先生，您好！

謝謝您的報價，由於P公司的報價較 貴公司低了一成，本館決定向P公司訂購這批圖書，無論如何，還是非常謝謝您的協助。

（省略問候語及下款）

chapter 10

Unit 10.2 Price Quotes, Place and Claim an Order

10.2.4 Decide Not To Order after Requesting a Quotation

Situation: The library plans to order some English books directly from an overseas dealer. The Acquisitions Librarian contacts the dealer through email.

Dear Mr. A,

Please send me a price quotation for the list of titles attached. Thank you.

Yours sincerely,

Dear Ms. B,

Thank you for your inquiry. I have enclosed the requested quotation in the attachment. If you have any questions, please feel free to contact me.

Yours sincerely,

Dear Mr. A,

Thank you for your reply. Since P Company's quotation is 10% lower than yours, we have decided to purchase the items from them. Thank you anyway for your assistance.

Yours sincerely,

Unit 10.3 視聽資料採購

情境：圖書館需要緊急採購一系列「畢卡索的故事」（*Life of Pablo Picasso*）DVD，作為某教授教學之用。由於此套DVD國內並無代理，採訪館員直接以email向國外出版商聯繫訂購事宜。

A先生，您好！

我是台灣愛河大學圖書館採訪館員B，由於本校老師急需 貴公司出版的「畢卡索的故事」（*Life of Pablo Picasso*）DVD，鑒於國內廠商並未代理此套DVD，我們希望直接向 貴公司訂購。以下問題麻煩回覆：
一、DVD公播版含稅及運費的價格為何？
二、付款方式為何？
三、郵寄需多少天？

（省略問候語及下款）

Unit 10.3 Acquire Media Materials

Situation: At the request of a professor, the library urgently needs to acquire the DVD series "*Life of Pablo Picasso.*" Since this DVD series is not available domestically, the Acquisitions Librarian contacts the overseas publisher directly.

Dear Mr.A,

I'm the Acquisitions Librarian B from Love River University Library in Taiwan. Since one of our professors urgently needs the DVD series "*Life of Pablo Picasso*," which is not available here in Taiwan, we would like to order them directly from your company. We have the following questions:
1. What is the price for the series with public performance rights, plus tax and shipping?
2. What is your preferred method of payment?
3. How long will it take to arrive?

Yours sincerely,

B小姐，您好！

謝謝您的來信。以下是對您問題的答覆：
一、本公司給教育單位的優惠折扣為8折，折扣後「畢卡索的故事」（*Life of Pablo Picasso*）公播版DVD一套3片，含稅及運費為US$220。
二、請以匯票付款，寄至我們公司的地址，並且註明要購買的DVD名稱及數量。我們公司的地址是－
　　45 Park Street
　　New Town, NJ XXXXX
　　USA
三、航空郵寄大約需要10天。

（省略問候語及下款）

A先生，您好！

謝謝您的回覆，近日內我們就會寄出美金220元的匯票，也麻煩您在收到匯票後儘速處理，謝謝！

（省略問候語及下款）

chapter 10

Dear Ms. B,

We were pleased to receive your inquiry. Here are the answers to your questions:
1. The discount terms we offer to all educational institutions is 20% off the publisher's price. The *Life of Pablo Picasso* series of 3 DVDs with public performance rights, including tax and shipping, is US$220 after the discount.
2. Please send a bill of exchange to our address shown below. Please include the title and the number of copies of the series requested. The address of our company is
45 Park Street
New Town, NJ XXXXX
USA
3. It takes approximately 10 days to send by air.

Yours sincerely,

Dear Mr. A,

Thank you for your reply. We will send a bill of exchange for US$220 in the next few days. After receiving the bill, please process the order as soon as possible. Thank you.

Yours sincerely,

技術服務業務用語 Technical Services

Unit 10.4 寄錯及更換圖書

情境：圖書館近日收到C出版公司寄的一箱書，其中有2本書寄錯，採訪館員以email聯繫退書及補寄。

A小姐，您好！

11月20日收到　貴公司訂單編號F77-245圖書共9冊，其中兩冊並非本館訂購的圖書：
1. No.0023 *Applied Calculus* (ISBN 0471881210)
2. No.0029 *Constitutional Law: Principles and Policies* (ISBN 73555787X)

同時，您少寄了另外兩冊書，明細如下：
1. *Chemistry: the Central Science*, by Theodore L. Brown, H. Eugene Lemay, Bruce E. Bursten, and Catherine J. Murphy (Hardcover - May 7, 2006, ISBN 0131096869)
2. *Business Law Today: the Essentials*, by Roger LeRoy Miller and Gaylord A. Jentz (Paperback - Sep 26, 2007, ISBN 0324654545)

近日內我們會將寄錯的書退回，也麻煩您儘快將缺寄的兩本書及正確的發票寄來，謝謝。

（省略問候語及下款）

Unit 10.4 Receive Wrong Items and Request Exchange ✉

Situation: The library has received a box of books from C Company. In the box there are two books that were not included in the original order. The Acquisitions Librarian writes to the dealer to inform her of the mistake and to ask for a replacement.

Dear Ms. A,

On Nov. 20th we received Order No. F77-245 for 9 books from your company. Unfortunately two of the titles received were not as requested:
1. No.0023 *Applied Calculus* (ISBN 0471881210)
2. No.0029 *Constitutional Law: Principles and Policies* (ISBN 73555787X)

In addition, two of our requested titles were not included in the shipment:
1. *Chemistry: the Central Science*, by Theodore L. Brown, H. Eugene Lemay, Bruce E. Bursten, and Catherine J. Murphy (Hardcover - May 2006, ISBN 0131096869)
2. *Business Law Today: the Essentials*, by Roger LeRoy Miller and Gaylord A. Jentz (Paperback - Sep 2007, ISBN 0324654545)

We will send the wrong titles back to you in the next few days. Please send us the correct titles and the updated invoice as soon as possible. Thank you.

Yours sincerely,

Unit 10.5 瑕疵書更換

情境：圖書館收到C出版公司的一箱書，其中有一本書嚴重缺頁，採訪館員以email聯繫補寄。

A先生，您好！

9月17日收到　貴公司訂單編號7963的圖書共4冊，其中一冊有嚴重缺頁情形，麻煩補寄，謝謝。書目資料如下：
No. 30005 *Cities and Growth : a Policy Handbook* / edited by Roger L. Kemp/published by McFarland & Company, c2008

（省略問候語及下款）

Unit 10.5 Request Replacement of Defective Books

Situation: The library receives a box of books from C Company. There are many pages missing in one of the books. The Acquisitions Librarian sends an email to ask for a replacement.

Dear Mr. A,

We received Order No. 7963 of 4 books on Sept. 17th and discovered that in one of the books many pages are missing. Please send us a replacement copy. Thank you. The bibliographical details are as follows:
No.30005 *Cities and Growth: a Policy Handbook* / edited by Roger L. Kemp/published by McFarland & Company, c2008

Yours sincerely,

Unit 10.6 發票金額錯誤 ✉

情境：C出版公司所寄的發票金額與原先報價不符，採訪館員以email聯繫更正補寄。

> A小姐，您好！
>
> 謝謝您寄來訂單編號10062的圖書共7冊，根據2008年3月6日您的email報價（請見附檔），這批圖書的總價應為US$511，而不是發票No. 08-7893上的US$578，麻煩更正後補寄正確的發票，謝謝。
>
> （省略問候語及下款）

Unit 10.6 Incorrect Total Amount of Payment ✉

Situation: Since the amount shown in the invoice sent by C Publishing Company is different from their quotation, the Acquisitions Librarian sends an email to ask for a correction.

Dear Ms. A,

Thank you for Order No. 10062 of 7 books. According to your quotation of March 6th , 2008 (see attached), the correct amount of payment should be US$511, not US$578 as shown on the invoice (No. 08-7893) you sent me. Please correct the error and send me the revised invoice. Thank you.

Yours sincerely,

Unit 10.7 遲未付款

情境：C出版公司遲遲未收到愛河大學的書款，A先生以email向採訪館員詢問。

B小姐，您好！

本公司於2007年11月21日寄出 貴館訂購的圖書一批（訂單編號B3051），至今仍未收到書款，麻煩您代為查詢遲遲未收到書款的原因，謝謝。

（省略問候語及下款）

A先生，您好！

經向本校會計部門查詢，的確是他們的疏忽，一直尚未付款，他們會儘快將書款匯出，很抱歉造成您的困擾，以後我們一定會多加注意。

（省略問候語及下款）

Unit 10.7 Late Payment

Situation: C Publishing Company has not received a payment from Love River University Library in quite awhile, so Mr. A sends an inquiry via email.

Dear Ms. B,

We sent the books you requested (Order No. B3051) on Nov. 21st, 2007, but haven't received your payment yet. Would you please investigate this matter for us and find out why the payment has not been sent? Thank you.

Yours sincerely,

Dear Mr. A,

I have checked with our Accouting Office and it is clear that they haven't made the payment yet. They apologize for the oversight and will send a bill of exchange as soon as possible. We are sorry for the delay. We will be more attentive to this in the future.

Yours sincerely,

Unit 10.8 資料庫議價

情境：11月初圖書館對所有資料庫及出版／代理廠商過去10個月的表現進行考核，Geography Online資料庫由於讀者使用率高，廠商服務態度也不錯，圖書館考慮續訂，採訪館員因此打電話與資料庫廠商代表聯繫，希望在合理範圍內，此資料庫可以調降訂價。

A館員：請問是B先生嗎？

B廠商代表：是的，我就是。

A館員：我是台灣愛河大學圖書館採訪館員A，目前我們正在進行資料庫續訂作業，希望知道 貴公司出版的Geography Online資料庫明年的續訂價格是多少。

B廠商代表：Geography Online資料庫明年的漲幅是12%，今年的價格是美金7,500元，加上12%，因此2009年的訂購價格是美金8,400元。

A館員：為什麼你們公司資料庫每年的漲幅都這麼高？事實上大多數圖書館的預算近年來都沒有增加，請問是不是有議價空間？

B廠商代表：很抱歉，對亞洲地區大學圖書館我們都是一樣的訂價、一樣的漲幅，調漲只是反應成本，過去一年Geography Online收錄的內容增加很多，另外像是增加工作人員等措施都會增加產品成本。

A館員：這一年 貴公司的訂戶一定也增加了，不是只有成本增加，相信你們的利潤也增加了。希望你們訂價可以更有彈性，如果價格不能更動，是不是可以增加授權使用人數？目前我們學校兩個license不夠用。

B廠商代表：這個我需要請示我們的業務經理，可不可以下週一再給您答覆？

chapter 10

Unit 10.8 Negotiate Subscription Fees for Electronic Databases

Situation: At the beginning of November, the library evaluates all the databases and the performance of publishers and vendors during the past 10 months. Since Geography Online has ranked among the top in terms of popularity and services, the library considers renewing the annual subscription. The Acquisitions Librarian phones the representative of the company to negotiate the subscription fee. She hopes to get a reasonable price reduction.

Librarian A: Is this Mr. B?

Representative B: Yes, speaking.

Librarian A: I'm A, the Acquisitions Librarian at Love River University Library in Taiwan. We are in the process right now of renewing database subscriptions. I would like to ascertain next year's subscription fee for Geography Online.

Representative B: Next year's rate increase for Geography Online is 12%. The subscription fee for this past year was 7,500 US dollars. Plus 12% of the inflation rate, it makes subscription fee 8,400 US dollars for the year of 2009.

Librarian A: Why is the annual rate increase for your databases always so high? It's a fact that most libraries have not had a budget increase in recent years. Is there any room for negotiation?

Representative B: I'm afraid not. The subscription fee and the rate increase are the same for all university libraries in Asia. The increased subscription fee is a reflection of our operating costs. In the past year, Geography Online has added more content. Activities such as hiring more staff have also increased our production costs.

技術服務業務用語 Technical Services

A館員：希望　貴公司可以了解多數大學圖書館面臨經費不足的問題，我們必須在經費有限的條件下，在資料庫之間做取捨。就麻煩您代為爭取，等候您的消息。

B廠商代表：謝謝您打電話來，下週一再向您報告。

A館員：謝謝。

chapter 10

Librarian A: I believe the number of your new subscribers has also increased in the past year. Although the cost of production has increased, we think your profit has increased, too. Hopefully your pricing policy can be more flexible. If the price is fixed, could you increase the number of simultaneous users allowed? At present 2 users are not enough for us.

Representative B: I'll have to talk to our Sales Manager about this issue. Can I call you back next Monday?

Librarian A: I hope that your company understands that most university libraries are under financial constraints. With a limited budget we have to be selective about which databases to keep. Please inform your colleagues about our situation. I'll wait for your answer.

Representative B: Thank you for calling. I'll get back to you next Monday.

Librarian A: Thank you.

Unit 10.9 期刊催缺

情境：英文期刊 *Statistics & Analysis* 為兩個月出版一次、每年出版6期的學術性刊物，圖書館至8月底，還沒有收到2008年6月出版的一期，期刊館員為此進行email催缺作業。

A小姐，您好！

我是台灣愛河大學圖書館期刊館員，由於圖書館至今尚未收到2008年6月份第34卷第3期的 *Statistics & Analysis*，麻煩代為查詢未收到的原因，本館的訂戶編號是W97002，謝謝。

（省略問候語及下款）

B小姐，您好！

謝謝您的來信，經我們查證2008年6月份第34卷第3期的 *Statistics & Analysis* 於6月15日準時出刊，根據本公司的電腦紀錄已於6月20日掛號寄出（掛號郵件編號32000547），應在幾週前就已寄到　貴館，麻煩您代為詢問當地的郵局此期刊是否已寄到。很抱歉造成　貴館的困擾，同時謝謝您的協助。

（省略問候語及下款）

chapter 10

Unit 10.9 Claim Journals Not Yet Received ✉

Situation: The English academic journal *Statistics & Analysis* is published bimonthly, 6 times a year. Since the library has not received the June 2008 issue by the end of August, the Serials Librarian writes an email to make a claim.

Dear Ms. A,

I'm the Serials Librarian at Love River University Library in Taiwan. We have not received the June 2008 issue of *Statistics & Analysis* vol.34, no.3. Would you please find out for us what has happened and rectify the situation? Our Subscription Number is W97002. Thank you for your help.

Yours sincerely,

Dear Ms. B,

Thank you for your email. After checking with my colleagues, we are sure that the June 2008 issue of *Statistics & Analysis* vol.34, no.3 was published on time on June 15th. According to our computer records, this specific issue was sent by registered mail on June 20th (Registered Mail No. 32000547). It should have arrived several weeks ago. Please check with your local post office to see if they have received it. Sorry about the delay and thank you for your assistance.

Yours sincerely,

技術服務業務用語 Technical Services

A小姐，您好！

經向本地郵局查詢，他們並未收到編號32000547的掛號信件，由於已有多位讀者詢問2008年6月份的 *Statistics & Analysis*，不知 貴公司是否可以在近日內補寄一期？謝謝。

（省略問候語及下款）

B小姐，您好！

對 貴館未能準時收到2008年6月份的 *Statistics & Analysis*，我們覺得很抱歉，我們會儘快補寄一份，希望您能順利收到。

（省略問候語及下款）

chapter 10

Dear Ms. A,

We confirmed with the local post office that the Registered Mail No. 32000547 has not arrived. Since the June 2008 issue of *Statistics & Analysis* has been requested by many patrons, would you please send the replacement copy in the next few days? Thank you.

Yours sincerely,

Dear Ms. B,

We are sorry that you did not receive the June 2008 issue of *Statistics & Analysis*. We will send the replacement copy as soon as possible. We hope it arrives safely.

Yours sincerely,

Unit 10.10　期刊停刊處理　✉

情境：C出版公司決定在出版2009年4月份*Mathematics & World*雙月刊之後即停止發行該期刊，C出版公司的業務人員以email通知愛河圖書館的期刊館員。

A小姐，您好！

本公司出版的*Mathematics & World*雙月刊預定發行至2009年4月即停刊。對於所有未到期的訂戶，我們致上十二萬分的歉意。至於如何處理今年剩餘的訂費，我們擬定了以下兩個方案供您選擇：
一、以2009年7-12月共2期*Applied Science Quarterly*取代，*Applied Science Quarterly*相關資訊請參閱網站http://www.tbcc.com/e-journal/ASQ_brief。
二、直接以匯票退還　貴館2009年1/2的訂費。

希望您能諒解本公司的決定，並像已往一般，繼續給予我們支持。

（省略問候語及下款）

Unit 10.10 Journal Ceases Publication ✉

Situation: The C Publishing Company decides to cease publishing the bimonthly journal *Mathematics & World* after the April 2009 issue. A sales representative from C Company sends an email to a serials librarian at Love River University Library to notify her of this decision.

Dear Ms. A,

Our company will cease publication of the bimonthly journal *Mathematics & World* after April 2009. We sincerely apologize for any inconvenience this may cause you. For the remaining portion of this year's subscription fee, we propose two options for you to choose from:

1. Substitute two issues of *Applied Science Quarterly* from July to December, 2009. For information about the *Applied Science Quarterly*, please go to the website, http://www.tbcc.com/e-journal/ASQ_brief.
2. Refund one half of the annual subscription fee of 2009 with a bill of exchange.

We hope you understand our decision and will keep supporting our publications in the future.

Yours sincerely,

B小姐，您好！

謝謝您3月5日的來信，對於 *Mathematics & World* 停刊的消息，我們覺得十分意外。經請示主管，我們決定採取第二方案，請以匯票退還1/2的年度訂費，匯票抬頭請寫明「愛河大學」。

（省略問候語及下款）

chapter 10

Dear Ms. B,

Thank you for the email dated March 5th. We are surprised by your decision to cease publication of *Mathematics & World*. After discussing the situation with our manager, we would like to go with the second option, which is the refund of one half of the annual subscription fee. Please make the bill of exchange payable to Love River University.

Yours sincerely,

Unit 10.11 國外贈書

情境：美國C大學圖書館擬淘汰一批圖書，由於該校與愛河大學為姐妹校，負責館藏淘汰業務的館員寫信詢問愛河圖書館是否願意接受捐贈，條件是需自行負擔運費。

A小姐，您好！

本館近日擬淘汰一批英文圖書（淘汰清單請見附檔），內容包含各類主題，如果　貴館對其中圖書有興趣，願意接受捐贈，請於11月25日前勾選書名，並回覆此信，唯贈書之寄運費用，　貴館需自行負擔。

（省略問候語及下款）

B先生，您好！

非常感謝您11月10日的來信及　貴館的捐贈圖書，我們十分樂意自行負擔運費，附檔為我們勾選後的書單，請查收。再次謝謝貴館的慷慨贈予。

（省略問候語及下款）

chapter 10

Unit 10.11 Gift Books from Overseas ✉

Situation: C University Library in the United States is weeding some of their collection. Since C University and Love River University are sister universities, a collection librarian from C University Library sends an email offering to donate the books to Love River University Library. Love River University will be responsible for the shipping costs.

Dear Ms. A,

Our library has weeded some English books from the collection (please see the attached list). The subjects of the books vary. If your library is interested in any of the titles and would like to accept them as gifts, please mark the titles and return the list to us by November 25th. Please note that you'll be responsible for the shipping costs.

Yours sincerely,

Dear Mr. B,

We are very grateful to receive your letter of Nov. 10th and would like very much to accept your books as gifts. Also, we are more than happy to pay for the shipping costs. We have marked the titles on the list that we would like to receive. Thank you again for your generous donation.

Yours sincerely,

Unit 10.12　外文書編目

情境：A館員編到一本俄裔美籍作家納博可夫（Vladimir Nabokov）的作品，她查了文學家傳記辭典及幾個美國學術圖書館的目錄，發現這位作家的某些作品在分類上並未和他的國籍一致，因此寫email去請教美國C大學圖書館編目館員。

B先生，您好！

我是台灣愛河大學圖書館的編目館員，很冒昧地請問您一個編目方面的問題：不知　貴館是將俄裔美籍作家納博可夫（Vladimir Nabokov）的作品歸入俄國文學或美國文學？

根據我查詢Dictionary of Literary Biography的結果，納博可夫是俄裔美籍作家，至於Melvyl（註：加州大學圖書館線上目錄）及OhioLINK是將納博可夫的作品歸入俄國文學及美國文學兩類。不知您的看法如何？非常感謝您的協助。

（省略問候語及下款）

chapter 10

Unit 10.12 Catalog Books in Foreign Languages ✉

Situation: Librarian A is cataloging a book authored by the Russian American writer, Vladimir Nabokov. She looks him up in dictionaries of literary biography and in the online catalogs of several U.S. academic libraries and finds that some of Nabokov's works are not consistently classified in terms of the writer's nationality. Librarian A writes an email to a catalog librarian at C University Library in the U.S. to ask for advice.

Dear Mr. B,

As a catalog librarian at Love River University Library in Taiwan, I'm writing this letter to seek your advice concerning the classification of works by the Russian American writer, Mr. Vladimir Nabokov. Do you classify his works as Russian literature or American literature?

According to the Dictionary of Literary Biography, Vladimir Nabokov is identified as a Russian American author, whereas in Melvyl and OhioLINK, Vladimir Nabokov's works are classified as both Russian literature and American literature. I would like to know your opinion about this issue. Thank you for your assistance.

Yours sincerely,

A小姐，您好！

謝謝您的來信。在美國絕大多數學術圖書館都是遵循國會圖書館的分類編目標準，也就是說，當一個作家以兩種不同的語文創作時，館員會依語文給予類號，因此納博可夫（Vladimir Nabokov）的俄文著作、譯作或評論歸入俄國文學（PG3476.N3或其他相關類號），而他的英文著作、譯作或評論則歸入美國文學（PS3527.A15或其他相關類號）。希望以上說明對您有所幫助。

（省略問候語及下款）

B先生，您好！

非常感謝您的回信，也謝謝您詳細的說明，釐清了我先前的疑慮。

（省略問候語及下款）

chapter 10

Dear Ms. A,

Thank you for your email. In the United States, most academic libraries follow the classification and cataloging standards of the Library of Congress. When an author writes in two different languages, the librarian assigns the call number according to the language of the work. So for Vladimir Nabokov's works in Russian and Russian translations or criticisms, the subject is Russian literature (PG3476.N3 or other related numbers). For his works in English and English translations or criticisms, they are classified under American literature (PS3527.A15 or other related numbers). I hope that you find my explanation helpful.

Yours sincerely,

Dear Mr. B,

Thank you so much for your reply. I really appreciate your detailed explanation. I now understand how to classify the author's works.

Yours sincerely,

第十一章
chapter 11

特殊狀況處理
Specific and Unexpected Situations

Unit 11.1 違規行為

11.1.1 攜帶食物入館

情境一：A同學剛剛買了早餐，準備到愛河圖書館唸書，當他走進圖書館大門時，被館員攔住。

B館員：同學，抱歉！請不要把食物帶入館內。
A同學：可是我沒有要吃啊！
B館員：抱歉，圖書館為了維護環境的整潔，禁止讀者帶食物及飲料進入，您必須先把食物處理掉才能進館。
A同學：這麼麻煩，我可以先放在服務台，等一下出來時再拿嗎？
B館員：抱歉，我們不代為保管任何物品。
A同學：可是圖書館地下1樓的輕食區不是可以吃東西嗎？
B館員：是的，但是必須是輕食區販售的飲食，而且只能在輕食區食用。
A同學：好吧，那我在外面把早餐吃完好了。
B館員：謝謝您的合作。

Chapter 11

Unit 11.1 Conduct Violating Library Rules

11.1.1 Bring Food into the Library
Situation 1: Student A has just bought his breakfast and is ready to go to the library to study. While entering the library gate, he is stopped by a librarian.

Librarian B: Hello there. I'm sorry, but you cannot bring food into the library.
Student A: But I'm not going to eat it!
Librarian B: I'm sorry, but in order to keep the library clean, we request that patrons not bring any food or drinks into the library. You'll have to finish eating or get rid of the food before entering the library.
Student A: That's a hassle! Can I leave it at the Information Desk and get it back when I'm ready to leave?
Librarian B: Sorry, we are not able to look after any items for the patrons here.
Student A: But people can eat in the Café on the ground floor, can't they?
Librarian B: Yes, but it has to be the food and drinks sold in the Café. Besides, you have to eat that food in the Café, too.
Student A: OK. Then I'll finish my breakfast outside the library.
Librarian B: Thank you for your cooperation.

情境二：A同學在期刊區吃麵包看雜誌，一位館員看到，因此向他走去。

B館員：同學，抱歉！圖書館內不可以吃東西，請您將麵包裝在背包裡，離開圖書館之前請您不要再拿出來。
A同學：可是，這只不過是塊麵包啊！
B館員：食物殘渣或是包裝很容易滋生蒼蠅、螞蟻、蟑螂或老鼠，這些昆蟲及動物會污染，甚至咬壞書籍。如果你要吃東西，請到地下1樓輕食區購買，並在輕食區食用。請您以後不要再帶食物進來圖書館。
A同學：好吧！
B館員：謝謝您的配合。

chapter 11

Situation 2: Student A is eating bread and reading a magazine in the Periodicals Area. A librarian sees it and walks towards him.

Librarian B: Hello there. I'm sorry, but we do not allow any food in the library. Please put the bread in your backpack and keep it there until you have left the library.

Student A: But, it is only bread!

Librarian B: Food crumbs or wrappings attract flies, ants, cockroaches and mice. These insects and animals can damage, or even consume books. If you want something to eat, you can always buy food and eat it in the Café on the ground floor. Please do not bring any food into the library next time.

Student A: OK.

Librarian B: Thank you for your cooperation.

Unit 11.1 違規行為

11.1.2 在館內打手機
情境：A同學到愛河圖書館靜讀區自修，突然手機響起，於是他接起電話。

B館員：抱歉！請不要在這裡使用手機。
A同學：對不起，我講一下就好。
B館員：抱歉！您必須立刻把手機關閉！
A同學：好的，我馬上關掉。請問圖書館為什麼不能使用手機，我講話很小聲啊？
B館員：為了不影響其他的讀者，必須請您把手機調整為震動模式或關機；如果不得已需要使用行動電話，您可以到手機室或其他指定的區域，如樓梯間或討論室等地方使用。
A同學：好的，我知道了，謝謝您。
B館員：謝謝您的配合。

chapter 11

Unit 11.1 Conduct Violating Library Rules

11.1.2 Use Mobile Phones in the Quiet Reading Area
Situation: Student A is reading in the Quiet Reading Area. Suddenly, his cell phone rings. He picks up his phone and starts to talk.

Librarian B: Hello, please do not use your cell phone here.
Student A: Excuse me. I only need to have a short conversation.
Librarian B: I'm sorry, but you have to turn off your phone right now.
Student A: OK. I'm turning it off. Why can't we use cell phones in the library? I talk very softly.
Librarian B: In order not to disturb other people you need to set your cell phone to vibrate or turn it off. If you have to use the phone, you need to go to the Cell Phone Room or other designated areas like the stairway or the discussion area.
Student A: OK. Now I know. Thank you.
Librarian B: Thank you for your cooperation.

Unit 11.1 違規行為

11.1.3 上色情網站
情境：A同學和B同學在資訊檢索區上網找資料，發現隔壁的C同學正在上色情網站，於是到流通台告知館員。

A同學：在資訊檢索區那邊有同學上色情網站。
D館員：好的，您可以告訴我那個人用的是幾號電腦嗎？
A同學：他用的是28號電腦，有掃瞄器的那台。
D館員：他的外型或衣著有什麼特徵嗎？
B同學：他穿咖啡色夾克，戴的是黑框眼鏡。
D館員：好的，我馬上會過去處理，謝謝你們！
B同學：不客氣。
（D館員走向資訊檢索檢索區。）
D館員：同學，請您立刻將開啟的網頁關閉，並且把您的學生證給我。
C同學：對不起，我只是一時好奇。
D館員：您違反了圖書館的規定，我們必須停止您的借書權利一個月。
C同學：對不起，我不知道這裡不能上這些網站。
D館員：這裡是公共場所，當然不能上色情網站。
C同學：好的，對不起，我知道了。這是我的學生證。

Unit 11.1 Conduct Violating Library Rules

11.1.3 Link to Porn Websites

Situation: Student A and Student B are surfing the web in the Information Access Area and observe that Student C in the next seat is viewing porn websites. They go to the Circulation Desk to report the incident.

Student A: A student in the Information Access Area is looking at porn websites.
Librarian D: Okay, can you tell me which computer he or she is using?
Student A: He is using computer no. 28, the one with a scanner.
Librarian D: Can you describe what he looks like or what he is wearing?
Student B: He is wearing a brown jacket and a pair of glasses with black frames.
Librarian D: OK. I'll go over there right now. Thank you for telling me about this.
Student B: You're welcome.
(Librarian D walks towards the Information Access Area.)
Librarian D: Please close this webpage immediately and give me your student ID card.
Student C: I'm sorry. I was just curious.
Librarian D: You have violated the library rules. We will have to suspend your borrowing privileges for a month.
Student C: I'm sorry. I didn't know I couldn't view those websites here.
Librarian D: This is a public area. Of course you can't view porn websites here.
Student C: OK. I realize that now. I'm sorry. Here's my student ID card.

特殊狀況處理 Specific and Unexpected Situations

Unit 11.1 違規行為

11.1.4 玩電腦遊戲
情境：A同學在資訊檢索區使用公用電腦玩線上遊戲，B館員發現後予以阻止。

B館員：同學，請您立刻關掉遊戲及網頁。
A同學：怎麼了？我在收集有關電玩的資料，這是我的報告主題。
B館員：不管怎樣這個區域都禁止玩線上遊戲，如果您要玩線上遊戲，請到多媒體電腦區使用。
A同學：這兩個區域有什麼差別嗎？
B館員：資訊檢索區的公用電腦是提供使用者查詢館藏及檢索資料的，這裡禁止玩線上遊戲或上聊天交友網站，這是圖書館的規定。
A同學：好吧，我去多媒體電腦區使用。
B館員：謝謝。

chapter 11

Unit 11.1 Conduct Violating Library Rules

11.1.4 Play Computer Games
Situation: Student A is playing computer games in the Information Access Area. Librarian B discovers this and stops him.

Librarian B: Sir, please stop the game and close the webpage.
Student A: How come? I'm collecting information about computer games on the Internet. That is the topic of my paper.
Librarian B: Patrons are not allowed to play computer games in this area, for any reason whatsoever. Please go to the Multimedia Studio if you want to play games.
Student A: What's the difference between these two areas?
Librarian B: The public computers in the Information Access Area are for people to search the library catalog or access digital information. Playing online games or using the social networking websites is prohibited. This is a library policy.
Student A: OK. Then I'll go to the Multimedia Area.
Librarian B: Thank you.

Unit 11.1 違規行為

11.1.5 攜未借圖書出館
情境：A學生正要走出愛河圖書館，門禁系統突然響起，館員請他到流通台。

B館員：同學，抱歉，可不可以麻煩您過來一下？
A學生：怎麼了？
B館員：很抱歉，您觸動了圖書安全系統，請問您的袋子裡是不是有書還沒辦理借閱手續？
A學生：沒有啊！這些書我都借了呀！
B館員：您方便給我您的包包，讓我檢查一下裡面的書嗎？
A學生：可以。
B館員：也麻煩您給我您的學生證，謝謝。
A學生：這裡。
B館員：在您的圖書館借閱紀錄上顯示您一共借了8本書，可是這裡有9本書，這一本*Gone Baby Gone*並沒有在您的紀錄裡。
A學生：真的嗎？讓我看看。啊！對了，真是抱歉！這本是我剛剛在書庫裡看的，不小心就把這本書也放進去包包裡了！
B館員：沒關係，那您要借這本書嗎？
A學生：不用，真是抱歉！對了，我同學上次沒有把未借的書帶出去，但走出圖書館時系統也是嗶嗶叫，請問是什麼原因？
B館員：那可能是因為您的同學帶著「百視達」等店的出租片或是書店剛買回的新書、文具或甚至化妝品等東西，有可能因為原來的店家沒有將這些物品消磁，而觸動了圖書館的安全系統。遇到這種情形，只要主動打開袋子讓我們檢查，就不會發生不必要的誤會。
A同學：原來如此，謝謝！
B館員：也謝謝您的配合。

chapter 11

Unit 11.1 Conduct Violating Library Rules

11.1.5 Take Out Books without Checking Out

Situation: The security alarm rings as Student A is walking out of the library. Librarian B asks him to come to the Circulation Desk.

Librarian B: Hi, excuse me. Would you please come over here for a moment?

Student A: What happened?

Librarian B: I'm sorry. The security alarm has been activated. Are there any books in your bag that have not been checked out?

Student A: No, I have checked out all of the books.

Librarian B: Would you please hand me your bag? I need to take a look.

Student A: OK.

Librarian B: Please also give me your student ID.

Student A: Here it is.

Librarian B: Thank you. I see in the record that you have checked out 8 books, but there are 9 books in your bag. The book *Gone Baby Gone* is not listed on your record.

Student A: Really? Let me see. Oh, yes. I'm sorry. I was reading this book in the Stacks Area and just put it in my bag without paying any attention.

Librarian B: That's OK. Do you want to check out this book?

Student A: No. I'm really sorry. By the way, the alarm beeped the last time a friend of mine left the library, but he didn't have any books that hadn't been checked out.

Librarian B: That might be because he carried a DVD rented from a store like Blockbuster or an item just bought from a store, like a book, stationary or even make-up. The salesperson in one of those stores forgot to demagnetize the item, so it activated the

特殊狀況處理 Specific and Unexpected Situations

chapter 11

library's security system. Whenever this happens, just open up your bag and let us take a look inside. That way there will not be any misunderstanding.

Student A: I see. Thank you.

Librarian B: Thank you for your cooperation.

Unit 11.2 緊急狀況

11.2.1 地震
情境:愛河圖書館於開館時間發生地震,館員因此進行緊急廣播。

A館員:各位讀者請注意,現在正發生地震,請各位儘量遠離書架,並且保持鎮靜,如果您要離開圖書館,請勿搭乘電梯,改使用各樓層兩側之緊急逃生門及樓梯離開圖書館,謝謝您的配合!

Unit 11.2 Emergency Situations

11.2.1 Earthquake

Situation: An earthquake occurs while Love River Library is open. The librarian makes an emergency announcement.

Librarian A: Attention please! There is an earthquake occurring now. Please keep away from the bookshelves and remain calm. If you want to leave the library, do not take the elevator. Please use the stairways located outside of the emergency exits on both sides of every floor to leave the library. Thank you for your cooperation.

Unit 11.2 緊急狀況

11.2.2 火災
情境：愛河圖書館於開館時間發生火災，館員因此進行廣播疏散。

A館員：各位讀者請注意，目前圖書館四樓發生火災，請各位讀者保持鎮靜，請勿搭乘電梯，請使用各樓層兩側之緊急逃生門及樓梯離開圖書館，謝謝您的配合！

Unit 11.2 Emergency Situations

11.2.2 Fire Alarm
Situation: There is a fire in Love River Library. The librarian makes an emergency evacuation announcement.

Librarian A: Attention please! There is a fire on the 4th floor of the library. Please remain calm and exit the library. Do not take the elevator. Please use the stairways, located outside of the emergency exits on both sides of every floor, to leave the library. Thank you for your cooperation.

Unit 11.2 緊急狀況

11.2.3 颱風臨時閉館
情境：颱風來襲，風雨達到停止上班上課的標準，愛河圖書館必須臨時閉館，館員進行緊急廣播。

A館員：各位讀者請注意，因為目前颱風強度轉強，學校已公布停止上班上課，圖書館將於15分鐘內閉館，請各位讀者儘速離開圖書館，並且在回家途中注意個人安全，謝謝您的配合！

Unit 11.2 Emergency Situations

11.2.3 Typhoon

Situation: A typhoon strikes Kaohsiung and the wind and rain intensify. The government declares a public holiday, so Love River Library has to close unexpectedly. The librarian makes an emergency announcement.

Librarian A: Attention please! Since the typhoon is getting stronger, the university has announced that today is a holiday. The library will close in 15 minutes. All patrons please leave the library as soon as possible and please pay special attention to your personal safety. Thank you for your cooperation.

Unit 11.2 緊急狀況

11.2.4 防空演習
情境:防空演習無預警進行,館員因此進行廣播。

A館員:各位讀者請注意,目前正進行防空演習,圖書館將暫時關閉所有照明設備,請各位讀者停留在原地,並且在解除警報前請勿離開圖書館,謝謝您的配合!

Unit 11.2 Emergency Situations

11.2.4 Air Defense Exercise

Situation: An air defense exercise is launched without notice. The librarian makes an emergency announcement.

Librarian A: Attention please! An air defense exercise is underway right now. The library is turning off all of the lights for now. Please stay where you are and do not leave the library until the exercise has been completed. Thank you for your cooperation.

Unit 11.2 緊急狀況

11.2.5 停電
情境：愛河圖書館突然停電，館員於是進行廣播。

A館員：各位讀者請注意，圖書館臨時停電，緊急照明設備已經啟動，請各位讀者不要慌張，儘量停留在您所在的樓層，等待電力恢復後再離開圖書館。如果您急需離開圖書館，請走樓梯，並小心行走。非常抱歉造成您的不便，謝謝您的配合與諒解！

Unit 11.2 Emergency Situations

11.2.5 Power Outage

Situation: A power outage occurs in Love River Library and the librarian makes an emergency announcement.

Librarian A: Attention please! There is a power outage in the library right now. The emergency lights have been activated. Please remain calm, stay where you're and leave the library after the power is restored. If you have to leave the library now, please take the stairway and watch your steps. Sorry about the inconvenience and thank you for your cooperation and understanding.

chapter 12

第十二章

讀者抱怨處理
Library Patron Complaints

Unit 12.1 逾期處理費

12.1.1 逾期處理費
情境：圖書館自動化系統故障，好幾天都無法正常發送逾期通知，A讀者恰好也忘了把到期的書歸還圖書館，等自動化系統修復後，A同學一連收到3封逾期通知，也累積了為數不小的罰款，他感到十分不滿，到圖書館流通台詢問。

A同學：小姐，圖書館最近系統故障，我到昨天才收到逾期通知，罰款是不是可以不用繳？
B館員：很抱歉，我們寄給您逾期通知的目的是提醒您還書，並不能作為繳或不繳罰款的依據。
A同學：可是這樣很不公平，如果系統正常運作，我一定會記得還書，自然就不需要繳那麼多罰款。
B館員：這一點我們很了解，系統故障也不是我們樂見的。真的很抱歉，在作業上，我們必須以書的到期日作為計算逾期處理費的根據，沒有辦法依據您有沒有收到逾期通知來決定是不是要繳逾期處理費。
A同學：可是我借了那麼多書，怎麼可能記得那一本書什麼時候到期？
B館員：如果您用自助借書機借書就會有收據，平常您也可以上網查詢個人的借閱紀錄，這樣就可以很清楚地看到那一本書什麼時候到期。
A同學：這次真的不能例外處理嗎？
B館員：很抱歉，真的不行。
A同學：真倒楣。
B館員：以後我們一定儘量避免發生系統故障的情形。

chapter 12

Unit 12.1 Overdue Fines

12.1.1 Overdue Fines

Situation: The library automation system has not been able to send overdue notices as usual because it is out of order. Coincidentally, Student A forgets to return the books he has borrowed from the library. When the system is back to normal, he receives three overdue notices successively. The overdue fines have accumulated to quite an amount. Student A is not happy about it and goes to the Circulation Desk to request information.

Student A: Miss, the library system has been out of order recently and I received this overdue notice just yesterday. Can I be exempt from the fines?

Librarian B: I'm sorry. The overdue notices the library sends you are courtesy reminders only. They can't be regarded as the deciding factor as to whether you should pay overdue fines.

Student A: But it is so unfair. If the system had been functioning properly, I would have remembered to return the books and wouldn't have to pay such a steep fine.

Librarian B: We understand that very well. Just like you, we also dislike seeing the system out of order. We are really sorry. From a practical perspective, the library has to calculate the fines according to the due date of the book. We can't decide if you should pay the fines based on whether you have received the overdue notice.

Student A: How can I remember when each book is due when I have borrowed so many books?

Librarian B: If you check out books at the Self Checkout System, you get

a printed receipt. As a routine, you might want to check your personal borrowing record online. By doing this you'll know exactly when each book is due.

Student A: Can you make an exception this time?
Librarian B: Sorry, we really can't.
Student A: This is just not my day.
Librarian B: We will try our best to prevent the system from being out of order in the future.

Unit 12.1 逾期處理費

12.1.2 賠償視聽資料
情境：A教授到媒體資源中心歸還一片DVD，B館員在檢查時發現片子已經嚴重損壞。

B館員：對不起，老師，這個片子有嚴重的刮痕。
A教授：我借的時候就已經是這樣了。
B館員：應該是不可能的，在借出DVD時，我們都會跟讀者確認片子是沒有問題的，有嚴重刮痕的片子，我們是不會借出去的。
A教授：可是我並沒有刮到它。
B館員：這一點我們就不清楚了，也許課堂上學生不小心刮到的。
A教授：我真的不記得有人把片子刮傷，我不覺得我應該負責。
B館員：很抱歉，這是圖書館的規定。
A教授：如果我不賠呢？
B館員：很抱歉，在繳清賠償費用前，您不能再由圖書館借出任何資料。
A教授：如果賠，要賠多少？
B館員：按照規定，您需要依定價賠償，另外，還要付賠償處理費。讓我查一下，……，這片DVD的公播版是3,600元，賠償處理費是200元，一共是3,800元。
A教授：怎麼這麼貴？太不合理了。
B館員：很抱歉，這裡要向老師解釋一下，大多數圖書館都儘量購買公播版的DVD，以免使用者觸犯著作權法，而公播版的DVD比家用版貴很多。
A教授：我可以買一片家用版的來賠嗎？
B館員：很抱歉，依規定，視聽資料必須依所遺失或損壞資料的定價來賠償，現在因為損壞的是公播版DVD，賠償的也必須是公播版DVD。
A教授：我覺得這樣真的非常不合理，我可以找你們館長談一談嗎？

Unit 12.1 Overdue Fines

12.1.2 Media Resources Replacement
Situation: Professor A returns a DVD to the Media Resources Center. Librarian B inspects it and discovers that it is badly damaged.

Librarian B: Excuse me, Professor. There are serious scratches on this DVD.
Professor A: It was like that when I borrowed it.
Librarian B: I'm sorry, but that is not likely to happen. Before checking out a DVD we always confirm with the patron that the DVD is in good condition. If there had been serious scratches, we would not have lent it out.
Professor A: But I didn't scratch it.
Librarian B: Well, we can't be sure about that. Maybe in the classroom one of your students scratched it by accident.
Professor A: I really can't recall an instance when someone damaged this DVD. I don't think I should be responsible for it either.
Librarian B: I'm sorry. This is the policy of the library.
Professor A: What if I don't pay for it?
Librarian B: I'm sorry, but if you do not pay for the replacement, you can't check out any more materials from the library.
Professor A: Well okay, then how much will I need to pay?
Librarian B: According to the policy you'll need to pay the list price. In addition, you also need to pay the handling fee for replacement. Let me check. The public performance rights for this DVD cost 3,600 dollars and the handling fee for the materials is 200 dollars. So, the total is 3,800 dollars.
Professor A: How come it is so expensive? That seems unreasonable!
Librarian B: I'm sorry. Let me explain. Most libraries try to purchase as

B館員：當然可以，不過館長一向非常尊重圖書館的規定，她一定會同意這樣的做法。
A教授：好吧，我改天再來處理這個問題，這片DVD今天先還給你。
B館員：謝謝您。

chapter 12

many DVDs with public performance rights as they can. This is so our users don't violate the copyright law. Materials with public performance rights are a lot more expensive than the home edition.

Professor A: Can I buy a home edition of the DVD as a replacement for the damaged DVD?

Librarian B: I'm sorry. The replacement policy requires that you pay the list price of the lost or damaged audio-visual material. Since the damaged DVD has public performance rights, the replacement has to be the same.

Professor A: I still think it is very unreasonable! May I talk to the Library Director?

Librarian B: Of course you may, but our Library Director always respects the library's policies. She will support our decision.

Professor A: OK. I'll come back another day to take care of this matter. Let me give you the DVD today.

Librarian B: Thank you.

Unit 12.2 圖書採購太慢

情境：A教授於學期開始不久後即推薦圖書館買一本書，學期快結束了，線上目錄上還不見這本書編目上架，因此對圖書館採購及編目效率很不滿意，打電話到圖書館，流通台的館員將電話轉到採訪組。

B館員：喂，圖書館採訪組，您好。
A教授：嗨，我是英文系的A，我想請問一下，我在剛開學時候推薦了一本書，到現在已經快3個月了，為什麼在館藏目錄上書還是不能外借？
B館員：您可以告訴我書名嗎？
A教授：*Teaching English in an Innovative Way*。
B館員：請等我查一下，……，的確我們在10月初就送出訂單了，不知道為什麼書一直沒到，我們需要向國內代理商查一下。
A教授：難道他們不會定期向你們報告嗎？你們害我整個學期都沒辦法用這本書。
B館員：真的很抱歉，廠商疏忽了，我們也沒有注意，我會儘快給您答覆。
A教授：你們這樣效率很差耶。
B館員：對不起，我們會改進。
A教授：請快一點，我寒假不在台灣。
B館員：我今天下班前就會給您回音，謝謝您。

chapter 12

Unit 12.2 Takes Too Long to Acquire Books

Situation: Professor A recommended a new book for purchase shortly after the semester started. The semester is almost over and he still doesn't see the book cataloged in the online catalog. Professor A thinks the library staff is not doing a good job acquiring and cataloging materials and feels dissatisfied, so he calls the library. The Circulation Desk forwards the phone call to the Acquisitions Department.

Librarian B: Hello, Acquisitions Department. May I help you?

Professor A: Hi, this is Professor A from the English Department. I have a question. At the beginning of this semester I recommended a book. It has been three months already and the book is still not available in the online catalog. Why is this?

Librarian B: Could you give me the title of the book?

Professor A: *Teaching English in an Innovative Way.*

Librarian B: Let me check. We did send out the order for this book at the beginning of October. I don't know why the book hasn't arrived yet. We need to check with our Taiwanese dealer.

Professor A: Don't they report to you regularly? Because of your delay, I wasn't able to use the book in my class at all during the entire semester.

Librarian B: I'm really sorry. The dealer isn't doing a good job. We didn't pay enough attention, either. I'll get back to you as soon as possible.

Professor A: You librarians are very inefficient.

Librarian B: I apologize. We will try to improve our service.

Professor A: Please be quick about this. I won't be in Taiwan during the winter vacation.

Librarian B: I'll get back to you before leaving the office today. Thank you.

讀者抱怨處理 Library Patron Complaints

Unit 12.3 開館時間太短 ✉

情境：A同學最近作業很多，考試也很多，可是每次在圖書館用功到晚上10點半，就會響起閉館音樂，雖然書還沒看完，30分鐘內還是必須離開圖書館，她覺得圖書館的開放時間很不理想，因此寫了一封信給校長。

敬愛的校長，

我是中文系三年級的學生A，寫信給您是希望向您表達作為一個愛河大學學生的一點心聲和請求。

我是一個住宿生，雖然宿舍也有自修室，但是校園裡最好的讀書場所是圖書館，我幾乎每天都向它報到。目前圖書館的開放時間是上午8:00到晚上11:00，這樣的開放時間實在太短了。每當我晚上在圖書館專心讀書或做作業的時候，就會被閉館音樂打斷，必須半小時內收拾書包離開。我知道有很多國外的大學圖書館都開放到凌晨，甚至有一些圖書館24小時開放，為什麼我們的圖書館不能向他們學習呢？我曾經向圖書館工作人員反應我的看法，但是他們說因為人力不足，也因為深夜使用圖書館的人很少，開放圖書館不合經濟效益，因此目前不考慮延長開館時間。可是我認為少數人的權益也應該受到重視，而且如果延長開放時間是世界潮流，為什麼我們不能克服困難，滿足師生的需求呢？

很抱歉在您繁忙的校務中，向您提出這樣的請求，誠懇地希望您能為一群真正用功好學的學生解決讀書場所的困難。

（省略問候語及下款）

Unit 12.3 Short Library Hours ✉

Situation: Student A has had to do a lot of homework and tests recently. Whenever she studies until 10:30 at night in the library, the music alert for library closure starts to play. Even though she hasn't finished her studies, she has to leave the library in 30 minutes. Student A thinks the library isn't open sufficient hours to meet student needs, so she writes an email to the President of the university.

Dear President,

My name is A and I'm a junior student in the Chinese Department. As a student at Love River University, I'm writing this letter to express my opinion and make a request.

I live in a dormitory. Although the dormitory has study halls, the best place to study on campus is actually in the library. I use resources in the library almost every day. Currently, the library is open from 8:00 a.m. to 11:00 p.m. This is too short. While concentrating on my studies or doing my homework at night in the library, I'm always interrupted by the music alert for library closure. After the music is played, I must get ready to leave the library in half an hour. I know many university libraries in other countries are open until after midnight; sometimes even for 24 hours a day. Why can't we learn from them? I discussed the situation with the staff in our library but they said the library can't stay open longer hours for now because there is insufficient staff. They also said that not many people use the library late at night, so it would not be economical. But, I think the library should pay more attention to the rights of minority groups of people. Besides, since it is the universal trend for libraries to maintain longer opening hours, why can't we overcome these difficulties and meet the needs of faculty and students?

讀者抱怨處理 Library Patron Complaints

（校長秘書將信轉給圖書館館長，請館長代為了解延長開館時間的困難所在及可行性，並代為回信。）

親愛的A同學，您好！

非常謝謝您對圖書館的重視與支持，我是愛河大學圖書館館長，校長特別囑咐圖書館針對您提出的要求做深入的了解，並予以回覆。

您來信建議圖書館延長開放時間，事實上在您之前有幾位師生也提出相同的建議，在慎重考慮目前圖書館的預算及夜間使用率之後，抱歉的是我們不得不告訴您：目前延長圖書館開放時間有其實施上的困難。目前我們考量的因素主要包括以下兩點：

一、無法支付額外的水電費用：由於近年石油價格持續調漲，水電費用隨之上升，目前圖書館照明及空調費用十分吃緊，而圖書館為一封閉的室內空間，一旦延長開放時間，勢必要支付更多水電費用，現階段有實施上的困難。
二、無法增加人力：近年圖書館業務量激增，除了傳統服務外，各項虛擬及資訊服務項目也不斷增加，但不論在館員或工讀生人力方面並沒有相對增加，若延長開館時間，人力支援會是一大問題。

chapter 12

Sorry to make this request while you're busy with all sorts of work. I sincerely hope you can help diligent students like myself by solving the problem about study space.

Sincerely yours,

(The President's Secretary forwards the letter to the Library Director and asks her to look into the pros and cons and the feasibility of extended open hours and reply to the student's request for him.)

Dear Ms. A,

Thank you so much for your attention and support. I'm the Library Director of Love River University Library. President B has asked the library to review your request and respond back to you.

In your letter you suggest that the library should remain open for longer hours. In fact several faculty members and students have made a similar request before. After thorough review of the current budget and the usage rate of the library at night, we are sorry to inform you that certain issues must be resolved before the library can adopt longer hours. The main factors we are currently evaluating are as follows:

1. The library can't afford additional utility costs. In the past few years, utility costs have gone up due to soaring oil prices. The electricity bill for lighting and air conditioning in the library is already pretty high. Since the library is an enclosed space, remaining open for longer hours leads to higher utility costs. It is difficult to implement longer hours in this case.

讀者抱怨處理 Library Patron Complaints

很抱歉在短期內圖書館確實無法延長開館時間,不得已的的情形下,建議您多多在週末不上課的時間來利用圖書館,或是在宿舍透過網路,隨時利用圖書館豐富的電子資源。我們會持續評估延長開館時間的可行性,也希望不久的未來,我們能夠解決經費及人力不足的問題。再次謝謝您的建議,有任何問題,歡迎與我們聯繫。

(省略問候語及下款)

chapter 12

2. The library can't afford the extra staff: The workload of the library has increased rapidly in the past few years. In addition to traditional services, the library is now providing various kinds of virtual and information services, but the number of staff and student helpers has not increased proportionally. The manpower problem will be an issue if the library opens longer hours.

I'm sorry, but the library won't be able to open longer hours in the near future. In this case, I would suggest that you make good use of the library during the weekend when you don't have any classes. Or, you can access our various e-resources from the dormitory anytime you like. We will continue to evaluate the feasibility of opening longer hours and hope the budget and manpower issues can be resolved in the near future.

Thank you again for your suggestion. Should you have any questions, please feel free to contact us.

Sincerely yours,

Unit 12.4 服務態度不佳 ✉

情境：A同學有一天因為不小心將未消磁的書帶出圖書館安全系統，負責門禁的工讀生請他進館來，將未借的書拿出來消磁，由於這位工讀生語氣不夠和緩，A同學覺得不滿，以email向館長投訴。

館長，您好！

我是本校國際企業系二年級的學生，希望投訴一件發生在圖書館的事件。

事情是這樣的，昨天下午一點多我由圖書館出來，突然安全系統響了起來，我這才想到剛才順手從書架上拿下來看的書還沒有借，我真的不是要偷書。這時候櫃台的工讀生大聲地叫我再刷卡進來，現場好幾位老師和同學都轉過頭來看我，他們一定以為我想偷書，讓我感覺很糗。請問圖書館工作人員一定要用這樣粗魯的態度對待讀者嗎？

並不是每一個沒有辦借書手續的人都是要偷書呀！圖書館可不可以加強工作人員的訓練？我不希望下次不小心又被工作人員當作賊。謝謝您。

（省略問候語及下款）

Unit 12.4 Bad Service Attitudes

Situation: One day Student A accidentally carries a book which had not been demagnetized through the library's security gate. The student assistant who is in charge of security asks her to return through the gate again. This is so the staff at the Circulation Desk can check out and demagnetize the book for her. Since the student assistant at the security gate didn't speak softly enough, Student A is embarrassed and writes an email to the Library Director to complain about the incident.

Dear Library Director,

I'm a sophomore student in the Department of International Business at Love River University and would like to file a complaint about what happened to me in the library.

I was coming out of the library after 1:00 p.m. yesterday when the security system beeped suddenly. That's when I thought about the book I'd just taken down from the bookshelf and forgotten to check out. I was not going to steal this book. At that moment, the student assistant at the counter loudly asked me to come in again. Many faculty and students in the area turned their heads to gawk at me. They must have thought that I was stealing the book. It was quite embarrassing. Does your staff have to treat the patrons in this fashion?

It is not always true that individuals who take books from the library without checking them out are thieves. Can you improve the training of your staff? I really don't want to be treated like a thief if I forget to check out books the next time. Thank you.

Sincerely yours,

讀者抱怨處理 Library Patron Complaints

親愛的A同學，您好！

謝謝您的來信，我真的很抱歉因為我們工作人員的態度不佳，而造成您有被羞辱的感覺。

我們在訓練新進館員及工讀生的時候，都會一再提醒大家良好服務態度的重要性，唯有尊重每一位讀者，讀者才會有賓至如歸的感覺。

我已經和當天值班的工讀生談過話，他表示當天並沒有認為您偷書，但講話的聲音的確大了些，也沒有適時向您解釋，以致造成您的誤會，他感到很抱歉。日後我們一定會更加叮嚀館內工作人員，以避免類似的事件再發生，也誠摯地希望您能原諒我們的疏忽，繼續支持圖書館，並常常光臨利用。

（省略問候語及下款）

chapter 12

Dear Ms. A,

Thank you for the email. I'm sorry that you feel humiliated because of the perceived inappropriate attitude of our staff.

In our staff orientations we always remind people of the importance of maintaining a good service attitude. Only by respecting every patron will we be able to provide a comfortable and welcoming environment in the library.

I have talked to the student assistant who was on duty that day. He said he did not think you were stealing the book, but admitted that his voice was a little too loud. He feels sorry about the misunderstanding and for not explaining this to you right away. In the future I will spend more time reminding our staff about this in order to prevent this kind of incident from happening again. I sincerely hope you'll forgive our mistake and keep supporting us. Please come to the library as often as before.

Sincerely yours,

Unit 12.5 施工噪音

情境：A同學在4樓碩博士論文區找資料，由於5樓正在施工，噪音讓他無法集中精神，他來到服務台投訴。

A同學：對不起，打擾一下，我知道圖書館已經貼了施工噪音的告示，但是我急著找資料，這個噪音讓我無法靜下心來，不知道是不是可以請他們在其他時間施工？像是閉館後或週末，以免干擾讀者利用圖書館。

B館員：很抱歉，施工單位有他們一定的工作進度，我們不方便干預，今天工人剛好在打除牆壁，噪音比較大，明天應該噪音就會小很多。我們需要在開學前完成5樓的改裝工程，所以不得不在這個時候施工。當初和施工單位溝通工程進度的時候，也儘量要求他們把噪音較大的工程集中在幾天內，或者在假日期間完成，以減少對大家的干擾。您要不要移到2樓或3樓？那兒的噪音會小一些。

A同學：可是我需要查找碩博士論文，只有4樓才有。

B館員：您要不要先利用「碩博士論文索引資料庫」或館藏目錄，確定您需要的論文排放位置？然後將論文拿到其他樓層閱讀，這樣也許可以減少您停留在4樓的時間。

A同學：好像也只有這樣了。為什麼圖書館總是有工程在進行？

B館員：很抱歉，這幾年資訊設備和團體討論區需求量大，為了提供給讀者更便利的使用空間和資訊設備，我們不得不將原有空間重新規劃和裝潢，造成不便，希望您能體諒。

A同學：也只能這樣了，不過還是希望以後你們能多從讀者的角度思考噪音的問題。

B館員：是的，我們下次會儘量改進，謝謝。

chapter 12

Unit 12.5 Noise Due to Construction Work

Situation: Student A is looking for materials in the Theses and Dissertations Area on the 4th floor. The noise from construction occurring on the 5th floor is very distracting for him. He goes to the Service Desk to report the situation.

Student A: Excuse me. I know the library has already put up a notice to apologize for the construction noise. However, since I urgently need to find some materials and I really can't concentrate, is it possible to ask the workers to work at some other time, like when the library is closed or during the weekend? That way they won't disturb people.

Librarian B: I'm sorry. The construction company has its own work schedule. It is not right for us to interfere. Today the workers are knocking down the walls, so it is noisier. Tomorrow it will be much better. Since the remodeling construction on the 5th floor must be finished before the semester starts, the workers need to work now. We did ask the company to work on the noisier jobs during a certain period of time or during the weekends to minimize the interference. Do you want to move to the 2nd or the 3rd floor? It is quieter there.

Student A: But I need to find several theses and dissertations. They are only on the 4th floor.

Librarian B: Do you want to use the Theses and Dissertations Index Database or the library online catalog to verify the exact location of the materials you want? Then you can take the material to other floors to read. It will reduce the amount of time you spend on the 4th floor.

Student A: It seems to be the only way to do it. Why is there always some

kind of construction going on in the library?

Librarian B: We are sorry. During these past few years there has been a tremendous need for more space to accomodate informational facilities and group discussion. In order to provide more convenient space and more informational facilities, we have had to redesign and remodel the library. I hope you understand about the temporary inconvenience caused by the construction.

Student A: What else can I do! In the future I sure hope that the library will examine the noise problem more from a user's position.

Librarian B: Yes, we will try to improve it next time. Thank you.

Unit 12.6 區域封閉時間延長

情境：圖書館裝訂期刊區因為颱風來襲，牆壁滲水，局部封閉了2週，但後來因為無法如期完工，封閉時間延長一週，A同學做作業需要利用過期期刊，覺得十分不滿，到服務台抱怨。

A同學：請問圖書館上次不是公告這個禮拜裝訂期刊區可以重新開放，為什麼又不開放了呢？

B館員：很抱歉，施工廠商當初估計2個禮拜可以完工，但是後來發現滲水的區域比原先預料的面積來得大，因此不得不延長封閉一週，我們已經在上個禮拜一寄發全校電子郵件，並且公告在網路上及施工現場，真的很抱歉。

A同學：可是我的報告需要用到幾篇過期期刊上的文章，可以讓我進去查一下嗎？

B館員：為了安全起見，這段時間讀者是不能進入施工區域的，而且目前大部分的書架都用帆布蓋起來了，要找期刊也很困難。您要不要試試看您需要的期刊有沒有電子版？或者也可以看看其他相關主題的電子期刊上有沒有您可以參考的資料？電子期刊上的文章都可以下載、列印。

A同學：可是我對電子期刊的使用方法不太熟悉。

B館員：若您需要，可以到3樓參考諮詢台找館員協助您。

A同學：好的，謝謝。

B館員：不客氣。

Unit 12.6 Extend Closure of Certain Library Areas

Situation: Due to the destructive power of a typhoon, the walls of the Bound Periodicals Area in the library are leaking. This area has been closed for two weeks, and because the construction repairs couldn't be finished on time, the closure period has been extended for another week. Since Student A needs to use back issues to do her project, she is unhappy and goes to the Service Desk to complain about the situation.

Student A: Didn't the library announce that the Bound Periodicals Area would reopen this week? Why it is still closed?

Librarian B: We are sorry. Originally the construction company estimated it would take 2 weeks to finish the work, but they discovered that the leaking area was bigger than originally expected. As a result, the closure period had to be extended for another week. Last Monday we sent an email to all faculty and students and put a notice on the library webpage and at the construction site. We are really sorry about the delay.

Student A: But I need to use a few articles in the back issues for my paper. Can I just go in and look at those for a few minutes?

Librarian B: No readers are permitted inside the construction area during this period because of safety issues. Besides, since most of the bookshelves are covered with canvas it is difficult to locate the journals. Do you want to check if the journal you need is available online? Or, do you want to check if there are articles in the e-journals in other related subjects? You can download or print out the articles from our e-journals.

Student A: But, I'm not familiar with e-journals.

Librarian B: If you would like, you can go to the Reference Desk on the 3rd

讀者抱怨處理 Library Patron Complaints

>　　floor to ask for help.

Student A: Yes, thank you.

Librarian B: You're welcome.

Unit 12.7 燈光閃爍

情境：A同學在教師指定參考資料區看書，天花板上的燈突然閃爍起來，讓他覺得看書很吃力，他就近走到服務台通知館員處理。

A同學：對不起，打擾一下，教師指定參考資料區有燈管在閃，不知道是不是可以麻煩修理一下？
B館員：好的，馬上會有工作人員去處理，謝謝您通知我們。
A同學：不客氣。

Unit 12.7 Light Bulb Blinking

Situation: Student A is studying in the Course Reserves Area. Suddenly, the light on the ceiling begins blinking rapidly. It is difficult for him to read, so he goes to the nearest Service Desk to notify the librarian.

Student A: Excuse me. There is a blinking light bulb in the Course Reserves Area. I'm wondering if somebody can fix it.
Librarian B: Yes, someone will be there right away. Thank you for notifying us.
Student A: You're welcome.

Unit 12.8 遺失錢包

情境：A同學因為上洗手間，離開座位幾分鐘，回來時背袋裡的錢包不翼而飛，她來到流通台，希望館員能夠協助尋找。

A同學：對不起，打擾一下，我剛才上了一下洗手間，回到座位，袋子裡的錢包就不見了，請問圖書館是不是有監視錄影？可不可以幫我找到偷錢包的人？
B館員：請問您坐在那個樓層？那個座位？
A同學：我坐在3樓參考資料區，靠近放英文字典的書架附近。
B館員：您大約是什麼時間離開座位？
A同學：大概是10:35。
B館員：什麼時間回到座位？
A同學：大約10:45。
B館員：雖然圖書館每個樓層都有監視錄影機，但是只裝在出入口等重點區域，我不確定是否拍到了偷錢包的人，您要不要跟我去辦公室看看？
（A同學跟隨B館員進辦公室看錄影畫面，由於錄影角度的關係，無法拍攝到A同學坐的位置。）
B館員：很抱歉，監視鏡頭沒有辦法拍到您坐的地方。
A同學：那麼可以看看附近其他的錄影畫面嗎？
B館員：可以的，可是如果沒有拍到您的座位，這樣就沒有直接的證據可以證明某個人在那段時間經過您的座位，或是拿了您的東西。
A同學：圖書館為什麼不能全面裝設錄影鏡頭？這樣如果讀者遺失東西，就可以很快地找到偷東西的人。
B館員：一來圖書館很大，全面裝設錄影鏡頭費用非常高，二來全面錄影會侵犯讀者的隱私權，我們必須非常謹慎。
A同學：我的錢包是在圖書館被偷的，你們真的不能幫忙找嗎？

Unit 12.8 Wallet or Purse Stolen

Situation: Student A leaves her seat for a few minutes to go to the restroom. When she comes back, the purse in her bag is gone. She goes to the Circulation Desk and hopes the staff can help find her purse.

Student A: Excuse me. I just went to the ladies' room for a few minutes and the purse in my bag was gone when I came back. Does the library have security cameras? Can you help me find the person who stole my purse?

Librarian B: May I know which floor you were on? And, at which seat you were sitting?

Student A: I was sitting in the Reference Collection Area on the 3rd floor, close to the bookshelves where the English dictionaries are located.

Librarian B: Approximately when did you leave your seat?

Student A: At about 10:35.

Librarian B: And what time did you come back?

Student A: Maybe 10:45.

Librarian B: Although there are security cameras on each floor of the library, we only set them up in important spots like entrances and exits. I'm not sure if we will have videotaped the person who took your purse. Do you want to go to the office with me and take a look?

(Student A follows Librarian B to the office to look at the videotape footage. Because of the angle of the camera, the seat where Student A was sitting can't be seen in the film.)

Librarian B: I'm sorry. The cameras didn't get a picture of the spot where you were sitting.

B館員：您可以留下姓名及聯絡方式，如果我們找到，會和您聯絡。另外，您要不要去學生事務處報個案？萬一有人在其他地方撿到，就知道要還給您。圖書館是一個公共場所，最安全的辦法還是將貴重物品隨身攜帶，我們能做的只是用標示提醒大家，這方面我們已經做了。

A同學：好吧，我留下我的email和手機號碼，等一下再去學生事務處報案。

B館員：麻煩您填一下這張表格。希望您能找回錢包。

A同學：謝謝您。

B館員：不客氣。

chapter 12

Student A: Then can we look at the picture frames of the areas nearby?

Librarian B: Yes, but since there are no pictures of your seat, there is no actual evidence to prove that someone was passing by or took your purse at that specific time period.

Student A: Why can't you set up cameras all over the library? That way whenever someone has something stolen, you can find the thief within a short period of time.

Librarian B: For one thing, the library is very big. It would be too expensive to install videotaping equipment to cover the entire library. Secondly, videotaping all the areas in the library would interfere with the privacy of our library users. We have to be very cautious.

Student A: My purse was stolen in the library. Aren't you going to help me find it?

Librarian B: You can leave your name and contact information. If it is found, we'll let you know. Do you want to report the incident to the Office of Student Affairs? In case someone finds it in another place on campus, he or she will know to whom the purse belongs. Libraries are public places. The safest approach is to carry all valuables with you at all times. The only thing we can do is to put up notices reminding users about this, and we have already done that part.

Student A: OK. I'll leave my email address and cell phone number. Later I'll also report the incident to the Office of Student Affairs.

Librarian B: Please fill out this form. I hope that you get your purse back.

Student A: Thank you.

Librarian B: You're welcome.

讀者抱怨處理 Library Patron Complaints

Unit 12.9 校外讀者太多

情境：時值期末考週，A同學在圖書館繞了一圈找不到座位可以讀書，但看見許多穿制服的高中生有位子可坐，心中不平，走到流通台向館員抱怨。

A同學：對不起，小姐，我不知道為什麼我們圖書館裡有這麼多高中生，我要準備期末考，在自己學校的圖書館卻找不到位子可以讀書，這樣真的很不合理。

B館員：真的很抱歉，您要不要去地下1樓的自修室看看有沒有空位？期末考期間我們已經限制同一時間內至多只有40位校外人士入館，因此大部分座位還是我們自己的學生在使用。

A同學：為什麼我們學校圖書館一定要開放給校外人士使用？

B館員：圖書館之間的合作非常重要，有一天您可能會需要其他圖書館的資料，其他大學的同學也可能需要我們圖書館的資料，大家互相合作、互通有無，可以運用的資源就增加了很多，對雙方都是有利的。

A同學：可是他們有時候只是來讀自己的書，並不是來利用我們圖書館的資料。

B館員：這一點我們就不能加以限制了。

A同學：圖書館可不可以再增加一些座位？

B館員：我會向館長反應，也許下次圖書館空間重新規劃的時候可以一併考慮。

A同學：好吧，我去其他地方看看有沒有座位。

B館員：謝謝您的諒解，希望您能找到位子。

chapter 12

Unit 12.9 Too Many Walk-in Visitors

Situation: It is the final exam week. Student A can't find any place to study after walking around the library, but recognizes many high school students, because of their uniforms, in a number of the seats. He feels that this is unfair and goes to the Circulation Desk to complain.

Student A: Excuse me, Miss. I don't know why there are so many high school students in our library. I need to study for an exam, but can't find a seat in our own library. It is so unfair.

Librarian B: I'm really sorry. Do you want to go to the Study Hall on the ground floor and see if there are any seats available? During the final exam week, we limit the number of walk-in visitors to forty at any one time, so most of the seats in the library are still available to our own students.

Student A: Why does our library have to be open to visitors?

Librarian B: It is important for libraries to cooperate with each other. One day you might need to use materials at other libraries and the students from other universities might need to use our collection. Cooperating with each other and participating in interlibrary loan increases the number of available resources. It is mutually beneficial.

Student A: But sometimes they only come to our library to read their own books, not to use our collection.

Librarian B: That is something we really can't regulate.

Student A: Can we increase the number of seats in the library?

Librarian B: I'll pass along this suggestion to our Library Director. Maybe we can take this into consideration when redesigning the library space.

Student A: OK. I'll go to the other floor to see if there are any seats available.

Librarian B: Thank you for your understanding. Hope you find a place to study.

讀者抱怨處理 Library Patron Complaints

Unit 12.10 館內有可疑人士

情境：A同學在女洗手間門口看到有個男人來回走動、行跡可疑，她來到服務台，向館員報告。

A同學：對不起，打擾一下，剛才我看到有一個男生在女洗手間門口徘徊，有點可疑。
BA館員：請問是在幾樓？
A同學：2樓。
B館員：您可不可以形容一下那個人的樣子？
A同學：他瘦瘦高高的，穿著格子上衣和卡其褲，年紀比較大，看起來不太像我們學校的學生。
B館員：您大概幾分鐘以前看到他在2樓廁所附近走動？
A同學：5分鐘以前吧！
B館員：他有什麼可疑的動作嗎？
A同學：他一直走來走去、東張西望，有時候會往女洗手間的方向看。
B館員：您知道他現在可能在那裡嗎？
A同學：我不確定。
B館員：您方不方便帶我去2樓看看他是不是還在？
A同學：好的。
（A同學和B館員來到2樓，沒有看到可疑人士。）
A館員：我們會加強巡邏各樓層的洗手間，同時也會調出錄影畫面來看，從現在起，我們會特別注意有這樣特徵的人。真的很謝謝您來通知我們。
B同學：不客氣，希望您們能趕快抓到這個人，免得我們上廁所的時候提心吊膽。
A館員：會的，我們會努力。

Unit 12.10 Suspicious Looking People in the Library

Situation: Student A sees a suspicious looking man walking back and forth outside the ladies' room. She goes to the Service Desk to report this behavior to the librarian.

Student A: Excuse me. I saw a suspicious looking man walking around outside the ladies' room just now.
Librarian B: On which floor was this?
Student A: On the 2nd floor.
Librarian B: Can you describe this man for me?
Student A: He is tall and thin, wearing a plaid shirt and khaki pants. He looks older and doesn't seem to be a student at our university.
Librarian B: About how long ago did you see him walking near the restroom on the 2nd floor?
Student A: About 5 minutes ago.
Librarian B: Did he do anything suspicious?
Student A: He kept walking back and forth and looking around. Sometimes he looked in the direction of the ladies' room.
Librarian B: Do you know where he might be now?
Student A: No.
Librarian B: Do you mind going back with me to the 2nd floor to see if he is still there?
Student A: No, I don't mind.
(Student A and Librarian B go to the 2nd floor and do not see the suspicious looking man.)
Librarian B: We will patrol the restrooms on every floor of the library more frequently than usual. We will also look through the video footage from the security cameras to see if we can get his picture. From

now on we will keep an eye out for the man you have described. Thank you very much for letting us know.

Student A: You're welcome. I hope you catch this guy soon so we don't feel worried when going to the restroom.

Librarian B: Yes, we will do our best.

第十三章
chapter 13

其他
Miscellaneous

Library Service English

Unit 13.1 如何捐書

情境：有一位愛河大學的校友有一些書想要捐給圖書館，因為不知道圖書館是否接受，於是打電話詢問。

B館員：愛河大學圖書館，您好。
A校友：您好，我是愛河的校友，我有一些書想要捐給圖書館，不知道圖書館接不接受？
B館員：您好，謝謝您。圖書館歡迎各方的捐贈，不過我們接受贈書有一些原則，請問您的這些書是屬於什麼類型的書？
A校友：有一些是電腦軟體方面的書，有一些則是小說。
B館員：嗯，根據我們的贈書原則，電腦類的書，因為時效性的關係，我們只收最近兩年出版的；如果是圖書館已經有的館藏，因為空間的考量，我們不收複本。小說類的書也是一樣的原則；不過，如果是租書店的那種羅曼史小說，不管圖書館有沒有複本，我們都不接受捐贈。
A校友：喔，好的，我知道了。我會把書再挑一挑，符合標準的書，我會郵寄過去，請問，要寄給圖書館的什麼單位？
B館員：非常感謝您的捐贈，麻煩您寄給圖書館典藏組。
A校友：好的，謝謝！再見。
B館員：謝謝您，再見。

Unit 13.1 Donate Books

Situation: A Love River alumna wants to donate some of her books to Love River Library. But she doesn't know if the library accepts gift books, so she calls the library to ask a librarian.

Librarian B: Love River Library. How can I help you?

Miss A: Hi, I'm a Love River alumna. I'd like to donate some books and I'm wondering if the library accepts gift books.

Librarian B: Sure, the library welcomes donations. However, there are policies for accepting book donations. Would you please tell me what kind of books you would like to donate?

Miss A: Some of them are about computer software and some are fiction.

Librarian B: Well, according to our policy we only accept computer books published during the past two years. This is to ensure that the collection in this subject area remains up-to-date. Plus, due to space limitations, if the library already has a copy of the book then we won't add a second copy. The same is true for fiction books, no second copies. Romance novels, like the ones from book clubs, are not appropriate for the library's collection.

Miss A: OK, I see. I'll select the books that meet your gift book policies and send them to you in the mail. To which department should I address the package?

Librarian B: Thank you so much for your donation. Please send it to the Collection Management Department.

Miss A: Alright. Thank you. Bye bye.

Librarian B: Bye bye.

Unit 13.2 教師授權機構典藏

情境：電機系A教授收到圖書館發出的email，說明圖書館正在推動「愛河大學機構典藏計畫」，希望學校教職員能夠將自己的學術論文授權給學校典藏，並開放在網路上公開存取。A教授不太清楚將已經發表的論文全文重複授權給愛河大學是否會違反著作權法。於是，他親自到圖書館詢問承辦的C館員。

A教授：您好，請問C館員在嗎？我是電機系的A老師，我有幾個關於機構典藏的問題想要請教他。
B館員：您好。他在辦公室，請稍等一下，我請他出來。
A教授：好的，謝謝您。
B館員：不客氣。
C館員：A老師，您好。我是C。
A教授：您好。前兩天我收到圖書館發出來的email，關於授權個人學術論文給學校的機構典藏，我有幾個疑問，想要釐清一下。
C館員：好呀，沒問題。您請說。
A教授：首先如果我的論文已經發表在Elsevier的期刊，我還可以授權給學校機構典藏嗎？這樣會不會因為重複發表而違反著作權法？
C館員：不會違法的，您可以放心授權給學校，除非您當初投稿的時候，和出版社所簽訂的合約中有明確的聲明不允許該篇論文授權給機構典藏。我們查過國內外大學機構典藏計畫的常見問題，這一點也是許多其他學術界人士的顧慮。請您放心，這是沒有問題的。
A教授：那就好，謝謝！不過，有沒有什麼方式可以查詢哪些出版商同意

chapter 13

Unit 13.2 Institutional Repository Project for Faculty Publications

Situation: Professor A from the Electrical Engineering Department receives an email message from the library regarding the launch of the Love River University Institutional Repository Project. Faculty members and staff are encouraged to submit their scholarly works to Love River University and these materials will be made freely and easily accessible via the Web. Professor A wonders if he will be violating copyright law if he submits his articles already published in academic journals to the University Repository. Therefore, he visits the library and asks Librarian C, who is responsible for this Project.

Professor A: Excuse me. Is Mr. C here? I'm A from the Double E Department and I need to talk with him about the Love River IR project.
Librarian B: Hi. He is in the office. I'll call him. Please wait a moment.
Professor A: Alright. Thank you.
Librarian B: You're welcome.
Librarian C: Hi, Professor A. My name is C.
Professor A: Hi. I received an email message from the libray about the submission of scholarly work to the University IR. I have some questions about this project.
Librarian C: Sure, no problem. Go ahead.
Professor A: First of all, I'm wondering if it is a violation of copyright law if I submit my articles which have already been published by Elsevier. Will this kind of duplicate submission violate copyright law?
Librarian C: No, it won't unless the copyright statement you signed with your publishers indicated that you're not allowed to deposit your work

其他 Miscellaneous

　　　　　作者授權機構典藏？
C館員：嗯，有的。您可以上網到SHERPA/ROMEO查詢出版社對於作者機構典藏的授權規定。網址是<u>http://www.sherpa.ac.uk/romeo</u>。
A教授：好的，請等一下，我抄一下。
C館員：您不用抄，您可以到圖書館網站，在首頁上方點選「機構典藏」，內容說明中就可以看到SHERPA/ROMEO的超連結。
A教授：好的，謝謝您。
C館員：不客氣，如果您還有其他問題，歡迎保持聯絡，您也可以打電話來，我的分機是1324。
A教授：好，謝謝，再見。
C館員：不客氣，謝謝您對這個計畫有興趣，再見。

in an IR. We have studied a lot of issues about IRs both in Taiwn and abroad and we found that your concern is the most common question from academic researchers. Please don't worry about it. You won't be breaking the copyright law.

Professor A: Good. Thank you. Can you tell me how to find information about the permission for copyright transfer agreement from the publisher?

Librarian C: Sure. You can check that out from a website called SHERPA/ROMEO. The URL is http://www.sherpa.ac.uk/romeo.

Professor A: Wait a moment please, let me jot down the website.

Librarian C: You don't have to jot it down. The URL of SHERPA/ROMEO is available on the library website. Click on the link for "Institutional Repository" at the top of the page.

Professor A: Great. Thank you.

Librarian C: You're welcome. If you have further questions, please feel free to contact me. My campus extention number is 1324.

Professor A: Alright. Thank you. See you.

Librarian C: You're welcome and thank you for your interest. See you.

Unit 13.3 寫作輔導中心

情境：經濟系的B同學今年畢業，系上要求同學畢業前需要完成一篇小型論文。由於他沒有論文寫作的經驗，老師課堂上的指導時間也相當有限，他覺得十分困擾。B同學曾聽朋友說愛河大學圖書館有個寫作輔導中心，於是打電話到圖書館寫作輔導中心詢問服務內容。

A館員：寫作輔導中心，您好。

B同學：您好，我是經濟系的學生，系上要求要寫一份畢業論文。我已經寫了一部份，可是教授似乎不太滿意，可是我也不知道是哪些地方有問題，不知道寫作輔導中心是否提供這方面的諮詢？

A館員：那麼，老師有沒有給您一些建議或評語？

B同學：有，可是，我還是不太清楚老師寫的意見，還有一些書目格式的問題。以前修課所寫的報告，其他老師都沒有這樣要求。

A館員：好的，既然您已經寫了一些內容，而且老師已經給您建議，那麼，就麻煩您把報告和老師的建議一起帶來寫作輔導中心。可是，您必須要先預約時間，我們有各個學科的研究生在這裡排班擔任寫作指導。您打算什麼時候來呢？

B同學：明天下午3點左右，可以嗎？

A館員：請稍等一下，我看一下排班表。可以，明天下午正好有經濟學研究所的研究生會來值班。他值班的時間是2:30-3:30。每次指導的時間以30分鐘為一個單位。如果前後都沒有人預約，您就可以先來或者時間到了繼續和他討論。目前這一個小時他都有空，我先幫您約3點。請一定要準時到，您要提早到也可以。請問您的姓名是？

chapter 13

Unit 13.3 Writing Center

Situation: Student B is a senior in the Economics Department. He must complete his undergraduate dissertation required by the Department. Since he doesn't have enough experience in writing academic papers and his advisor doesn't have the time to provide adequate individual advice, Student B is in trouble. He learns from his friends that there is a Writing Center in Love River University Library. Therefore, he calls the Writing Center and asks for detailed information about their services.

Librarian A: Writing Center. How can I help you?

Student B: Hi. I'm a student in the Economics Department. I have to write an undergradauate dissertation to fulfill the graduation requirement. I have written some paragraphs, but my advisor does not seem very satisfied with it. However, I have no idea what's wrong with my writing. Do you provide help for this type of problem in the Writing Center?

Librarian A: Well, did your advisor give you any suggestions or comments?

Student B: Yes, but I just don't understand his comments and I have difficulty with citation styles. Instructors that I've had for other courses were not as demanding with their writing assignments.

Librarian A: Alright. Since you have written something and your advisor has already given you some feedback, please bring all of them to the Writing Center. I think we can work with you. It is necessary to make a reservation because the tutors on duty are graduate students from different colleges and departments. When would you like to come over?

Student B: Tomorrow afternoon around 3:00. Is this ok?

B同學：好的，我的名字是B。對了，請問寫作輔導中心在那一層樓？
A館員：在3樓。
B同學：謝謝您！
A館員：不客氣。
B同學：再見。
A館員：明天見。

Librarian A: Just a second, please. Let me check the schedule. Sure, you may come over then. A graduate student from the Economics Department will be on duty tomorrow afternoon from 2:30 to 3:30. Each student may sign-up for half an hour per session. If there is no one signed up before or after your appointment, you may either come earlier or stay later to continue the discussion with the tutor. So far, based on the schedule, he will be available for the whole hour. I'll make the reservation for you. Please do come on time; it's okay if you arrive early. Now, may I have your name to make the appointment?

Student B: Sure, my name is B. By the way, which floor is the Writing Center on?

Librarian A: It is on the 3rd floor.

Student B: Thank you.

Librarian A: You're welcome.

Student B: Bye bye.

Librarian A: See you tomorrow.

參考資料 Reference

中文圖書

1. 大杉邦三著（2001）。卓加真、李菽蘋譯。會議英語隨身書（Conference English: for better international communication）。台北市：寂天文化。
2. 李德竹（1997）。圖書館學暨資訊科學詞彙（二版）。台北市：文華。
3. 潘華棟、陳兆能主編（2006）。圖書館英語：圖書館日常用語。澳門：澳門大學圖書館；上海：上海交通大學圖書館。
4. LiveABC互動英語教學集團編譯（2006）。LiveABC互動英語會話百科：生活與休閒。台北市：希伯崙。
5. Taylor, Shirley著（2003）。劉秋枝譯。現代英文商業書信（Gartside's model business letters & other business documents, 5th ed.）。台北市：台灣培生教育。
6. Woods, John著（2005）。朱文宜譯。商務英文書信範例2500。台北市：寂天文化。

日文圖書

古林洽子、松本和子、高田宜美、田中理恵子、塚田洋、ジョン・A.トカーズ著（1996）。図書館員のための英会話ハンドブック：国内編。東京都：日本図書館協会。

附錄
Appendix

I. 表格舉隅 Sample Service Request Forms
1. 眷屬借書證申請表 Faculty and Staff Spouses & Dependents Application Form

愛河大學圖書館眷屬借書證申請表
Love River University Library Card Application for Faculty and Staff Spouses & Dependents

申請人姓名 Faculty / Staff Name		申請日期 Date	
服 務 單 位 Department		證號 LRU ID No.	
職稱 Position			
電話 Phone No.	(O)		(H)
E-Mail			
通 訊 地 址 Mailing Address			
眷 屬 姓 名 Authorized Person		關係 Relationship	

—以下由館員填寫—　　　—Library Internal Use Only—

承 辦 人 Library Staff	
領 取 日 期 Pick up Date	
備　　　註 Remarks	

註：
1. 眷屬借書證之申請，限本校教職員工之配偶與16歲及16歲以下之子女。
2. 繳交眷屬照片一張，俾便製作借書證。
3. 眷屬借書冊數為20冊，借期為4週。
4. 可線上辦理或親自到館辦理續借2週。

Note:
1. A faculty or staff member may apply for a library card for his/her spouse and children under age 16.
2. The user must submit a passport-sized photo for use in making the library card.
3. A maximum of 20 items may be checked out with 4-week loan periods .
4. Items may be renewed online or at the Circulation Desk for further 2 weeks.

2.長期借閱申請表 Request Form for Long-Term Loan Period

愛河大學圖書館館藏資料長期借閱申請表
Love River University Library Request Form for Long-Term Loan Period

申請人： Name：	系所/單位： Department：	借書證號： LRU ID No.
職稱 Position：		申請日期 Date：
申請理由 Purpose： □研究計畫用資料 Research □教學用資料 Teaching		計畫編號 Project No.:_____ 結案日期 Project Deadline： _____ / _____ / _____

課程/計畫名稱 Course/Project Title：

借閱期限 Loan Period 開始日期 Start:_____ / _____ / _____ 結束日期 End: _____ / _____ / _____	E-Mail： 聯絡電話 Phone No.：

申請長期借閱之圖書資料 List of Requested Materials

序號 No.	書名/資料名 Title	登錄號 Barcode	備註 Note
1			
2			
3			
4			
5			
6			
7			
8			
9			
10			

承辦人： Library Staff:	申請人簽收： Applicant Signature:

表格未完，請續下頁>

備註：
1. 長期借閱資料冊/件數：圖書10冊，多媒體資料5件，不與個人可借冊/件數併計。借閱媒體資源中心資料以4週為限，圖書資料借期以一學期之內或研究計畫期間為限。
2. 不得續借，逾期歸還依圖書館相關規定處理。
3. 指定參考資料、參考工具書、期刊（含合訂本）及學報等資料不得申請長期借閱。
4. 申請人須妥善保管所借圖書資料，遺失或毀損概依圖書館相關規定賠償。
5. 圖書館得視需要臨時催還長期借出之資料。

Notes:
1. Limits by material types for Long-Term Loan Period: Books -- 10 volumes for a semester or the project period; Multimedia materials -- 5 items for 4 weeks.
2. Renewals are not available. Overdue fines and replacement fees follow the regular borrowing policy.
3. The following may not be checked out on Long-Term Loan Period: course reserves, reference works, periodicals (bound periodicals included) & college / university journals.
4. The borrower is responsible for the safety and the condition of the checkouts.
5. The library reserves the right to recall checked out items in the event of urgent requests.

3.委託代借申請表 Proxy Borrower Authorization Form

愛河大學圖書館館藏圖書資料委託代借申請表
Love River University Library Proxy Borrower Authorization Form

申請日期 Date：_____

委託人（簽章）： Borrower (Sign.)	借書證號： LRU ID No.
聯絡電話： Phone No.	E-Mail：
被委託人（簽章）： Proxy Borrower (Sign.)	借書證號： LRU ID No.
聯絡電話： Phone No.	E-Mail：

茲委託上述被委託人代借圖書資料，列表如下：
I hereby authorize the above named proxy borrower to check out the following items from the Love River University Library.

書名 Title	登錄號 Barcode	備註 Note
1.		
2.		
3.		
4.		
5.		
6.		
7.		

合計共　冊 Total No. of Items Checked Out: _____

備註：被委託人請攜帶本人身份證件、委託人之借書證與此委託書，親自至流通台辦理外借。

Note: The proxy borrower must present his/her personal ID card, the borrower's library card, and this form at the Circulation Desk in order to check out library materials.

4.教師指定參考資料申請表 Course Reserves Request Form

<table>
<tr><td colspan="3" align="center">愛河大學圖書館
_____學年度第_____學期　教師指定參考資料申請表</td></tr>
<tr><td colspan="2">科系：</td><td>授課教師：</td></tr>
<tr><td colspan="3">課程名稱：</td></tr>
<tr><td colspan="2">E-Mail:</td><td>連絡電話：</td></tr>
<tr><td rowspan="3">1.</td><td colspan="2">資料名稱：</td></tr>
<tr><td colspan="2">資料類型：□圖書／期刊　　□VHS／DVD／VCD影片
　　　　　□CD／錄音帶　　□CDROM／磁片　　　　□其他</td></tr>
<tr><td colspan="2">自行提供：□是　　　　□否　　　　□不上磁，不貼條碼，不貼書標</td></tr>
<tr><td rowspan="3">2.</td><td colspan="2">資料名稱：</td></tr>
<tr><td colspan="2">資料類型：□圖書／期刊　　□VHS／DVD／VCD影片
　　　　　□CD／錄音帶　　□CDROM／磁片　　　　□其他</td></tr>
<tr><td colspan="2">自行提供：□是　　　　□否　　　　□不上磁，不貼條碼，不貼書標</td></tr>
<tr><td rowspan="3">3.</td><td colspan="2">資料名稱：</td></tr>
<tr><td colspan="2">資料類型：□圖書／期刊　　□VHS／DVD／VCD影片
　　　　　□CD／錄音帶　　□CDROM／磁片　　　　□其他</td></tr>
<tr><td colspan="2">自行提供：□是　　　　□否　　　　□不上磁，不貼條碼，不貼書標</td></tr>
<tr><td rowspan="3">4.</td><td colspan="2">資料名稱：</td></tr>
<tr><td colspan="2">資料類型：□圖書／期刊　　□VHS／DVD／VCD影片
　　　　　□CD／錄音帶　　□CDROM／磁片　　　　□其他</td></tr>
<tr><td colspan="2">自行提供：□是　　　　□否　　　　□不上磁，不貼條碼，不貼書標</td></tr>
<tr><td rowspan="3">5.</td><td colspan="2">資料名稱：</td></tr>
<tr><td colspan="2">資料類型：□圖書／期刊　　□VHS／DVD／VCD影片
　　　　　□CD／錄音帶　　□CDROM／磁片　　　　□其他</td></tr>
<tr><td colspan="2">自行提供：□是　　　　□否　　　　□不上磁，不貼條碼，不貼書標</td></tr>
</table>

填表說明：
1. 每一課程請單獨填列。本表不敷使用時，請自行影印。
2. 提供之資料若為影印資料，請自行裝訂成冊，連同本表送回圖書館，本館將於學期結束之後歸還教師。
3. 本表可親自繳交至圖書館或以WORD檔案格式email至abc@mail.loveriver.edu.tw，主旨請註明「指定參考資料」。
4. 非本館館藏之資料，為防止遺失及方便借閱，本館將加貼磁條、條碼及書標，請授課教師見諒。若不欲加貼，請勾選不上磁、不貼條碼、不貼書標。
5. 教師指定參考資料的陳列原則上以一學期為限，在每學期期末考結束一週後即撤回書庫或歸還教師，但可配合任課教師的教學需求而調整，請事先註明。
6. 當年度期刊不得列為指定參考資料。
7. 若有疑問，請洽圖書館分機3208，A先生。　　　　經手人：

Love River University Library Course Reserves Request Form
Academic Year: _____ ☐ Spring Semester   ☐ Fall Semester

Department:	Instructor:

Course Title:

E-Mail:	Phone No.:

1.
- Title:
- Item Format: ☐ Book / Periodicals   ☐ VHS / DVD / VCD
  ☐ CD / Audiocassette   ☐ CDROM / Disk   ☐ Others
- Personal Collection: ☐ Yes   ☐ No   ☐ No Magnetic Strip, No Barcode, No Labels

2.
- Title:
- Item Format: ☐ Book / Periodicals   ☐ VHS / DVD / VCD
  ☐ CD / Audiocassette   ☐ CDROM / Disk   ☐ Others
- Personal Collection: ☐ Yes   ☐ No   ☐ No Magnetic Strip, No Barcode, No Labels

3.
- Title:
- Item Format: ☐ Book / Periodicals   ☐ VHS / DVD / VCD
  ☐ CD / Audiocassette   ☐ CDROM / Disk   ☐ Others
- Personal Collection: ☐ Yes   ☐ No   ☐ No Magnetic Strip, No Barcode, No Labels

4.
- Title:
- Item Format: ☐ Book / Periodicals   ☐ VHS / DVD / VCD
  ☐ CD / Audiocassette   ☐ CDROM / Disk   ☐ Others
- Personal Collection: ☐ Yes   ☐ No   ☐ No Magnetic Strip, No Barcode, No Labels

5.
- Title:
- Item Format: ☐ Book / Periodicals   ☐ VHS / DVD / VCD
  ☐ CD / Audiocassette   ☐ CDROM / Disk   ☐ Others
- Personal Collection: ☐ Yes   ☐ No   ☐ No Magnetic Strip, No Barcode, No Labels

Instructions:
1. One form per course. Please photocopy the form as needed.
2. Please bind personal photocopied articles together before submitting them to the library. They will be returned after the semester ends.
3. You may submit this request in person or by email to abc@mail.loveriver.edu.tw (subject: Course Reserves)
4. To ensure security and appropriate checkout procedure, any material from personal collection will be magnetized and a barcode and a label will be attached. If you disagree with this procedure, please check "No Barcode, No Magnetic Strip, No Labels" on the form.
5. All reserve items will be returned to the general collection or to the instructor when the semester ends. If you have any special requests, please inform the library in advance.
6. Current periodicals are not available for course reserve requests.
7. For further inquiries, please contact Mr. A at ext. 3208.

II. 導覽腳本 Library Tour Script

加州大學爾灣分校（University of California Irvine）
Langson圖書館Podcast導覽腳本（中譯）

歡迎光臨加州大學爾灣分校Langson圖書館。為了順利進行今天的圖書館導覽，在導覽開始時請您站在圖書館二樓的大廳，面對大片的玻璃展示櫃，背對圖書館的入口。Langson圖書館是1965年由建築師William Pereira先生設計的，為校內八幢最古老的建築之一。圖書館的館藏及服務支援本校在藝術、人文、教育、社會科學、社會生態學及商管方面的研究與教學。

在左手邊，您可以看到流通台，在這裡您可以啟用您的借書證，也可以辦理借還書；另外，流通台也存放指定參考資料，當教授希望他的學生讀某一本書或某一篇期刊文章時，通常會將書或文章列為指定參考資料，也就是說，這些資料至多只能外借兩小時，如此一來，班上每位同學都有機會可以借到。有些指定參考資料有電子版，您可以上圖書館網站的「指定參考資料」網頁查看進一步細節。

繞過流通台，另一端是館際合作櫃台，如果有同學或教職員需要一本校內圖書館沒有的書或期刊，他可以透過館際合作櫃台提出申請。負責館際合作業務的館員會幫忙查出那一所大學有這本書或這本期刊，然後請對方將書或期刊文章寄過來。

在您的正前方可以看到一個展示櫃，在這個展示櫃中，我們會輪流展出圖書館的特藏及檔案資料，請記得來圖書館的時候，也來這裡看看有沒有新展示的資料喔。

在您的右手邊有一面玻璃牆，沿著牆是固定的書架，書架上放了很多新到館的小說。玻璃牆的另一邊是現期期刊區，這裡陳列了最新的學術期刊、一般雜誌及國內外出版的報紙；過期報紙的微縮捲片也放在這個區域。這裡也有舒適的椅子和書桌，您可以很舒服地在這裡閱讀！

我們參觀的下一站是一樓。往右邊走，在現期期刊區旁邊您可以搭電梯向下

本導覽腳本獲美國加州大學爾灣分校圖書館授權引用及中譯
Reprinted and translated with permission of Langson Library, University of California Irvine

Langson Library Podcast Tour Transcript

Welcome to UC Irvine's Jack Langson Library. To begin this tour, you should be standing in the lobby on the second floor of the building, looking toward the large glass display cases, and facing away from the entrance. The Langson Library is one of the eight original buildings on campus, designed by architect William Pereira in 1965. This library contains the collections and services that support research and teaching in the Arts, Humanities, Education, Social Sciences, Social Ecology, and Business & Management.

To your left, you'll see the Loan Desk. This is where you can go to activate your library card and check out and return books. This is also where you'll find course reserves material. When professors want their students to read a certain book or journal article, they'll often put it on reserve, which means that each item has a brief, 2-hour loan period, so each student in the class has a chance to check it out. Also, some reserve materials are available electronically. Check the Course Reserves section on the Libraries homepage for more information.

Around the far corner of the Loan Desk, you'll find the Interlibrary Loan desk. If students, faculty or staff members need a book or journal that we don't have here at UCI, they can request it through Interlibrary Loan. Our Interlibrary Loan staff will locate the item at another university, and have it delivered here.

Looking straight ahead, you should see an exhibit case. The library showcases materials from our Special Collections and Archives on a rotating basis, so be sure to check out these exhibits when you visit.

To your right is a glass wall with built-in bookcases, which is where we keep

一層樓，這段時間請暫停播放mp3，出了電梯，往前走幾步之後，再繼續我們的參觀行程。

現在請暫停您的mp3 player。

您現在在圖書館的一樓。這一層樓您所看到的電腦，任何人都可以使用，不需要證件，也不用登記。這些WindowsXP電腦中已安裝了Explorer瀏覽器、Firefox瀏覽器、Microsoft Office作業系統及其他軟體。這一層樓有很多電源插座，您讀書的時候可以很方便地使用手提電腦。

圖書館的參考資料區在您的左手邊，因為參考資料，像是百科全書和字典，都只能在圖書館內使用，許多同學會利用館內各樓層的影印機影印需要的資料。在各樓層也有網路印表機，您可以在一、二、三、四樓的購卡機上購買預付卡之後使用影印機或印表機。

在電梯的右邊，您可以看到參考諮詢台。當您有研究問題時，可以來這裡尋求協助，態度親切的參考館員會熱心地幫忙您，不用害羞！此外，如果您需要研究方面的個別服務，可以和參考館員預約半小時、一對一的研究諮詢時間。

參考諮詢台的正對面是多媒體資源中心，這裡存放了所有非印刷資料，也就是DVD、錄影帶、CD和其他形式的媒體資料。這裡有電視機及耳機可以觀看影音資料，電腦中安裝有先進的軟體，同學和教職員也可以向多媒

new fiction. On the other side of the glass wall is the current periodicals area. This section of the library houses the latest issues of academic journals and popular magazines, as well as domestic and international newspapers. Older issues of newspapers are also stored on microfilm in this area. There are some comfy chairs and study tables in there, too, so make yourself at home!

The next part of this tour will take you down to the first floor. Pause your mp3 player while you take the elevator to your right, next to the current periodicals area, and go one floor down. Once you get out of the elevator, take several steps forward, and resume the tour.

Please pause your mp3 player now.

You are now on the first floor of the library. The computer workstations you see on this floor are available for anyone to use-- no ID or sign-up necessary. These Windows XP PCs feature Internet Explorer, Firefox, the Microsoft Office suite, and more. There are also a number of outlets available on this floor- perfect for keeping your laptop plugged in while you study.

The library's reference collection is located to your left. Because reference materials such as encyclopedias and dictionaries can only be used inside the library building, many students make copies of the information they need using one of the copy machines located throughout the library. Networked printers are also available on each floor of the building. You can use these copiers and printers by purchasing a pre-paid card from dispensers located on the first, second, third, and fourth floors of the building.

To the right of the elevators, you'll see the Reference Desk. This is where you go to get your research questions answered. Friendly librarians are eager to help you out, so don't be shy! And, if you're in need of personalized research help, make a half-hour, one-on-one Research Consultation appointment with a

體資源中心借用手提電腦無線上網，使用手提電腦需要出示加州大學爾灣分校證件。

這一層樓最左側是東亞圖書資料區，這裡有各種主題的中文、日文及韓文資料。

我們參觀行程的下一站是地下室，您可以搭電梯往下一層樓，出了電梯，請向右走幾步，您會來到一張大書桌和幾台電腦前面的開放空間。
現在請暫停您的mp3 player。

歡迎您來到最近才剛裝修完成的地下室。除了四樓之外，地下室是另一個圖書館中規劃為靜讀區的空間，至於一樓和三樓則適合團體討論。這一層樓有政府出版品、大型資料、過期雜誌和學術期刊。

請注意看一下附近的書架，您會發現它們和一般書架有點不同！這裡大多數書架和書架之間並沒有什麼空間。密集式書架是為了節省圖書館空間而設計，它讓圖書館有較多空間可以存放增加的館藏。您不妨再往前走幾步，經過書桌旁，走到標示著「P」的密集書架，試著操作看看。

當您走到書架前面時，看看靠您最近、可以走進去的書架走道在那裡，走過去看看走道上是不是有人或物品在那裡；如果沒有，您可以按一下「停止／重設」按鍵，當按鍵上的綠燈亮了時，您可以走到想要取書的書架，

librarian.

Directly across from the Reference Desk is the Multimedia Resources Center. This is where we house everything that isn't in print. In other words, DVDs, videos, CDs and other types of media. There are televisions with headphones for viewing video, and computers loaded with advanced software. Students, staff, and faculty can also check out wireless laptops from the Multimedia Resources Center. Use of this facility requires a UCI ID.

To the far left side of this floor, you'll see the East Asian collection, which contains Chinese, Japanese, and Korean language materials covering a variety of subjects.

The next tour stop is the basement. Take the elevator one floor down. When you exit the elevator, proceed several steps to your right, until you're standing in an open area in front of a large study table and several computers.

Please pause your mp3 player now.

Welcome to the recently renovated library basement. In addition to the fourth floor, this is one of the officially designated quiet study areas in the building, whereas the first and third floors are best for group study. On this floor, you'll find government publications, oversized materials, and older issues of magazines and journals.

Take a look at the nearest bookshelves on this floor, and you might notice that these shelves are a little different from the usual! There's no space in between most of the shelves. Compact shelving is designed to save space in the library, allowing more room for our collections to keep growing. Take a few steps past the study table toward the shelves that are labeled with the letter P, and try using the compact shelving.

按下其中一個有箭頭的按鍵,書架就會開始移動!

這是今天參觀行程的最後一站,除了剛才看到的部分外,還有一些事想要告訴您。圖書館大部分的書是放在三樓和四樓,日後您有時間可以自己去探索。三樓還有東南亞檔案資料,那裡收藏了由柬埔寨、寮國及越南來到美國的難民及移民史料,尤其是關於東南亞國家人民移入橘郡及加州的史料。另外,不要錯過了五樓的特藏及檔案資料,這裡有許多珍本書及手稿,包括西元1623年印行的第一對開本莎士比亞劇本集,請務必要光臨這一個樓層,尤其是當您需要尋找第一手研究資料的時候。在您找圖書或期刊文章時,如果需要協助,也別忘了詢問圖書館館員!希望您還喜歡今天的圖書館之旅,也期待加州大學爾灣分校Langson圖書館可以成為您的第二個家。

Once you're standing in front of the shelves, go to the nearest open aisle. Check to see that it's clear of any people or obstructions, and press the stop/reset button. When you see the green light on the button panel, you can proceed to the shelf you want to access, press one of the arrow buttons on that shelf, and watch the shelves move!

This is the last stop on your library tour, but there are a few more things we'd like to share with you. The majority of our books are located on the third and fourth floors, but you can explore those areas on your own, at your leisure. The third floor also features the Southeast Asian Archive, which documents the experiences of refugees and immigrants from Cambodia, Laos, and Vietnam in the United States, with a special focus on Southeast Asians in Orange County and California. Also, don't miss the library's Special Collections and Archives, located on the fifth floor. Lots of rare books and manuscripts are kept there, including a First Folio edition of Shakespeare's plays, printed in 1623. So be sure to stop by, especially if you're looking for primary sources for your research. And remember, if you need help finding a book or article, ask a librarian! We hope you've enjoyed this tour and will make the library your home away from home here at UCI.

III. 問卷調查 Sample Survey

Prairie View A&M University圖書館使用者滿意度問卷（中譯）

1. 圖書館對您而言，重要性如何？
   ☐ 極為重要　☐ 非常重要　☐ 有些重要　☐ 不太重要　☐ 完全不重要

2. 您的身份是（可複選）：
   ☐ 大一　　　　☐ 大二　　　　　☐ 大三　　　　　☐ 大四
   ☐ 教師　　　　☐ 護理學院學生　　　　　　　　　☐ 研究生
   ☐ 行政主管　　☐ 西北校區教職員生　☐ 行政職員　☐ 社區民眾

3. 您的年齡是：
   ☐ 18－22歲　☐ 23－30歲　☐ 31－45歲　☐ 46 歲以上

4. 您的性別是：
   ☐ 女性　　　☐ 男性

5. 您屬於何種族：
   ☐ 非洲裔／黑人　☐ 波多黎各人　　☐ 亞洲裔　　☐ 墨西哥裔
   ☐ 印地安人　　　☐ 夏威夷／太平洋島嶼原住民
   ☐ 白人　　　　　☐ 其他拉丁美洲裔　　　　　　☐ 其他

6. 您所屬系科是：
   ☐ 農業與人文科學學院　☐ 工學院　　　　☐ 大學部不分科
   ☐ 建築學院　　☐ 少年犯罪與心理學院　　☐ 行政職員
   ☐ 文理學院　　☐ 護理學院　　　　　　　☐ 教育學院
   ☐ 商學院　　　☐ 遠距學程　☐ 醫學院預科班　☐ 其他

7. 您通常都是哪一天來圖書館？（可複選）
   ☐ 星期一　☐ 星期二　☐ 星期三　☐ 星期四　☐ 星期五
   ☐ 星期六　☐ 星期日　☐ 很少去圖書館

本問卷調查獲美國Prairie View A&M University圖書館授權引用及中譯
Reprinted and translated with permission of Prairie View A&M University Library

Prairie View A&M University Library User Satisfaction Survey

1. How important is the Library to you?
   ☐ Extremely Important   ☐ Very Important   ☐ Somewhat Important
   ☐ Not Very Important   ☐ Not Important at All

2. Which of the following best describes you (select all that apply)?
   ☐ Freshman   ☐ Sophomore   ☐ Junior
   ☐ Senior   ☐ Faculty Member   ☐ Nursing School Student
   ☐ Graduate Student ☐ Administration   ☐ Northwest Campus
   ☐ Staff Member   ☐ Community Member

3. What is your age?
   ☐ 18 - 22   ☐ 23 - 30   ☐ 31 - 45   ☐ 46 +

4. Gender?
   ☐ Female   ☐ Male

5. What is your ethnicity?
   ☐ African American / Black   ☐ Puerto Rican   ☐ Asian American / Asian
   ☐ Mexican American / Chicano   ☐ Native American
   ☐ Native Hawaiian / Pacific Islander   ☐ White / Caucasian
   ☐ Other Latino   ☐ Other

6. What College / School are you affiliated with?
   ☐ College of Agriculture and Human Sciences   ☐ College of Engineering
   ☐ University College   ☐ School of Architecture
   ☐ College of Juvenile Justice and Psychology ☐ University Staff
   ☐ College of Arts and Sciences   ☐ College of Nursing
   ☐ College of Education   ☐ College of Business

8. 您通常在哪裡做研究或找資料寫報告：（可複選）
   □ 在PV校區　□ 在校外，利用遠端連線設定　□ 其他校區　□ 以上皆非

9. 您最喜歡在什麼時間查資料做研究？（可複選）
   □ 週一至週五上午6:00-9:00　　　　□ 週末上午6:00-9:00
   □ 週一至週五上午10:00-中午12:00　□ 週末上午10:00-中午12:00
   □ 週一至週五下午1:00-4:00　　　　□ 週末下午1:00-4:00
   □ 週一至週五下午5:00-9:00　　　　□ 週末下午5:00-9:00
   □ 週一至週五晚上10:00-凌晨2:00　　□ 週末晚上10:00-凌晨2:00
   □ 週一至週五清晨3:00-5:00　　　　□ 週末清晨3:00-5:00

10. 您最常使用圖書館的哪個或哪些空間？（可複選）
    □ 流通台　　□ 參考諮詢台　　□ 期刊區　　　　□ 展覽藝廊
    □ 特藏區　　□ 書庫　　　　　□ 政府出版品區

11. 您今天（或上一次）來圖書館最主要的原因是什麼？（可複選）
    □ 上課或討論功課　　□ 參加特定活動　　□ 找資料做研究
    □ 自修　　　　　　　□ 小組研討　　　　□ 外借圖書資料
    □ 用電腦　　　　　　□ 收Email　　　　 □ 社交活動

12. 圖書館典藏的圖書資料，對您而言有用嗎？
    □ 總是有用　　　　□ 經常有用　　　　□ 有時有用
    □ 總是沒有用　　　□ 不曾使用過

13. 圖書館所訂購的紙本期刊，對您而言有用嗎？
    □ 總是有用　　　　□ 經常有用　　　　□ 有時有用
    □ 總是沒有用　　　□ 不曾使用過

14. 圖書館的視聽館藏，對您而言有用嗎？
    □ 總是有用　　　　□ 經常有用　　　　□ 有時有用
    □ 總是沒有用　　　□ 不曾使用過

☐ Distance Education ☐ Undergraduate Medical Academy
☐ Other

7. What days do you usually visit the Library (select all that apply)?
   ☐ Monday   ☐ Tuesday   ☐ Wednesday   ☐ Thursday
   ☐ Friday   ☐ Saturday   ☐ Sunday
   ☐ I rarely visit the Library

8. Do you usually do research (select all that apply):
   ☐ On the PV Campus   ☐ Remotely via Online Access
   ☐ At Another Campus   ☐ None of the Above

9. What is your preferred time of day to do research (select all that apply)?
   ☐ Weekdays 6 - 9 AM   ☐ Weekends 6 - 9 AM
   ☐ Weekdays 10 - 12 Noon   ☐ Weekends 10 - 12 Noon
   ☐ Weekdays 1 - 4 PM   ☐ Weekends 1 - 4 PM
   ☐ Weekdays 5 - 9 PM   ☐ Weekends 5 - 9 PM
   ☐ Weekdays 10 PM - 2 AM   ☐ Weekends 10 PM - 2 AM
   ☐ Weekdays 3 - 5 AM   ☐ Weekends 3 - 5 AM

10. What areas of the Library do you use the most (select all that apply)?
    ☐ Circulation   ☐ Reference   ☐ Periodicals   ☐ Art Gallery
    ☐ Special Collections / Archives   ☐ Book Stacks
    ☐ Government Documents

11. What activity is your primary reason for visiting the Library today (or the last time you visited the Library; please select all that apply)?
    ☐ For a class or meeting   ☐ Special Event   ☐ Research
    ☐ Quiet Study   ☐ Group Study   ☐ Check out a book/video
    ☐ Use a Computer   ☐ Check Email   ☐ Socialize

15. 圖書館有充足的全文電子資源可以滿足您研究上的需要嗎？
　　□ 總是可以　　　　□ 經常可以　　　　□ 有時可以
　　□ 總是無法　　　　　　　　　　　　　□ 不曾使用過

16. 您所需要的資料在圖書館容易找得到嗎？
　　□ 總是找得到　　　□ 經常找得到　　　□ 有時找得到
　　□ 總是找不到　　　□ 不曾找過

17. 當找不到資料或者有問題的時候，您通常會到哪裡詢問？（可複選）
　　□ 流通台　　　□ 期刊服務台　　　□ 參考諮詢台
　　□ 服務台　　　□ 其他

18. 當您需要自修的時候，在圖書館裡找得到一個安靜的地方嗎？
　　□ 總是找得到　　　□ 經常找得到　　　□ 有時找得到
　　□ 總是找不到　　　□ 不曾找過

19. 您使用圖書館電子資源時（包含由家中使用遠距學程），連結路徑容易找到，而且容易使用嗎？
　　□ 總是找得到，而且容易使用　　□ 經常找得到，而且容易使用
　　□ 有時找得到，而且容易使用　　□ 總是找不到　　□ 不曾找過

20. 對於圖書館的參考諮詢時間、工作人員和參考資源，您感到滿意嗎？
　　□ 總是滿意　　□ 經常滿意　　□ 有時滿意　　□ 總是不滿意
　　□ 沒使用過這項服務

21. 對於圖書館流通台的工作人員和資源，您感到滿意嗎？
　　□ 總是滿意　　□ 經常滿意　　□ 有時滿意　　□ 總是不滿意
　　□ 沒使用過這項服務

22. 對於圖書館教師指定參考資料區的開放時間、工作人員和資源，您感到滿意嗎？
　　□ 總是滿意　　□ 經常滿意　　□ 有時滿意　　□ 總是不滿意
　　□ 沒使用過這項服務

12. Are the Library's book collections useful to you?
    ☐ Always   ☐ Often   ☐ Sometimes   ☐ Never   ☐ Not Applicable

13. Are the Library's print journal collections useful to you?
    ☐ Always   ☐ Often   ☐ Sometimes   ☐ Never   ☐ Not Applicable

14. Are the Library's audiovisual collections useful to you?
    ☐ Always   ☐ Often   ☐ Sometimes   ☐ Never   ☐ Not Applicable

15. Does the Library have sufficient full text electronic resources to meet your research needs?
    ☐ Always   ☐ Often   ☐ Sometimes   ☐ Never   ☐ Not Applicable

16. Is the information that you need easy to find in the Library?
    ☐ Always   ☐ Often   ☐ Sometimes   ☐ Never   ☐ Not Applicable

17. Where do you request assistance from when you cannot find the information you need (select all that apply)?
    ☐ Circulation   ☐ Periodicals   ☐ Reference Desk
    ☐ Information Desk   ☐ Other / Does Not Apply

18. Can you find a quiet study area in the Library if you need one?
    ☐ Always   ☐ Often   ☐ Sometimes   ☐ Never   ☐ Not Applicable

19. Are the Library's electronic resources (including access from home for Distance Education) easy to find and use?
    ☐ Always   ☐ Often   ☐ Sometimes   ☐ Never   ☐ Not Applicable

20. Are you satisfied with the Reference hours, staff and resources?
    ☐ Always   ☐ Often   ☐ Sometimes   ☐ Never   ☐ Not Applicable

23. 對於圖書館政府出版品書區的開放時間、工作人員和資源，您感到滿意嗎？
    ☐ 總是滿意　　　☐ 經常滿意　　☐ 有時滿意　　☐ 總是不滿意
    ☐ 沒使用過這項服務

24. 對於圖書館特藏區的開放時間、工作人員和資源，您感到滿意嗎？
    ☐ 總是滿意　　　☐ 經常滿意　　☐ 有時滿意　　☐ 總是不滿意
    ☐ 沒使用過這項服務

25. 對於圖書館服務台的開放時間、工作人員和資源，您感到滿意嗎？
    ☐ 總是滿意　　　☐ 經常滿意　　☐ 有時滿意　　☐ 總是不滿意
    ☐ 沒使用過這項服務

26. 對於圖書館行政辦公室開放時間、工作人員和資源，您感到滿意嗎？
    ☐ 總是滿意　　　☐ 經常滿意　　☐ 有時滿意　　☐ 總是不滿意
    ☐ 沒使用過這項服務

27. 對於圖書館四樓展覽廳的開放時間、工作人員和展品，您感到滿意嗎？
    ☐ 總是滿意　　　☐ 經常滿意　　☐ 有時滿意　　☐ 總是不滿意
    ☐ 沒使用過這項服務

28. 您對圖書館的電腦滿意嗎？
    ☐ 總是滿意　　　☐ 經常滿意　　☐ 有時滿意　　☐ 總是不滿意
    ☐ 沒使用過這項服務

29. 對於圖書館期刊區的開放時間、工作人員和期刊資源，您感到滿意嗎？
    ☐ 總是滿意　　　☐ 經常滿意　　☐ 有時滿意　　☐ 總是不滿意
    ☐ 沒使用過這項服務

30. 圖書館的設備（如：微縮單片閱讀機、微縮捲片閱讀機或影印機）狀況良好而且容易使用嗎？
    ☐ 總是良好，而且容易使用　　☐ 經常良好，而且容易使用
    ☐ 有時良好，而且容易使用　　☐ 總是故障　　　☐ 不曾用過

21. Are you satisfied with the Circulation staff and resources?
   ☐ Always   ☐ Often   ☐ Sometimes   ☐ Never   ☐ Not Applicable

22. Are you satisfied with the Reserves hours, staff and resources?
   ☐ Always   ☐ Often   ☐ Sometimes   ☐ Never   ☐ Not Applicable

23. Are you satisfied with the Government Documents hours, staff and resources?
   ☐ Always   ☐ Often   ☐ Sometimes   ☐ Never   ☐ Not Applicable

24. Are you satisfied with the Special Collections / Archives hours, staff and resources?
   ☐ Always   ☐ Often   ☐ Sometimes   ☐ Never   ☐ Not Applicable

25. Are you satisfied with the Information Desk hours and staff?
   ☐ Always   ☐ Often   ☐ Sometimes   ☐ Never   ☐ Not Applicable

26. Are you satisfied with the Administration hours, staff and resources?
   ☐ Always   ☐ Often   ☐ Sometimes   ☐ Never   ☐ Not Applicable

27. Are you satisfied with the Fourth Floor Exhibit Space hours, staff and resources?
   ☐ Always   ☐ Often   ☐ Sometimes   ☐ Never   ☐ Not Applicable

28. Are you satisfied with the computers in the Library?
   ☐ Always   ☐ Often   ☐ Sometimes   ☐ Never   ☐ Not Applicable

29. Are you satisfied with the Periodicals hours, staff and resources?
   ☐ Always   ☐ Often   ☐ Sometimes   ☐ Never   ☐ Not Applicable

30. Is the equipment (microfiche, microfilm, copiers) in good working order

31. 對於圖書館的新網站，您感到滿意嗎？
   □ 總是滿意　　□ 經常滿意　　□ 有時滿意　　□ 總是不滿意
   □ 沒使用過

32. 您曾經參加過圖書館舉辦的資源利用指導或在課堂上安排過這類課程嗎？
   □ 有　　□ 不曾　　□ 不曾，但計畫未來參加或安排
   □ 此問題不適用於本人

33. 圖書館的開館時間對您而言，適合嗎？
   □ 是的，我很滿意現在的開館時間。
   □ 還好，不過我喜歡晚上開放長一些時間。
   □ 還好，不過我喜歡週末開放長一些時間。
   □ 還好，不過我喜歡上午早一些開館。

34. 當您要找研究主題的時候，您會使用以下哪一個（些）方法？（可複選）
   □ 找參考館員　　　　　　　　　□ 到書架瀏覽
   □ 查詢電子資料庫（例如：EBSCO, ProQuest等）　□ 查詢線上目錄
   □ 網路／搜尋引擎　　　　　　　□ E-Mail或線上留言給圖書館
   □ 打電話到參考諮詢台　　　　　□ 以上皆非

35. 整體而言，您對圖書館的滿意程度為何？
   □ 非常滿意　　□ 滿意　　□ 不太滿意　　□ 不滿意
   □ 沒意見

36. 有沒有其他的服務是目前沒有提供，可是您希望圖書館考慮新增的？（例如：傳真機，彩色影印機或掃瞄器）
   請說明：＿＿＿＿＿＿＿＿＿＿＿＿＿＿＿＿＿＿＿＿＿＿＿＿＿＿＿

37. 請利用以下空白處，提出您想要給圖書館的其他建議或意見：

and easy to use?
☐ Always ☐ Often ☐ Sometimes ☐ Never ☐ Not Applicable

31. Are you satisfied with the Library's new web site?
☐ Always ☐ Often ☐ Sometimes ☐ Never ☐ Not Applicable

32. Have you attended or arranged for a Library Research Instruction class?
☐ Yes   ☐ No
☐ No, but I plan to in the future   ☐ Not Applicable

33. Are the hours the Library is open useful to you?
☐ Yes, I'm satisfied as they are
☐ Yes, but I'd like more hours at night
☐ Yes, but I'd like longer weekend hours
☐ Yes, but I'd like more hours in the morning

34. Which of the following do you use when researching a topic (select all that apply)?
☐ Reference Librarians   ☐ Shelf Browsing
☐ Databases (EBSCO, ProQuest)   ☐ Online Catalog
☐ Internet / Search Engine   ☐ E-mail / Ask-A-Librarian
☐ Calling the Reference Desk   ☐ None of These

35. Overall, how satisfied are you with the Library?
☐ Very Satisfied   ☐ Usually Satisfied
☐ Seldom Satisfied ☐ Not Satisfied   ☐ No Opinion

36. Are there any other additional services the Library does not currently provide that you would like us to consider? (example - fax machine, color copier / scanner)

37. Please add any additional comments in the space below:

IV. 公告舉隅 Sample Library News Items and Announcements
1. 自動化系統主機維護 Maintenance on Library Server

標題：10/17圖書館系統停機及服務異動公告

圖書館將於10月17日零時至10月18日上午9時進行新舊主機系統轉換作業，作業期間服務調整如下：
1. 館藏目錄、線上預約／續借、個人借閱查詢、遠端使用電子資料庫認證等服務暫停
2. 流通台不提供借還書服務
3. 媒體資源中心閉館

服務恢復不另行通知，造成不便，敬請見諒。

Subject: Library Server Maintenance

Date: 10/17/2007 0:00 AM ~ 10/18/2007 9:00 AM
Duration: 1 day and 9 hours
Love River U Library will be performing maintenance on the library server on Wednesday, October 17th, from midnight until 9:00 a.m., Thursday, October 18th. During this time all the relevant online services, including WebPAC search, Online Book Request, Renewal, View Personal Record and Authentication for Remote Access, will be temporarily inaccessible. On October 17th the Circulation Desk will be unable to check out or check in any library materials. Also, the Media Resources Center will be closed. No further notice will be sent or posted when services resume.
Thank you for your understanding!

2.國定假日閉館 Closed on National Holidays

標題：中秋節閉館

2007年9月24日（星期一）及25日（星期二），適逢中秋節連續假期，圖書館閉館兩日。

Subject: Library Closure Dates

Love River U Library is closed for the consecutive holidays of Moon Festival from Monday, Sept. 24th to Tuesday, Sept. 25th.

標題：圖書館春節期間閉館

農曆春節期間，圖書館於1月24日至2月1日閉館。

Subject: Library Closed during the Lunar New Year Holidays.

The library is closed from Jan. 24th through Feb. 1st for the Lunar New Year holidays.

3.消毒閉館 Closed for Sanitization

標題：3月11日(星期日)圖書館開館時間異動

3月11日（星期日）全校進行消毒作業，時間為上午8時至中午12時。為配合消毒作業，圖書館延至下午1時開館。不便之處，敬請見諒。

Subject: Library Opening Hours Change on March 11th, 2007

The Library Building is scheduled for sanitization on Sunday, March 11th. The opening of the library will be postponed until 1:00 p.m. Sorry for the inconvenience.

4.其他 Miscellaneous

標題：響應地球日停電1小時

愛河大學全校響應4月22日地球日實施節能減碳措施，共同為減少地球暖化而努力。圖書館於當天中午12:00—13:00暫時關閉所有空調、照明設備及電梯。不便之處，敬請見諒。

Subject: Lights Out for One Hour on Earth Day

Responding to the campus-wide action to reduce CO2 on Earth Day 2008, all lights, air-conditioners, and elevators in the library will be turned off between noon and 1:00 p.m. Thank you for your understanding and let's help reduce global warming!

標題：圖書館照明設備暫時關閉

因舉行萬安防空演習，圖書館照明設備於5月22日中午12:00至12:30暫時關閉。不便之處，敬請見諒！

Subject: Library Lighting System Off at Noon on May 22nd, 2007.

Because of the annual "Wan An" air-defense exercise, all lights in the Library Building will be turned off between 12:00 and 12:30 p.m. Thank you for your understanding!

進入本館後個人貴重物品應自行保管,若有遺失,本館不負賠償之責任。

Library patrons should properly secure all personal valuable belongings. The Library does not accept any liability for any loss of them.

V.標示舉隅 Sample Library Signs

1.影印機／印表機故障 Copier / Printer Out of Order

此影印機故障,請前往三樓或五樓影印區使用。

This copier is out of order. Please use the ones on the 3rd or 5th floor.

如果您不確定影印機如何使用,請洽1樓流通台。

If you are not sure how to use this copier, please ask for help at the Circulation Desk on the 1st floor.

2.網路斷線 Network Disconnected

網路斷線中,造成不便,敬請見諒。

Network is disconnected. Sorry for the inconvenience.

3.電梯維修 Elevator under Maintenance

此電梯維修中,請使用右側電梯。造成不便,敬請見諒。

This elevator is under maintenance. Please use the one on your right. Thank you for your understanding.

VI. 活動辦法 Library Events
1. 換書活動 Book Swap & Raffle

2008愛河圖書館週「集點換愛書」活動

主旨：透過與其他人換書，建立分享好書的觀念；並以書會友，拉近愛
　　　書人距離，藉以提升校園閱讀風氣。
主辦單位：圖書館
對象：本校教職員工生

辦法：
一、收書時間：11月3日(一)至11月28日(五) 每日開館時間內
　　收書地點：圖書館1樓參考服務台

二、活動辦法：
　　於收書時間內，攜帶欲交換分享的圖書至圖書館1樓參考服務台換
　　取點券（點券請妥善保存至12月換書活動期間），憑券參加抽獎活
　　動，並可於圖書交換時間內來館換書。

三、收書原則：以下資料不收（依工作人員判定為準）
　　(一) 違反著作權法、無版權圖書
　　(二) 宣傳品、小冊子
　　(三) 宗教經書
　　(四) 缺頁、破損、髒污、塗畫註記圖書
　　(五) 2005年之前出版的電腦書
　　(六) 高中及高中以下教科書
　　(七) 期刊、雜誌等連續性出版品
　　(八) 視聽資料
　　(九) 暴力或色情內容
　　(十) 其他本館認定不宜者

Love River University Library Week 2008
Book Swap & Raffle

To celebrate Library Week 2008 and promote reading, Love River University Library is organizing a book swap. All students, staff, and faculty members are encouraged to share their favorite books with others.

Collect your book(s)
Please bring your book(s) to the Reference Desk, located on the first floor of the library. You'll receive a coupon worth one point for every book you share. You are welcome to share as many books as you'd like. Be sure to keep your coupon(s) in a safe place because in December 2008 you can exchange them for books, get a cloth mini bag or a tote bag as a gift, and enter the raffle.

* Date: Nov. 3rd – 28th (Mon-Fri), 2008 / during library hours

* Venue: Reference Desk, 1st floor, Love River University Library

* Criteria: The following types of materials are NOT eligible for this event:
  1. Publications violating copyright law
  2. Pamphlets / flyers
  3. Religious publications, i.e. Sutra / Testament
  4. Books with scribbled notes or other defacement
  5. Computer application books published prior to 2005.
  6. Textbooks for secondary and elementary schools
  7. Periodicals, magazines
  8. Audio-visual materials
  9. Publications with violent or sexual content
  10. Other inappropriate materials (based on librarian's judgment)

四、圖書計點原則：每本圖書兌換一點。

五、圖書交換時間及實施地點：
12月1日(一)～3日(三) 每日16:00 - 18:30
圖書館1樓展覽廳

六、換書方式：
(一) 換書時間內，憑換書點券進入會場挑選圖書，交予會場工作人員核算後，即完成交換手續。每張點券限使用一次。
(二) 一點換取一冊書。
(三) 若未能在活動期限內換書，視同放棄換書點券。
(四) 活動中禁止任何金錢交易行為。

七、參加者可獲得小環保袋，集10點以上者可獲大環保袋，於換書時間內在活動場地領取，每人限領一份。

八、活動結束後剩餘圖書，由本館統籌處理。

九、憑換書點券可參加抽獎，每人不限張數，換越多，得獎機會越高！
iPod shuffle 2GB　　1名
3M 精緻檯燈　　　　1名
8G 隨身碟　　　　　5名
圖書禮券300元　　　15名

Swap your book(s)

Please bring your coupon(s) to exchange books. One coupon for one book! Please show your coupon to be admitted to this event. Participants may also use their coupons to enter the raffle. The more coupons you have, the better chance you'll have of winning a prize. The library retains the right to determine the use of any remaining books.

*Date: Dec. 1st – 3rd (Mon-Wed), 2008 / 16:00-18:30
*Venue: Exhibition Area, 1st Floor, Love River University Library

Prizes for the Raffle
   iPod shuffle 2GB (x1)
   3M Desk Lamp (x1)
   Flash USB (8G) (x5)
   Book voucher valued at $300 (x15)

2.講座活動 Lecture

《看電影學英文》系列活動之一～ 李天志老師談「慾望城市」

　　圖書館於本學期推出「看電影學英文」系列活動，透過本校英文系教師對電影的分析與探討，讓學生從電影中熟悉英美各國文化，並提升英語文能力。第一場演講的講者是愛河大學英文系李天志老師。

　　李天志老師為大家分析在HBO頻道連播六季（1998-2004）、榮獲艾美獎和金球獎肯定的熱門影集【慾望城市】的電影版，內容精采，請大家別錯過這個難得的機會，參加者還有機會抽中「慾望城市」音樂CD等獎品，敬請踴躍報名參加。

時間：4月8日 15:30-17:00
地點：圖書館六樓數位學習中心
講者：李天志老師
報名網址：http://library.loveriver.edu.tw/att_online/

Learning English through Movies part I - the Film *Sex and the City*

To help viewers learn English more authentically through its cultural aspects, the library has organized a series of events with the theme of "Learning English through Movies." Instructors from the Department of English are invited to review the film after watching it together with the audience. The film "*Sex and the City*" will be the inaugural event of this series. At the end of the event, a raffle will be conducted. Prizes include soundtrack CDs of the film. Please see the details below.

*Speaker: Mr. Andrew Lee (English Department)
*Date: April 8th, 2009 / 15:30-17:00
*Venue: Digital Learning Center, 6th Floor, Love River University Library
*Online Registration: http://library.loveriver.edu.tw/att_online/

VII. 感謝狀 Certificates of Appreciation
1. 義工 Volunteer

愛河大學

感謝狀

AAA女士
於西元二〇〇八年三月至西元二〇〇九年五月
擔任愛河大學圖書館志工，
熱心服務，無私奉獻，
特頒此狀，以資感謝。

校長 ○○○

2009年6月15日

Love River University

CERTIFICATE OF APPRECIATION

In recognition of Ms. AAA's dedication and outstanding volunteer services to
Love River University Library from March 2008 to May 2009,
we present this certificate with our gratitude.

June 15, 2009

President

2.捐贈 Gift

誌　謝

＿＿＿＿＿＿＿＿先生／女士

謝謝您所捐贈的＿＿＿＿＿＿＿，由於您的慷慨捐助，使得本館館藏日益豐富，您對愛河圖書館的支持我們長銘於心！

愛河大學圖書館館長

○○○

西元　　年　　月　　日

Donation Acknowledgment

Date: ＿＿＿＿＿ / ＿＿＿＿＿ / ＿＿＿＿＿

Thank you for your generous donation. Your gift ＿＿＿＿＿＿＿＿＿＿＿＿＿＿＿＿＿＿ contributes significantly toward enhancing the collections at Love River University Library. As a donor of library materials, you are one of our most valued supporters of this institution.

Gratefully,

———————————

AAA

Director, Love River University Library

VIII.授權書 Author Permission Forms
1.演講活動錄影授權書 Video & Audio Recording Permission Form

愛河大學 錄影授權同意書

演講名稱：＿＿＿＿＿＿＿＿＿＿＿＿＿＿＿＿＿＿＿＿＿
主 講 者：＿＿＿＿＿＿＿＿＿＿＿＿＿＿＿＿＿＿＿＿＿
所屬系/所/中心/行政單位（機構名稱）：＿＿＿＿＿＿＿＿＿

茲授權愛河大學將本人於愛河大學進行之上述演講，以電子形式儲存、製作與利用（例如演講全程影音錄製與製作、演講中所使用之資料數位化並以光碟形式、或與電腦網路連結等方式整合），提供讀者基於個人非營利性質之線上學習與檢索、閱讀、列印等，得不限時間與地域，為教學與學術研究等目的之參考。

立授權書人聲明對上述授權之著作擁有著作權，得為此授權。唯本授權書為非專屬性之授權，立授權書人對上述授權之著作與教材內容仍有著作權。

立授權書人：　　　　　　　　　　　　　（簽名或蓋章）
身分證字號：
通訊地址：
聯絡電話：
E-Mail：

年　　　月　　　日

Love River University
Video and Audio Recording Authorization Form

Title of Work: _____
_____

Name(s) of Presenter(s): _____
Affiliated Department（Institute）: _____

I, the undersigned, give permission for my presentation at Love River University (hereafter referred to as LRU) to be photographed, videotaped, audio taped, or otherwise preserved. I have full right, power and authority to grant to LRU and its library a non-exclusive license to archive my presentation as entitled above in digital formats, and to make it accessible in whole or in part in all forms of media in perpetuity including electronic access. I further understand that the recording of my presentation will be used by LRU for non-profit, educational and/or research purposes only.

I retain all other ownership rights to the copyright of this presentation, as well as the right to use partial or full content of this presentation in the future.

Signature:
Passport Number:
Postal Address:
Telephone Number:
E-Mail Address:

Date(Y/M/D):

2.機構典藏作者授權書 Permission Form for Institutional Repository

愛河大學著作授權書

著作名稱：_____
作　　者：_____
所屬系/所/中心/行政單位（機構名稱）：_____
類別：□學位論文　　□教師校內研究計畫報告　　□升等著作
　　　□國科會計畫研究　□其他_____ (請填寫)

　　立書人基於資源共享、合作互惠、回饋社會及促進學術研究之理念，同意無償、非專屬授權愛河大學（以下簡稱愛大）將立書人以上著作，不限地域、時間及次數，以紙本、光碟、網路或其它方式收錄、編輯、重製、發行或陳列展示，以提供讀者個人非營利性質之檢索、瀏覽、下載或列印。非專屬授權意指愛大所取得者為非獨占性的使用權，立書人仍可將相同的權利重複授權予他人。

　　立書人保證以上著作為立書人所創作，立書人有權為本授權書之各項授權，且未侵害任何第三人之智慧財產權。如有聲明不實，而導致愛大違反著作權法或引起版權糾紛，立書人願負一切法律責任。

立書人：　　　　　　　　　　　　　　　　　　　(簽名)
身份證字號：
通訊地址：
聯絡電話：　　　　　　　　　　傳真：
E-Mail：

　　　　　　日期：　　　　　年　　　　月　　　　日

Love River University
Publications Archives and Collection Project
Author Permission Form

Title of Work: _____

Name(s) of Author(s): _____

Affiliated Department（Institute）: _____

Type of Work:　☐ Thesis/Dissertation　　☐ Research Project Report
　　　　　　　☐ Faculty Promotion　　　☐ Gov. Grants Project Report
　　　　　　　☐ Other _____ (Please indicate)

I agree that submission of a copy of my work as entitled above to Love River University (hereafter referred to as LRU) enhances equal access to scholarly publications and fulfills the goals of resource sharing and collaboration in the scholarly community worldwide. I hereby have full right, power and authority to grant to LRU the non-exclusive, royalty-free right to archive, modify, reproduce, distribute, and display this work as entitled above in any format such as in print, on disc, on the internet, or other formats for any individual to search, browse, download, and print solely for non-profit use. I retain all other ownership rights to the copyright of this work and to use all or part of this work in future works.

I attest that this work is my (or our) original work and warrant that it does not infringe on any copyright or other rights held by third parties.

Signature:
Passport Number:
Postal Address:
Telephone Number:　　　　　　　　　Fax Number:
E-Mail Address:

Date(Y/M/D):

IX. 電子郵件通知 Announcements via Email
1.電子資料庫試用 Free Database Trials

標題：Testing & Education Reference Center
　　　(留學資訊與考試資源中心)試用

內容：
本資料庫完整收錄Peterson出版的美加及墨西哥地區的留學資訊和留學考試測驗題庫。留學資訊包括大學、研究所、遠距線上課程以及其他在職進修課程的選校指南。留學考試內容收錄各項留學測驗的線上模擬題本。使用者可以線上註冊，申請個人帳號密碼進行模擬測驗。歡迎踴躍試用！

試用網址：http://infotrac.galegroup.com/itweb/terc_asia?id=lrul
期限：97年5月15日止
試用期間若有任何問題與建議，請與圖書館A先生聯絡（分機3152或 lib@mail.loveriver.edu.tw）

Subject: Free Trials: Finding School Information and Test Preparation

The Testing & Education Reference Center provides access to school information for colleges, graduate schools, distance learning programs, and special career programs in the United States, Canada, and Mexico. Online practice exams for college and graduate school admissions are also available. Users can register for a personal account to take mock exams.

Trial site: http://infotrac.galegroup.com/itweb/terc_asia?id=lrul
Trial Period Ends on May 15th, 2008
Should you have further inquiries or any comments, please contact Mr. A at ext. 3152 or email to lib@mail.loveriver.edu.tw

2.展覽活動通知 Announcement for an Upcoming Exhibition

標題：《愛河大學圖書館十年回顧展》即將在圖書館展出

誠摯地邀請全校師生參觀《愛河大學圖書館十年回顧展》，一起見證圖書館的成長，重溫你我共同寫下的歷史、一同走過的足跡。

本展覽同時採實體及虛擬展示方式，精選十年來圖書館空間設備、推廣活動、學術研討、國際化及館員學習等方面的成長軌跡，以影像為主、文字為輔的方式呈現。現場並播放珍貴的擴館工程紀錄片，錯過這次，可能還要再等十年，讓我們一起回顧過去、展望未來。

展出時間：98年5月4日至6月30日，圖書館開館時間內
展出地點：圖書館五樓展覽藝廊
網路展覽：http://lib.loveriver.edu.tw/misc/10yearCelb

Subject: A Cordial Invitation to the Exhibition *A Visual Story of Love River University Library: 2000-2009*

We are pleased to invite you to explore an exhibition of the history of LRU Library over the past ten years, *A Visual Story of Love River University Library: 2000-2009*. From the historical but colorful pictures, the development of our library is visualized. Besides printed materials, a well-edited documentation film on a series of expansion constructions is shown. Anyone missing this exhibition might need to wait for another 10 years. Together let's look back on the past and anticipate the future.

Venue: Library Gallery, 5th Floor, Love River University Library
Exhibition Periods: Library Hours, May 4th, 2009 - June 30th, 2009
Virtual exhibition: http://lib.loveriver.edu.tw/misc/10yearCelb

X.圖書館管理營運辦法 Library Policies
1.圖書館借書規則 Borrowing Policies

愛河大學圖書館借書規則

愛河大學圖書館（以下簡稱本館）為有效管理館藏圖書資料，以達到方便讀者借用的目的，特訂定愛河大學圖書館借書規則（以下簡稱本規則）。

第 一 條　本館所藏圖書以提供本校教職員工生使用為主，兼任教師、短期及臨時聘雇人員、退休教職員工、校友及館際互借單位等依相關辦法或館際互借契約得申辦借書證。借書人具雙重身分者，擇一種身分辦理，不得重複申領借書證。

第 二 條　教職員工憑教職員工證，學生憑學生證辦理借書，其他身份之校外讀者依有效借書證件辦理借書。借書證件限本人使用，禁止轉借或冒用他人身份借書，如有轉借或冒用情事，本館得以停止其人借書權利三個月。如因此致使本館圖書遭受損失者，原持證人應負賠償責任。

第 三 條　借書證應妥善保存，如有遺失，應立即向本館掛失。掛失前如因借書證遺失，而造成本館圖書損失者，原持證人應負賠償責任。

第 四 條　珍善本書、特藏資料、期刊、報紙、參考工具書、教師指定參考資料及縮影資料等概不外借。

第 五 條　借書冊數及借期規定如下：
　　　　　一、專任教師、客座教師借書總數以五十冊為限，借期八週。
　　　　　二、研究生借書總數以四十冊為限，借期八週。
　　　　　三、職員工借書總數以三十冊為限，借期八週。
　　　　　四、兼任教師借書總數以三十冊為限，借期八週。
　　　　　五、大學部學生借書總數以二十冊為限，借期四週。
　　　　　六、退休教職員工、校友、推廣教育班師生、短期及臨時聘雇人員借書總數以十冊為限，借期四週。

Love River University Library Borrowing Policies

This borrowing policy serves as a guideline to assist staff in managing the library collection effectively so as to better serve users when checking out library materials.

Section 1. Eligibility of Library Users

The Love River University Library collection focuses on supporting the learning, teaching and research needs of enrolled students, faculty and staff of the university. They may borrow circulating materials from the general collections. Per LRU policy the following individuals must obtain a valid library card or reciprocal borrowing card: part-time instructors, temporary and short-term staff, retired full-time faculty and staff, alumni, and users from other institutions.

Section 2. Library Card

All eligible users are required to present a university ID or valid library card. Individuals are not allowed to borrow the ID of another person to check-out library materials. Anyone who lends his or her card to another person will have their library borrowing privileges suspended.

Section 3. Loss of Library Card

Your Love River University card is also your library card. Report your lost or stolen card immediately to any Circulation Desk staff member to prevent its unauthorized use. Card holders will be held responsible for any library materials damaged or lost before the library card is reported lost.

Section 4. Non-Circulating Materials

Rare books, items from Special Collections, periodicals, newspapers, reference works, course reserves, microfilms, and other materials classified as non-circulating may not be checked out from the library.

第 六 條　借書到期如欲續借，應於到期日前五日內（含到期日）辦理續借。續借可線上辦理、電話辦理或親自到館辦理，續借以兩次為限，若該書有人預約，則不接受續借。

第 七 條　讀者得預約圖書，每人預約冊數上限為五冊。預約書到館逾五日，預約人尚未借書者，視為放棄預約，本館不予保留，依序通知下一位預約者或直接上架。

第 八 條　本館實施催還制度，借書人所借圖書有其他讀者預約時，若到期日尚存十五日或十五日以上，系統將自動將到期日修正為第十四日，借書人若未在十四日內歸還，一律視為逾期。

第 九 條　已借出之圖書如因列為教師指定參考書或其他必要原因，本館得隨時要求借書人歸還，借書人應於本館通知日起七日內歸還，借書人若未在七日內歸還，一律視為逾期。

第 十 條　借書人所借圖書逾期歸還時，除停止其借書權利外，每逾一日每冊（件）需繳新台幣五元逾期處理費；限隔夜借閱之圖書資料，每逾一小時每冊（件）需繳五元逾期處理費。借書人歸還圖書及繳清逾期處理費後，即恢復其借書權利。

第 十一 條　教職員工離職、學生離校前須還清所借圖書，如有逾期情形，須繳清逾期處理費，始得辦理離職離校手續。

第 十二 條　借書人應妥善愛護所借圖書，如有遺失或污損情事，需負賠償責任，依「愛河大學圖書館館藏資料賠償辦法」處理。

第 十三 條　本規則經行政會議通過後實施，修正時亦同。

Section 5. Borrowing Privileges by Category of Library Users

This section of the policy describes the various categories of library users and defines their loan period for library materials from the general collections.

5.1 Full-time faculty and visiting scholars currently employed may borrow up to 50 items of circulating library materials for eight weeks.

5.2 Graduate students currently enrolled may borrow up to 40 items of circulating library materials for eight weeks.

5.3 Staff members currently employed may borrow up to 30 items of circulating library materials for eight weeks.

5.4 Part-time faculty members currently employed may borrow up to 30 items of circulating library materials for eight weeks.

5.5 Undergraduate students currently enrolled may borrow up to 20 items of circulating library materials for four weeks.

5.6 Retired full-time faculty and staff members, alumni, instructors and students in the Continuing Education Center, temporary and short-term staff may borrow up to 10 items of circulating library materials for four weeks.

Section 6. Renewals

A book checked out by a user from the circulating collection may be renewed two times unless another user has placed a hold on it. If books are not overdue, renewals may be accomplished during the five days before the due date in person, by phone or online.

Section 7. Holds

A library user may place a hold on a circulating book which is currently checked out by another user. The maximum number of holds allowed is five per user. When books placed on hold are returned to the library, the individual who requested the hold must pick up the book within five days. Otherwise, the book will be transferred to the next user placing a hold or will be re-shelved as usual.

Section 8. Recalls

Any book checked out by a user, including faculty and staff, may be recalled after two weeks. If the due date is more than 15 days from the date the recall was placed, the library system will automatically adjust the due date to 14 days. Fines may be imposed for items that are recalled but not returned.

Section 9. Urgent Recalls

Books requested by faculty for course reserves or other reasons may be recalled at any time. The books must be returned to the library within seven days after the recall date shown on the recall notice. Fines may be imposed for items that are recalled but not returned.

Section 10. Fines for Overdue Materials

Fines are charged for circulating materials returned after the due date. For materials from the circulating collection, the overdue fine is $5 per day per item. For materials with overnight loan periods, the overdue fine is $5 per hour per item. Library users with overdue items or unpaid fines cannot check out additional items until the overdue items are returned and the fines are paid.

Section 11. Returning Materials

All library checkouts must be returned upon a student's graduation or withdrawal and upon a university employee's resignation. Should overdue fines be assessed, all fees must be paid.

Section 12. Loss and Damage

The library user is responsible for damaged or lost books and materials on the basis of the Love River University Library Policy for Lost or Damaged Materials.

Section 13. This policy and amendments thereof take effect after the approval of the University Administration.

2.圖書委員會設置辦法 Library Committee

愛河大學圖書委員會設置辦法

第一條　為集思廣益，共謀本校圖書館業務之發展，特設置愛河大學圖書委員會（以下簡稱本會）。

第二條　本會設委員若干人，由圖書館館長、每一學院兩位圖書委員代表及兩位學生代表組成。圖書館館長為當然委員兼召集人，學院圖書委員代表由該學院院長推薦，學生代表由學生會推選研究所及大學部各一位擔任，除當然委員外，其餘委員任期為一年，可連任一次，任期一年。

第三條　本會任務如下：
　　　　一、圖書資料發展方向之確定。
　　　　二、圖書資料重要制度及章則之研議。
　　　　三、圖書資料經費之分配與運用。
　　　　四、其他有關之建議事項。

第四條　本會每學期以召開一次會議為原則，必要時得召開臨時會議。如有需要，得邀請有關單位主管列席。

第五條　本辦法經校務會議通過後實施，修正時亦同。

Love River University Library Committee Policy

Section 1. The Library Committee is authorized to promote collection development and to review policies and procedures for Love River University Library.

Section 2. The Library Committee shall consist of the Director of the Library, two members of the teaching faculty from each college and two student representatives. The Director of the Library is an ex-officio member and convener. Faculty members shall be selected each year by the Dean of each college. The two student representatives shall consist of one graduate student and one undergraduate. All committee members may renew for an additional term of one year except for the ex-officio.

Section 3. Library Committee Objectives

3.1 To affirm the collection development policy for library materials.

3.2 To advise on library collection policies.

3.3 To provide consultations on the allocation or execution of the library materials budget.

3.4 To comment or advise on the strategic operation and direction of the Library.

Section 4. The Library Committee will meet at least once per semester. If necessary, additional meetings will be scheduled, or heads of administrative sections may be invited to sit in the audience.

Section 5. This policy and amendments thereof take effect following the approval of University Board members.

3. 媒體資源中心使用規則 Media Resources Center Circulation Policies

愛河大學圖書館多媒體資源中心使用規則

第 一 條　愛河大學圖書館（以下簡稱本館）多媒體資源中心（以下簡稱本中心）為便利讀者使用本中心資料、資源及設備，進行教學、研究、學習及休閒活動，特訂定「愛河大學圖書館多媒體資源中心使用規則」（以下簡稱本規則）。

第 二 條　凡本校教職員工、學生、校友及持有本館有效借書證之讀者均得於本中心使用設備及館藏，唯僅本校教職員工生可外借多媒體資料。

第 三 條　本中心館藏外借件數、借期、續借、逾期處理費及賠償規定如下：
　　　　　一、專兼任教師、客座教師及研究人員借閱總數以十件為限，借期四週，可續借一次。
　　　　　二、職員工及學生借閱總數以五件為限，借期四週，不得續借。
　　　　　三、多媒體資料不接受預約，亦不實施催還制度。
　　　　　四、多媒體資料每件每逾一日需繳逾期處理費二十元，不足一日者以一日計。
　　　　　五、多媒體資料件數與圖書冊數合併計算，借閱多媒體資料逾期，等同於借書逾期，在未歸還圖書或多媒體資料，並繳清逾期處理費前，不得借書或多媒體資料。
　　　　　六、讀者於借閱多媒體資料時應自行檢查資料狀況，如有損壞情形應告知工作人員，資料一旦借出，如有毀損情形，最後一位借用人需負賠償責任。
　　　　　七、借閱多媒體資料如有遺失或損壞情形，依「愛河大學圖書館館藏資料賠償辦法」處理。

第 四 條　讀者使用多媒體資料，應確實遵守著作權法相關規定，如觸

Love River University Library Media Resources Center Circulation Policies

Section 1. Purpose

This policy serves as a guideline to facilitate user access to materials and facilities in the Media Resources Center (hereafter referred to as MRC) for purposes of instruction, research, learning, and leisure.

Section 2. Eligibility of MRC Users

The MRC at Love River University Library is open for on-site use to anyone holding a valid ID card from the university or a library-issued library card. Only students currently enrolled, and faculty and staff members currently employed by the university are permitted to borrow materials from the MRC.

Section 3. Borrowing Privileges and Overdue fines by Category of MRC User

This section of the policy describes the various categories of MRC users and defines the loan periods, renewals, overdue fines and replacement fees for MRC materials.

3.1 Faculty members, visiting scholars and researchers currently employed by the university may borrow up to 10 MRC items for four weeks, with one renewal.

3.2 Staff members currently employed and students currently enrolled may borrow up to five MRC items for four weeks. Renewal is not allowed.

3.3 MRC materials may not be placed on hold or recalled.

3.4 Fines are charged for checked-out MRC materials returned after the due date. The overdue fine is $20 per day per item.

3.5 Users with overdue items from either the MRC or from the general library collections or with unpaid fines cannot check out additional items until the overdue is returned and the fine is paid.

3.6 Borrowers should inspect the condition of MRC materials before

　　　　　犯法律，借用人須負所有法律責任。

第 五 條　不得擅自搬動各項多媒體器材及拷貝、轉錄多媒體資料，亦不得占用座位自習。

第 六 條　請勿攜入個人持有的多媒體資料或器材。

第 七 條　請勿攜帶背包、食物、飲料（含白開水）進入本中心。

第 八 條　讀者應愛惜使用本中心各項器材及設備，因不當使用而造成器材及設備受損時，應負賠償責任。

第 九 條　本中心大、小團體欣賞室採預約制，其申請及使用依「愛河大學圖書館多媒體資源中心團體欣賞室借用管理規則」辦理。

第 十 條　本規則經圖書館館務會議通過後公布實施，修正時亦同。

checking out an item. If an item is found to be damaged, please inform MRC staff. Once an item has been checked out, the borrower is responsible for any damage to the checkout and also for replacement of the item.

3.7 The MRC user is responsible for damaged or lost materials on the basis of the Love River University Library Policy for Lost or Damaged Materials.

Section 4. Copyright Law

Users are held responsible for adhering to the copyright law in any use of MRC materials.

Section 5. Inappropriate Use of Facilities or Materials

It is prohibited to move any MRC equipment around, to occupy any seat, to make copies of AV materials, or to convert the format of AV materials into others without prior permission.

Section 6. Personal Copy of AV Materials or Equipment

Personal copies of audio-visual materials or viewing equipment are not allowed in the MRC.

Section 7. Personal Belongings and Food

Personal bags, food or drinks, including water, are not allowed in the MRC.

Section 8. Loss and Damage

Borrowers will be held responsible for any loss or damage, due to inappropriate operation, to all equipment that they use.

Section 9. Use of Group Viewing Rooms

An advance reservation is required for the use of MRC group viewing rooms. For request procedures and access policy, please refer to MRC Group Viewing Rooms in Love River University Library Borrowing Policies.

Section 10. This policy and amendments thereof take effect after the approval of Library Staff members.

國家圖書館出版品預行編目資料

圖書館服務英文＝Library Service English /
文藻外語學院・圖書館團隊著；謝慧貞, 王愉文英
譯. --初版. -- 臺北縣中和市：
Airiti Press, 2009.07　　面；　公分

ISBN 978-986-85182-3-0 (平裝)
1. 大學圖書館 2. 英語 3. 詞彙 4. 會話

024.7　　　　　　　　　　98009249

圖書館服務英文 Library Service English

策　　劃／李文瑞	發行者／華藝數位股份有限公司
作　者／文藻外語學院・圖書館團隊（王愉文・向永輝・宋綺年・林洋聖・林意屏・許世原・郭弘志・黃明莉・賈玉娟・趙育群・鄭仲蓓・謝慧貞，以上依姓氏筆劃排列）	地址／台北縣永和市成功路一段80號18樓
	電話／(02)2926-6006
	傳真／(02)2231-7711
	Email／press@airiti.com
	帳戶／華藝數位股份有限公司
中文撰稿／謝慧貞・王愉文・趙育群	銀行／國泰世華銀行　中和分行
英　　譯／謝慧貞・王愉文	帳號／045039022102
英文審定／Sandi Edwards	

出　版　者／文藻外語學院、Airiti Press Inc.
總編輯／張　芸　　責任編輯／呂環延
封面及內頁設計／楊美娟
法律顧問／立暘法律事務所　歐宇倫律師

ISBN／978-986-85182-3-0
出版日期／2009年7月初版　2010年11月第四刷
定價／新台幣NT$550元

©Airiti Press Inc. 版權所有・翻印必究